OFF THE BEATEN PATH® SERIES

Maryland and Delaware

FIFTH EDITION

by Judy Colbert

Guilford, Connecticut

Cover and text design by Laura Augustine
Maps created by Equator Graphics © The Globe Pequot Press
Art on page 171 by M. A. Dubé; all other art by Carole Drong, rendered from photographs by Judy Colbert.

Library of Congress Cataloging-in-Publication Data

Colbert, Judy.
Maryland and Delaware off the beaten path : a guide to unique places / by Judy Colbert.—5th ed.
p. cm.—(Off the beaten path series)
Includes index.
ISBN 0-7627-0930-8
1. Maryland—Guidebooks. 2. Delaware—Guidebooks. I. Title.
F179.3.C65 2001
917.5104'44—dc21 2001018955

Manufactured in the United States of America
Fifth Edition/First Printing

Dedicated to Ben and Rockzana

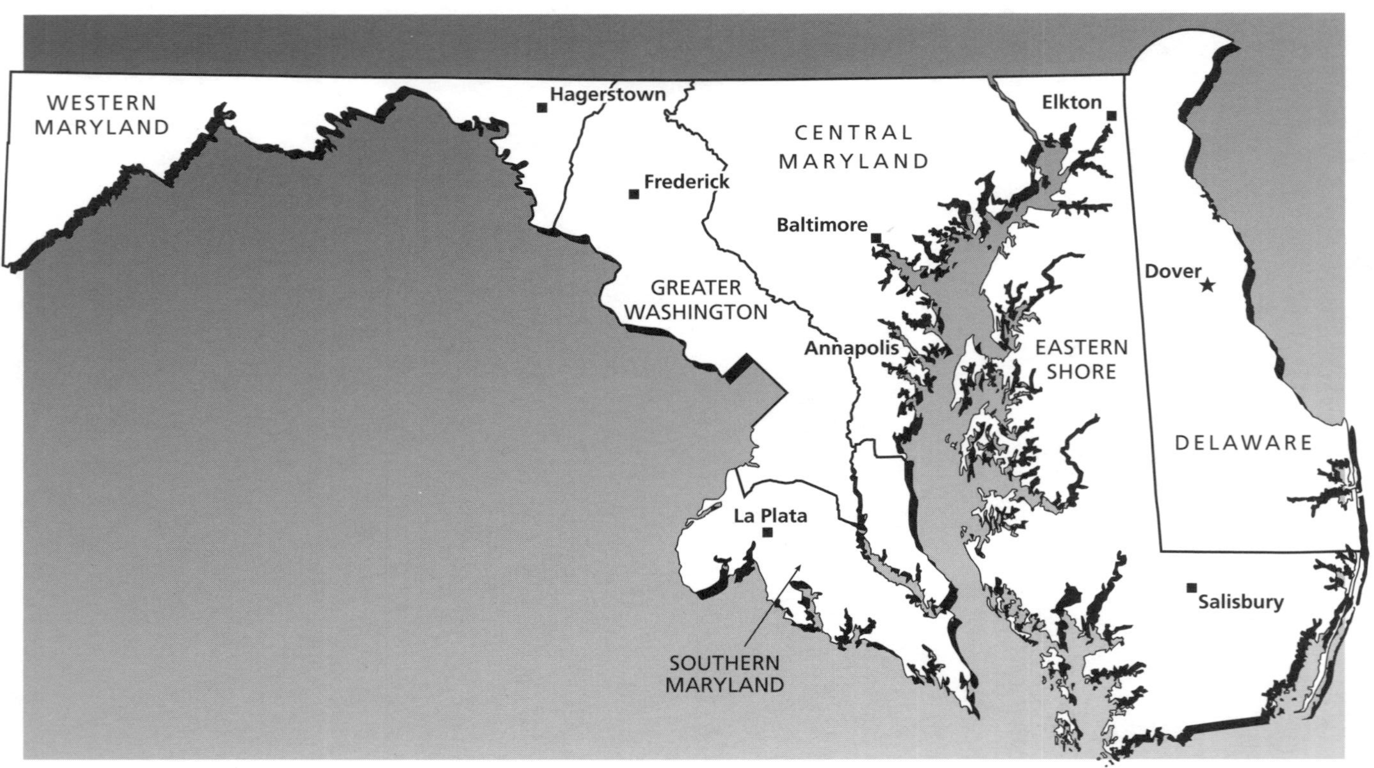
WESTERN MARYLAND
Hagerstown
Frederick
CENTRAL MARYLAND
Elkton
Baltimore
GREATER WASHINGTON
Annapolis
EASTERN SHORE
Dover
DELAWARE
La Plata
Salisbury
SOUTHERN MARYLAND

Contents

Introduction vii
Western Maryland 1
Central Maryland 31
Greater Washington 81
Southern Maryland 119
Eastern Shore 141
Delaware 195
Index 229
About the Author 236

Introduction

Welcome to *Maryland and Delaware: Off the Beaten Path,*® fifth edition, where you'll find some of the best food, the most unusual attractions, the friendliest people, the most incredible history, the most wonderful scenery and natural resources, and the best way to spend a few hours off the interstate.

Maryland is often called America in Miniature because the state goes from the seashore (the Atlantic Ocean and the Chesapeake Bay) on the east to the mountains (the Appalachians) on the west. The mountains are not high compared to the Rockies (Backbone Mountain in Garrett County is the tallest, at 3,360 feet), but they provide fair downhill and excellent cross-country skiing. The seashore is among the finest in the East. In one day you can go from one to the other and theoretically ski in the morning and the afternoon; snow skiing one direction, water skiing the other. About the only clime we don't have here is desert, yet there are sand quarries.

Not everything in Maryland, however, is miniature. The National Aquarium in Baltimore is one of the world's largest. The collection at the Walter's Gallery, also in Baltimore, is world renowned. Maryland also has the nation's largest white oak tree (see Talbot County), one of the nation's largest hydroelectric generating stations at Conowingo (see Cecil County), the largest colony of African black-footed penguins in the United States (Baltimore City Zoo), one of the largest and finest public libraries in the U.S. at the Enoch Pratt Free Library (Baltimore City), and the largest wooden dome in the country built without nails (Annapolis). Well, the list continues, but you get the idea.

Maryland is also called the Free State (road signs say KEEP THE FREE STATE LITTER FREE), and if you ask residents, they'd probably cite the freedom of worship advocated by the state's founders. Others might point to Maryland's alliance with the northern states during "the war" and its intolerance of slavery (at least in some parts of the state). These historical facts are true, but the name dates from 1917, when the state opposed prohibition on the grounds that it was a states' rights issue.

In the summer of 2000, Maryland introduced its Scenic Byways program, celebrating the "roads less traveled." From the mountains to the seashore, thirty-one byways have been designated, encompassing 1,797 miles. The average length of a byway is 60 miles and takes seventy minutes to drive, but lots of side trips are possible. The shortest is 5 miles, along the Historic National Seaport route, and the longest is 170 miles along the Historic National Road route. As part of this program, 800 new SCENIC BYWAYS signs were erected, a state map was created, and a free 192-page book titled *Maryland Scenic Byways* was published. For additional information, contact the state highway administration communications office at (410) 545–0303 or (800) 323–6742.

Maryland is also involved with the Gateways Network, coordinated by the National Park Service in partnership with the Chesapeake Bay program. A Gateway is an entrance to the byways and water trails in the National Park Service program. Among the first Chesapeake Bay Gateways in Maryland, Washington, D.C., Virginia, Pennsylvania, and New York, are twelve Gateway sites, one Gateway hub, two regional information centers, seven water trails, and one land trail. And, that's just the beginning. Pick a Maryland Gateway and you may visit the Barge House Museum (Annapolis), the Blackwater National Wildlife Refuge (Cambridge), Jefferson Patterson Park and Museum (St. Leonard), and the Monocacy River Water Trail. For additional information, stop by www. chesapeakebay.net/gateways.htm.

As with other places around the country, the demand for telephone numbers has increased exponentially in the past few years. Maryland has four area codes divided in an overlay pattern. Generally, 301 and 240 codes are for the western, suburban Maryland (around Washington, D.C.), and southern Maryland counties. Similarly, 410 and 443 are for Annapolis, Baltimore, and Eastern Shore areas. All local calls require the entire ten-digit number (area code and phone number). Only long-distance calls require the number 1 before the ten-digit number.

In addition to showcasing Maryland's attractions, this book also explores Delaware, which has been called Small Wonder for its diminutive size and its natural beauty. Only 96 miles in length, the state borders the Atlantic Ocean and Delaware Bay on the east and Maryland to the west and south. Delaware proudly boasts the fact that there is no sales tax. That's why you'll find so many outlet stores and other good shopping venues, from small shops to sprawling malls, throughout the state.

The area code for Delaware is 302, and you needn't dial it for local calls within Delaware.

I hope you enjoy reading and using this book as much as I enjoy discovering *Maryland and Delaware: Off the Beaten Path®*.

Fast Facts about Maryland

Maryland Tourism

Maryland Office of Tourism, 217 East Redwood Street, Baltimore 21202; (800) 543–1036, (410) 767–3400; www.mdisfun.org.

Allegany County Convention and Visitors Bureau, Western Maryland Station Center, 13 Canal Street, Cumberland 21502; (301) 777–5905; www.mdmountainside.com.

Annapolis and Anne Arundel County Visitors Bureau, 26 West Street, Annapolis 21401; (410) 280–0445; info@visit-annapolis.org; www. visit-annapolis.org.

Baltimore Area Convention and Visitors Association, 100 Light Street, Baltimore 21202; (410) 659–7300. Visitors Center at the Constellation Pier, Inner Harbor (walk-in queries); (800) 282–6632; www.baltimore.org.

Baltimore County Convention and Visitors Bureau, 118 Shawan Road, Hunt Valley Mall, Hunt Valley 21030; (410) 329–1001, (800) 570–2836; info@visit.bacomd.com; www.visitbacomd.com.

Calvert County Department of Economic Development and Tourism, 176 Main Street, Suite 101, Prince Frederick 20678; (301) 855–1880 (D.C.), (410) 535–4583, (800) 331–9771; cced@chesapeake.net; www.co.cal.md.us/cced.

Caroline County Economic Development Commission, 218 Market Street, Denton 21629; (410) 479–4188, (410) 479–2230.

Carroll County Office of Tourism, 210 East Main Street, Westminster 21157; (410) 848–1388, (800) 272–1933; www.carr.org/tourism.

Cecil County Tourism, 1 Seahawk Drive, Suite 114, North East 21901; (410) 996–6290, (800) CECIL–95; www.seececil.org

Charles County Tourism, Box B, La Plata 20646; (301) 645–0558, (301) 870–3000 (D.C.), (800) 766–3386; tourism@govt.co.charles.md.us; www. govt.co.charles.md.us.

Dorchester County Tourism, 2 Rose Hill Place, Cambridge 21613; (800) 522–TOUR, (410) 228–1000; www.tourdorchester.org; info@tourdorchester.org.

Tourism Council of Frederick County Inc., 19 East Church Street, Frederick 21701; (301) 663–8687, (800) 800–9699; www.visitfrederick.org.

Garrett County Chamber of Commerce, 15 Visitors Center Drive, McHenry 21541; (301) 334–1948, (800) 800–5557; GCTourism@garrett.ncin. com; www.gcnet.net/gctourism/gct.html.

Discover Harford County Tourism Council Inc., 121 North Union Avenue, Suite B, Havre de Grace 21078; (410) 939–3336, (800) 597–2649.

Howard County Tourism, P.O. Box 9, Ellicott City 21041; (410) 313–1900, (800) 288–TRIP; www.howardcountymdtour.com.

Kent County Tourism, 400 High Street, Chestertown 21620; (410) 778–0416; www.kentcounty.com.

Conference and Visitors Bureau of Montgomery County, 12900 Middlebrook Road, Suite 1400, Germantown 20874; (800) 925–0880; www.cvb montco.com.

Ocean City Office of Tourism/CVB, 4001 Coastal Highway, Ocean City 21842; (800) OC–OCEAN; www.ocean-city.com.

Prince George's County Conference and Visitors Bureau Inc., 9200 Basil Court, Suite 101, Largo 20774; (301) 925–8300, (888) 925–8300; visitor _info@co.pg.md.us.

Queen Anne's County Office of Tourism, Department of Business and

Jousting in Maryland

The state sport is jousting, the oldest equestrian sport in the world, with men and women competing. Like other sports and competitions, jousting originated as a test of a man's occupational skills. In Maryland, the challenge in jousting is not to toss a man off his horse, but to spear a series of metal rings while riding on a horse.

The 80-yard course has three arches from which rings are suspended; in each round, the size of the rings decreases. These are not huge rings to begin with: The largest ring is 1¾ inches in diameter and the smallest is ¼ inch.

There are numerous jousting tournaments throughout the year. The schedule usually starts in April and continues through to the Maryland State Championship and the Nationals in October. Events may take place in Hagerstown, Frederick, St. Mary's City, Easton, Denton, Trappe, Port Republic, Lily Pons, Clear Spring, Chestertown, and Havre de Grace. Each tournament has its pageantry and fun, its food and its partying. Usually there is an admission charge, which often is used to benefit a charitable organization. Call the Maryland Jousting Tournament Association at (410) 795–5067 for a schedule of events.

Tourism, 425 Piney Narrows Road, Suite 3, Chester 21619; (888) 400–RSVP, (410) 604–2100; tourism @qac.org, www.qac.org.

St. Mary's County Division of Travel and Tourism, P.O. Box 653, Governmental Center, Washington Street, Second Floor, Leonardtown 20650; (301) 475–4411, (800) 327–9023; www.saintmaryscountymd.com/decd.

Trivia

The state's official fossil, the four-ribbed snail, is of an extinct invertebrate that ranged in size from microscopic to 3 or 4 inches in diameter. Fossils can be found at the Cliffs of Calvert, in the Choptank and St. Mary's areas.

Somerset County Tourism, P.O. Box 243, Princess Anne 21853; (410) 651–2968, (800) 521–9189; www.skipjack.net/le_shore/visitsomerset.

Talbot County Office of Tourism, Easton Airport, U.S. Route 50, Easton 21601; (410) 770–8000; www.talbotcounty.md.

Hagerstown/Washington County Convention and Visitors Bureau, Elizabeth Hager Center, 16 Public Square, Hagerstown 21740; (301) 791–3246; www.marylandmemories.org.

Wicomico County Tourism, P.O. Box 2333, Salisbury 21802; (410) 548–4914, (800) 332–TOUR; www.wicomicotourism.org.

Worcester County Tourism, 113 Franklin Street, Unit 1, Snow Hill 21863; (410) 632–3110, (800) 852–0335; econ@ezy.net; www.skipjack.net/le_shore/visitworcester.

Other Web Sites and Information

Maryland Department of Natural Resources; www.dnr.state.md.us

Farmers Markets; www.mda.state.md.us/market/fmd.htm

Maryland Fall Foliage Hotline, (800) LEAVES–1

Maryland Welcome Centers

The Welcome Centers offer maps, local traffic conditions (major road construction), brochures about the area and the rest of the state, and assistance in planning your trip.

All Welcome Centers are open daily from 9:00 A.M. to 5 P.M. except Thanksgiving, Christmas, New Year's Day, and Easter. The eateries at the Chesapeake House are open for extended hours, with the Burger King open twenty-four hours a day.

Youghiogheny Overlook Welcome Center, I–68 East, mile marker 6 (east of West Virginia state line), P.O. Box 297, Friendsville 21531; (301) 746–5979.

I–70 West Welcome Center, I–70 West, mile marker 39 (just east of the Washington County–Frederick County line), General Delivery, Myersville 21773; (301) 293–4161.

I–70 East Welcome Center, I–70 East, mile marker 39 (just east of the Washington County–Frederick County line), P.O. Box 419, Myersville 21773; (301) 293–2526.

U.S. 15 Welcome Center, U.S. 15, 1 mile south of Pennsylvania, P.O. Box 695, Emmitsburg 21727; (301) 447–2553.

I–95 South Welcome Center, I–95 South, mile marker 37 (just south of Route 32), P.O. Box 288, Savage 20763; (301) 490–2444.

I–95 North Welcome Center, I–95 North, mile marker 37 (just south of Route 32), P.O. Box 1058, Savage 20763; (301) 490–1333.

Chesapeake House Welcome Center, I–95 North/South, mile marker 97 (includes fast-food restaurants, gift shop, and country market), P.O. Box 785, Perryville 21903; (410) 287–2313.

State House Visitors Center, State Circle, Annapolis 21401; (410) 974–3400.

Crain Memorial Welcome Center, U.S. 301 North, 12480 Crain Highway (just north of the Govenor Nice Memorial Bridge), Newburg 20664; (301) 259–2500.

U.S. 13 Welcome Center, U.S. 13 North, 144 Ocean Highway (just north of the Virginia state line), Pocomoke City 21851; (410) 957–2484.

Bay Country Welcome Center, U.S. 301 North/South, 1000 Welcome Center Drive, Centreville 21617; (410) 758–6803.

BWI Airport Welcome Center, BWI Airport, Terminal Building, Baltimore 21240; (410) 691–2878.

Bicycling Information

Bicyclists are prohibited from riding bicycles on Maryland Transportation Authority toll facilities, including bridges, tunnels, and approach roads. Understanding that this can be an oops in your travel plans, the Authority offers the following services as a courtesy to bikers:

Authority personnel will transport bikes and bikers across the Thomas J. Hatem (U.S. Route 40, Susquehanna River) and Harry W. Nice (U.S. Route 301, Potomac River) Bridges for the normal toll fee when time, personnel, and equipment permit. Call (410) 575–6650 for the Hatem Bridge, and (301) 259–4444 for the Nice Bridge, Monday through Friday 8:00 A.M. to 4:30 P.M. Try to give them at least an hour's notice.

Major Maryland Newspapers

The *Capital,* 2000 Capital Drive, Annapolis 21401; (410) 268–5000 (editorial), (410) 268–4800 (circulation), (301) 261–2200 (Washington, DC); www.capitalonline.com

Washington Post, 1150 Fifteenth Street, Washington, DC 20071; (202) 334–6000 (editorial), (202) 334–6100 (circulation); www.washingtonpost.com

Baltimore Sun, 501 North Calvert Street, Baltimore 21278; (410) 332–6000; www.sunspot.com

The *Star Democrat,* 29088 Airpark Drive, Easton 21601; (410) 820–6505; www.stardem.com

Public Transportation

Amtrak, (800) USA–RAIL; www.amtrak.com

Baltimore Washington International Airport (BWI), (800) 435–9294, (410) 519–0000, or (301) 261–1000; www.bwiairport.com

Washington Metropolitan Area Transit Authority (WMATA), (202) 637–7000; www.wmata.com

Fast Facts about the Old Line State

Area (land): 10,455 square miles (27,077 square kilometers), forty-second in size

Capital: Annapolis

Largest city: Baltimore

Number of counties: twenty-three, plus Baltimore City

Highest elevation: Backbone Mountain, 3,360 feet (1,024 meters)

Lowest elevation: sea level, along the Atlantic Ocean

Greatest distance from north to south: 124 miles (199 kilometers)

Greatest distance from east to west: 238 miles (383 kilometers)

Coastline: 31 miles (50 kilometers) of Atlantic Ocean coastline, 3,190 miles (5,134 kilometers) of Chesapeake Bay coastline

Population: 5,219,125 (2000 estimate), nineteenth among the states

Population density: 459 persons per square mile

Population distribution: 81 percent urban, 19 percent rural

Median family income: $43,628 (1999)

Statehood: April 28, 1788 (seventh state)

Nickname: the Old Line State, the Free State, America in Miniature

State flower: black-eyed Susan

State tree: white oak

State motto: *Fatti maschii, parole feminine* (Manly deeds, womanly words)

State bird: Baltimore oriole

State fossil shell: *Ecphora quadricostata*

State dog: Chesapeake Bay retriever

State reptile: diamondback terrapin (*Malaclemys terrapin*)

State fish: Striped bass (rockfish, *Morone saxatilis*)

State crustacean: Maryland blue crab (*Callinectes sapidus*)

State insect: Baltimore checkerspot butterfly (*Euphydryas phaeion*)

State dinosaur: *Astrodon johnstoni*

State boat: skipjack

State song: "Maryland, My Maryland"

State sport: jousting

State folk dance: square dancing

State theaters: Center Stage, Baltimore; Olney Theater Center, Olney (summer theater)

State drink: milk

Trivia

The Maryland flag was adopted in 1904. The red and white section is the coat of arms of the Crossland family, the first Lord Baltimore's relatives on his mother's side. The black and gold design is the coat of arms for the Calvert family, Lord Baltimore's relatives on his father's side.

Fast Facts about the Chesapeake Bay

At 200 miles long by 25 miles wide at some points, covering about 4,400 square miles, the Chesapeake Bay is five times as large as the State of Maryland. It is the largest estuary in the United States.

The bay holds about 19 trillion gallons of water.

The average depth of the bay is just 21 feet, but at Bloody Point, near Kent Island on the upper Eastern shore, the water is 174 feet deep.

More than 3,000 species of plants and animals, including 295 types of fish, live in the bay. It is the biggest producer of crabs in the country.

Forty-eight rivers and one hundred small tributaries flow into the bay, with the Susquehanna River contributing about 50 percent of the bay's fresh water.

The population of the Chesapeake Bay watershed, which stretches over six states, is 15.5 million.

Historians debate whether Viking explorer Thorfinn Karlsfennias (in the Eleventh century), Italian sailor Giovanni da Verrazano (in 1524), or Spanish explorer Pedro Menendez de Aviles (in 1566) was the first European in the bay.

The name Chesapeake is derived from the Native American word *Tschiswapeki.* Earlier names included "Great Waters," "Mother of Waters," and "Great Shellfish Bay."

The biggest problem endangering the bay is pollution, in the form of nitrogen and phosphorus.

Thomas Point Shoal Lighthouse, built in 1875, is the most photographed lighthouse on the Chesapeake.

Climate Overview

Maryland enjoys, if that's the word, hot and humid summers (temperatures are sometimes in the 90s) and cold and snowy winters. An average of 16 inches of snow falls each year in the Baltimore–Washington, D.C. corridor. In 1997–1998, there was only 0.1 inch of snow, while a few years earlier there were 70 inches of the white stuff (if this is Friday it must be snowing, or if it's snowing, it must be Friday).

Keep in mind, of course, that there's more likely to be snow in the mountainous western part of the state (it gets an average of 83 inches of snow annually, more than Anchorage, Alaska), while the Eastern Shore is almost snowless. Summer temperatures will usually be ten to twenty degrees cooler in the mountains than at the beach.

Actually, the weather can be quite pleasant most of the year, and the state has at least its share of seasons, with beautiful spring blossoms, showy summers, fall foliage, and winter wonderlands. The Chesapeake Bay is large enough to create its own weather systems.

Fast Facts about Delaware

Delaware Tourism Office, 99 Kings Highway, Dover 19901; (302) 739–4271, (800) 441–8846, www.visitdelaware.net.

Bethany–Fenwick Chamber of Commerce, Box 1450, Bethany Beach 19930; (302) 645–6838, (302) 539–2100, (800) 962–7873; www.bethanyfenwick.org.

Brandywine Valley Tourist Information Center, Route 1, Longwood Gardens 19348; (800) 228–9933, (610) 388–2900.

Delaware Memorial Bridge Information Center, I–295 at the Delaware Memorial Bridge, P.O. Box 71, New Castle 19720; (302) 571–6340.

Delaware State Chamber of Commerce Visitors Center at Bridgeville, Route 13, Box 69, Bridgeville 19933; (302) 337–8877.

Dagsboro Area Chamber of Commerce, P.O. Box 380, Dagsboro 19939; (302) 732–3777.

Delaware State Visitor Center, Duke of York and Federal Streets, Dover 19903; (302) 739–4266.

Delmar Chamber of Commerce, P.O. Box 416, Delmar 19940; (302) 846–3336; www.delmar.de.us.

Greater Georgetown Chamber of Commerce, 140 Layton Avenue, Box 1, Georgetown 19947; (302) 856–1544; home.ce.net/coc/georgetown.

Kent County Convention and Visitors Bureau, 9 East Loockerman Street, Suite 203, Dover 19901; (302) 734–1736, (800) 233–KENT; www.visitdover.com.

Laurel Chamber of Commerce, P.O. Box 696, Laurel 19956; (302) 875–9319.

Lewes Chamber of Commerce and Visitors Bureau, 120 Kings Highway, Lewes 19958; (302) 645–8073; www.leweschamber.com.

Greater Milford Chamber of Commerce, 11 North DuPont Highway, Box 805, Milford 19963; (302) 422–3344; www.milford-de.com/ccgm.

Millsboro Chamber of Commerce, Village Green Complex, 317 Main Street, Millsboro 19966; (302) 934–6777.

Historic New Castle Visitors Bureau, P.O. Box 465, New Castle 19720; (800) 758–1550, (302) 322–8411; www.hsd.org.

Chamber of Commerce of Milton, 104 Federal Street, Milton 19968; (302) 684–1101.

Rehoboth Beach–Dewey Beach Chamber of Commerce, 501 Rehoboth Avenue, Rehoboth Beach 19971; (302) 227–2233, (800) 441–1329; www.beach-fun.com.

Greater Seaford Chamber of Commerce, 1200 West Stein Highway, Second Floor, Box 26, Seaford 19973; (302) 629–9690; www.ce.net/coc/seaford.

Selbyville Chamber of Commerce, P.O. Box 1150, Selbyville 19975; (302) 436–5526.

Smyrna Visitors Center, 5500 DuPont Highway, Smyrna 19977; (302) 653–8910.

Sussex County Convention and Tourism Commission, P.O. Box 240, Georgetown 19947; (302) 856–1818, (800) 357–1818; www.visitsoutherndelaware.com.

Greater Wilmington Convention and Visitors Bureau, 100 West Tenth Street, Suite 20, Wilmington 19801; (302) 652–4088, (800) 422–1181; www.wilmcvb.org.

Major Delaware Newspapers

Newark Post, 153 East Chestnut Hill Road, Newark 19713; (302) 737–0724.

News-Journal, 950 West Basin Road, New Castle 19720; (302) 324–2700.

Philadelphia Inquirer, 440 North Broad, Wilmington 19801; (302) 654–6033.

Public Transportation

Philadelphia International Airport; (215) 492–3000.

Amtrak, (800) USA–RAIL; www.amtrak.com.

Salisbury/Ocean City Regional Airport, (410) 548–4827.

Fast Facts about the First State

Area (land): Delaware ranks forty-ninth in the nation, with a total area of 1,982 square miles (5,133 square kilometers)

Capital: Dover

Trivia

According to the Graduate College of Marine Studies at the University of Delaware, there are as many as sixty-two species of shark roaming the eastern waters of North America, including the Delaware and Maryland coasts. Typical mid-Atlantic sharks include the common hammerhead shark, the atlantic mako shark, the sand shark, the smooth dogfish shark, the spiny dogfish shark, and the sandbar shark.

Largest city: Wilmington

Number of counties: three

Highest elevation: 447.85 feet (136.5 meters) above sea level, in New Castle County

Lowest elevation: sea level, along the Atlantic Ocean

Greatest distance from north to south: 96 miles (154.46 kilometers)

Greatest distance from east to west: 35 miles (56.3 kilometers)

Coastline: almost 300 miles (482.7 kilometers)

Population: 754,000 (1999 estimate) forty-sixth among the states

Population Density: 34.5 persons per square mile

Population distribution: 73 percent urban, 27 percent rural

Statehood: December 7, 1787 (first state)

Nicknames: the First State, Small Wonder, Blue Hen State

State flower: peach blossom

State tree: American holly

State motto: Liberty and Independence

State bird: blue hen chicken

State song: "Our Delaware"

State bug: ladybug

State fish: weakfish (a.k.a. sea trout, gray trout, yellow mouth, yellowfin trout, and tiderunner)

State beverage: milk

State mineral: sillimanite

State colors: Colonial blue and buff

Climate Overview

Delaware's climate is moderate year-round. Average monthly temperatures range from 75.8 to 32.0 degrees. The average temperature in the summer months is 74.3 degrees. About 57 percent of the days are sunny. Annual precipitation is approximately 45 inches. Temperatures along the Atlantic Coast are about 10 degrees warmer in winter and 10 degrees cooler in summer than the rest of the state. The average growing season varies from 170 to 200 days.

The prices and rates listed in this guidebook were confirmed at press time. We recommend, however, that you call establishments before traveling to obtain current information.

Western Maryland

Western Maryland's three counties—Garrett, Allegany, and Washington—are a combination of farmlands, rugged mountains, sedate streams, and white-water rivers.

The products of farms and iron furnaces needed to be transported to customers between Wheeling, West Virginia, and the East Coast. So through this territory came the National Pike, which now is Alternate Route 40. It was the first road across the country funded by the federal government. This was long before President Eisenhower dictated there would be a national system of interstate highways. Along the road are many of the original mile markers, white metal (although they look like stone) obelisks that stand about 3 feet high.

Garrett County

Perhaps Garrett County is best known for ***Deep Creek Lake,*** the largest lake in Maryland (all Maryland lakes were made by humans). In 1925 a dam 1,300 feet long and 62 feet high was constructed to provide hydroelectric power, and the lake resulted. It is fed by Deep and Cherry Creeks, seven stream runs, and two glades. In 1999 the state announced that it was buying the lake for $7.8 million to ensure the area remains available as a recreation site. Deep Creek Lake State Park, 898 State Park Road, Oakland 21561, is open from sunrise to sunset. Phone (301) 387–7067.

Trivia

The Garrett County Chamber of Commerce, knowing how to promote its county's treasures, offers a Fly Fishing in Western Maryland *brochure, which includes information about the rivers, streams, and Deep Creek Lake, as well as what lures to use and when. Call (800) 800–5557 or (301) 334–1948.*

Just 13 feet from the shores of Deep Creek Lake is the ***Lake Pointe Inn,*** a fine bed-and-breakfast inn with sweeping views of the lake and mountains. The oldest house on the lake, it dates from the late 1800s, although it enjoyed a restoration in 1995. Each of the nine rooms has individually controlled heat, telephone with a private number, private bath, and down comforter and pillow. One

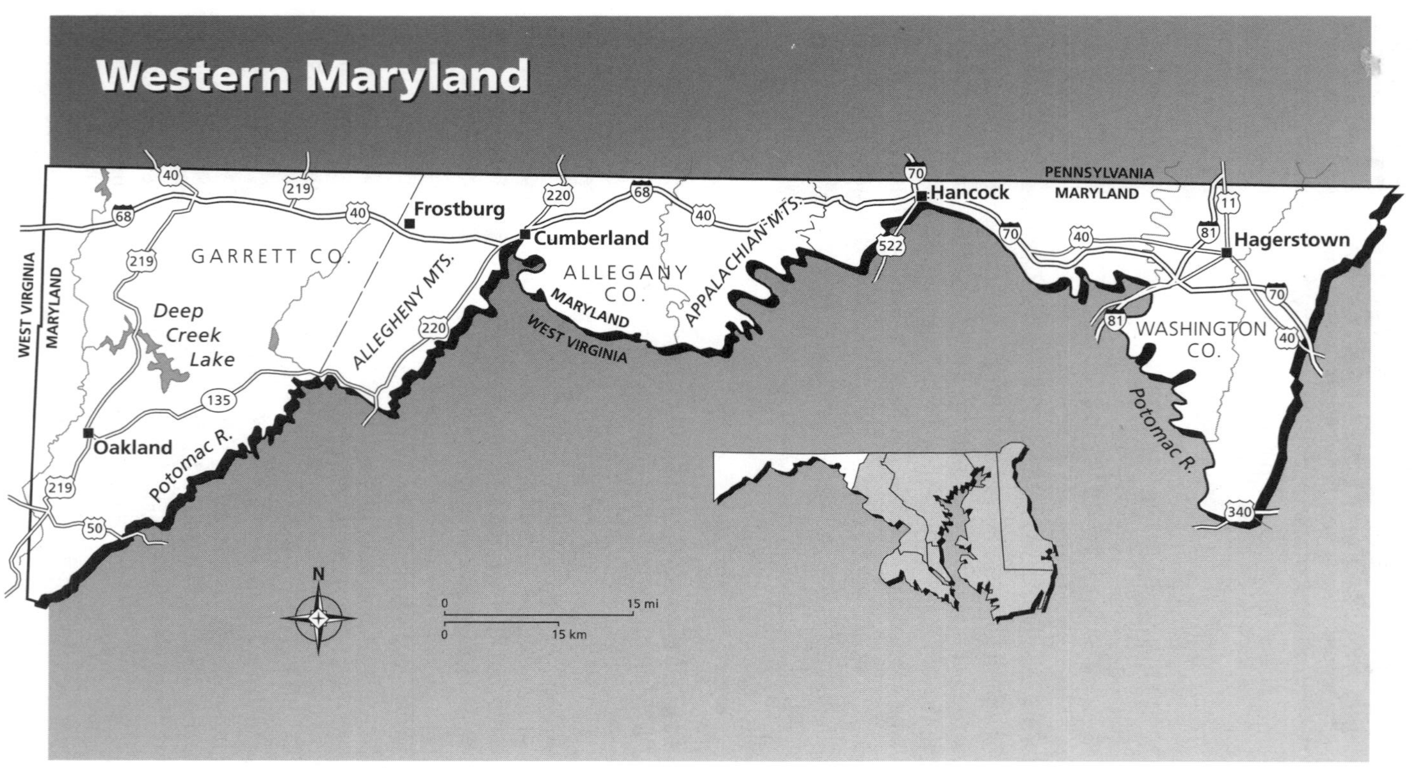
Western Maryland
PENNSYLVANIA
MARYLAND
Frostburg
Cumberland
Hancock
Hagerstown
GARRETT CO.
ALLEGANY CO.
WASHINGTON CO.
ALLEGHENY MTS.
APPALACHIAN MTS.
Deep Creek Lake
Oakland
Potomac R.
MARYLAND
WEST VIRGINIA
40
219
68
220
522
70
11
81
340
135
50
N
0
15 mi
0
15 km

room is handicapped accessible. Enjoy an evening by the stone fireplace in the Great Room or a lazy afternoon on the wraparound front porch. A light dinner is available upon request (give at least three days' notice), for an additional charge. The inn is at 174 Lake Pointe Drive, McHenry 21541. Call (301) 387–0111 or (800) 523–LAKE, or log on to www.deepcreekinns.com.

Judy's Favorite Attractions in Western Maryland

Antietam Battlefield

LaVale Toll Gate House

Sideling Hill Exhibit area

Washington County Museum of Fine Arts

Western Maryland Scenic Railroad

Rafters on the ***Upper Youghiogheny River*** (or Upper Yough, pronounced "yock") fight their way over Gap and Bastard Falls and through rapids with names like Charlie's Choice, Rocky III, Cheeseburger, and Meat Cleaver. In the 9-mile ride there are twenty Class IV and V rapids (the top of the scale being class VI) and a downhill drop of 100 to 120 feet per mile. These rapids can provide some tough but exhilarating times; an experienced guide is a necessity.

When the White Water Canoe/Kayak World Championships were held in the United States for the first time in 1989, they were held on nearby Savage River, another popular rafting place. Then, in 1992, the river was the site of the canoe and kayak team Olympic trials.

Other recreational pastimes in Garrett County include water sports, skiing (downhill and cross-country), hiking, camping, golfing, horseback riding, hunting, and mountain biking. The mountains in this area receive about 83 inches of snow a year, more than Anchorage, Alaska. which makes for good downhill skiing at Wisp (Deep Creek Lake) and extraordinary cross-country skiing.

Within the more than 70,000 acres of public land, Garrett County has cleared and marked trails in Germany State Park, 6 miles of maintained trails around Herrington Lake, and an additional 6 miles of primitive trails. Deep Creek and Swallow Falls State Parks have marked hiking trails that are suitable for cross-country skiing. Ski rentals are available at Herrington Manor State Park (301–334–9180) and New Germany State Park (301–895–5453).

Trivia

The **Our Fathers House Log Church** *near Altamont is among the last log churches in the eastern United States still in use. Reportedly, the church was constructed for $50. (301) 334–1948.*

In La Vale you will find the only remaining tollhouse (circa 1836) in Maryland.

The ***La Vale Toll Gate House*** shows life as it was when the National Road (Route 40) came this way. There's a neat sign showing the tolls for various animals, pedestrians, and wagons. This is the only remaining toll gate on the National

Trivia

Garrett County has the state's highest mountain (Backbone, at 3,360 feet), the longest waterfall (Muddy Creek Falls, at 52 feet), and the largest lake (Deep Creek, with a length of 12 miles and a 65-mile shoreline).

Road in Maryland. The furnishings are fascinating as well; be sure to ask about the "courting candle."

The House is at 14302 National Highway, La Vale 21502, and is open 1:30 to 4:30 P.M. Saturday and Sunday May through October, and by appointment. Call (301) 729–3047 for more information.

Paralleling the Potomac River to Cumberland was the Chesapeake and Ohio Canal. The canal was part of George Washington's dream of a water system that would unite the Atlantic with the Ohio River. The canal is now a National Historical Park. The 184½-mile towpath is used year-round by nearly four million hikers, cyclists, paddlers, anglers, picnickers, and nature enthusiasts who enjoy seeing the restored aqueducts and canal locks and communing with nature. Canal Place, $45 million plan that will once again fill the canal with water, provide barge rides, restaurants, shops, a museum, and more is in the works. Scheduled for completion by 2005, it should bring lots of tourists and locals to this historic site.

In the meantime, Canal Place coordinates activities and events, including the C&O CanalFest, keeping the story of the canal alive. For more information, contact the Canal Place Preservation and Development Authority, Western Maryland Railway Station, 13 Canal Street, Room 301, Cumberland 21502. Call (301) 724–3655 or (800) 989-9394 (Maryland only); or e-mail: info@canalplace. org.; TTY/TDD: (800) 735–2258.

Trivia

If you'd like to see the historical marker for the 3,360-foot highest point in the state on Backbone Mountain, take Route 50 east of Redhouse and you'll be at the crest of the Alleghenies.

Railroads superseded the canal as an efficient means of transportation. Today I–81, I–68, and I–70 provide the lifelines connecting this part of the state with the rest of the country. The geographic features that isolated western Maryland for so many years also made it attractive to vacationers; residents from Washington, D.C., and Baltimore traditionally have come here to escape the summer heat. Here you will find traces of Amish and Scottish culture, of hardy stock and friendly people. You will note some wealth, both in property and in cultural heritage. As yet, you will not find hundreds of thousands of tourists. You will find hospitality, tranquillity, perseverance, a dedication to remembering the "old ways," and beautiful mountain scenery.

Reportedly western Maryland has the only town in the country named ***Accident.*** The story is that George Deakins was given a land grant for 600 acres in 1751 by King George II. Deakins sent two engineers on separate missions to find his paradise. By accident, each selected the same plot, starting at the same tall oak tree. Deakins called this plot "The Accident Tract," and the name endures; locals wouldn't have it any other way. Most noted by visitors are the Accident Garage, the Accident Fire Department, and the Accident Professional Building.

The ***Drane House,*** built in the late eighteenth century, just east of Accident, is one of the few original frontier plantation homes remaining in this area. A key to Accident's past, it has been restored and is open for free tours upon request. The Drane House is on Old Cemetery Road, Accident 21520. Call the Accident Town Hall, Monday, Wednesday, and Friday, at (301) 746–6346.

Vacationers have been seeking respite in Garrett County for hundreds of years, and traces of that history can be found throughout the county. The Shawnee Indians summered here. People from the sun-baked, humid cities of Washington and Baltimore came here to enjoy the cool mountain climate as early as 1851. That is when the Baltimore and Ohio Railroad ran its line to Oakland, which would become the county seat. The train no longer stops in Garrett County, but the Oakland station, an outstanding and picturesque Queen Anne structure built in 1884, remains.

Oakland is the county seat, so you're most likely to find a variety of interests addressed here.

The ***Oakland Post Office mural*** at 22 South Second Street, Oakland 21550 (301–334–3151) was created by Robert Gates in 1942; it portrays a buckwheat harvest. Gates also did the mural in the Bethesda Post Office, which depicts the Montgomery County Farm Woman's Cooperative Market.

There is such an interesting blend of history here, from Native American to Civil War, and such an interest in genealogy, that you might want to spend a few hours at the ***Garrett County Historical Museum,*** with its exhibits portraying the history of the county's residents. There's a large genealogy library here too.

Trivia

In 1989 Frank "Doc" Custer sent 3,200 of his white pine and balsam fir Christmas trees to the Bahamas. This was the first time that a Maryland grower had exported trees outside the United States. Custer planted his first tree in 1956, and his Mountain Top Tree Farm, outside Oakland, is one of the largest tree farms in the state. As you drive around the county and spot perfect trees for your next holiday season, remember it may be going to Nassau to brighten up the holidays for someone who misses snow and cold weather.

Trivia

Presidents Grant, Garfield, Harrison, and Cleveland attended services in the St. Matthew's Episcopal Church in Oakland. (301) 334–2510.

There is no admission fee to the museum (contributions are accepted, though), which is located at 107 South Second Street, Oakland 21550. Generally, it's open daily from 11:00 A.M. to 4:00 P.M. Call (301) 334–3226.

About 10 miles out of Oakland off Cranesville Road is the Nature Conservancy's ***Cranesville Sub-Arctic Swamp***, covering more than 500 acres (plus more in West Virginia). This natural phenomenon is a remnant of a boreal forest that produces growth normally found in arctic regions. So, you geologists, biologists, and nature lovers can see many rare species of flora and fauna. Although the ice sheet or glaciers of the last Ice Age (15,000 years ago) didn't reach this far south, they did lower the temperatures here, making this area a suitable habitat only for northern or colder clime plants and animals. They stayed this far south, even though the colder weather retreated north, because of a natural phenomenon known as a frost pocket, due to the cool air in the high mountains.

Among the plants you'll find here are the tamarack or larch (*Larix laricina*) and the tiny, round-leaved sundew (*Drosera rotundifolia*), an insectivorous plant. Additionally, this is the only significant site in Maryland where you can see creeping snowberry (*Gaultheria hispidula*). There are nineteen different plant communities, from shrubby wetlands to hardwood forest, in Cranesville.

One of the animals you might see is the northern water shrew (*Sorex palusyris punculatus*), and among the state-rare breeding birds are the golden-crowned kinglet, alder fly-catcher, Nashville warbler, and the saw-whet owl.

In 1965, Cranesville Swamp became one of the first National Natural Landmarks to be designated by the National Park Service. It's open to the public for photography, nature study, birding, and walking, with four color-coded marked trails (with interpretative signs) through the woods to a 1,500-foot boardwalk. The trails start from either the drive into the swamp or from the parking lot, and all trails lead to the boardwalk. Please stay on the trails and the boardwalk so you don't take a chance of harming the plants.

Pets, even on a leash, are not allowed, nor is smoking or all-terrain vehicles. Remove nothing except your trash. Camping and fires are not allowed either.

Trivia

The town of McHenry was settled about 1805 by Col. James McHenry, aide to Gen. George Washington, signer of the Declaration of Independence, and the man for whom the Baltimore fort was named.

Do wear sensible shoes, sunblock, insect repellent, and socks pulled up over your pants' cuffs to protect against chiggers, mosquitoes, ticks, poison ivy, and poison sumac. Bring field glasses and a good field guide to help you enjoy your visit.

Understand that the roads into the swamp are not paved. So, although the swamp can be gorgeous under a snow cover, you may need a four-wheel drive vehicle to get there. Although open to the public during daylight hours, the conservancy likes you to call ahead of time to tell them you'll be wandering along their boardwalks. The number is (301) 656–8673.

Grover Cleveland and his bride, Frances Folsom, stayed in the three-story, fourteen-room "Cottage Number Two," now "Cleveland Cottage," near the ***Deer Park Hotel*** for their fifteen-day wedding trip in 1886. The Deer Park Hotel was built in 1873 by the Baltimore and Ohio Railroad when John W. Garrett (for whom the county was named) was company president. None of the hotel's main structure remains because it was razed in 1942, but some of the foundation is still visible. About 5 miles east of Oakland, on Route 135, turn south on Deer Park Hotel Road and proceed ½ mile, then drive east on the loop at Pennington Cottage to reach the hotel.

Solomon Sterner opened the ***Casselman Inn,*** Main Street, Grantsville 21536, in 1824 to take in travelers from the National Pike. As is usual with restaurants, inns, and hotels along the pike, this one is on the north side, or the side that westbound travelers would be on. The phone number is (301) 895–5055.

When the nearby ***Casselman Bridge*** on alternate Route 40 East was built in 1813, it was the largest single-span stone-arch bridge in America. Gracefully curving 50 feet above the river, it was constructed so that the Chesapeake and Ohio Canal could travel beneath its span. The canal never came this far, but the bridge carried traffic for 125 years. It is now closed to motorized traffic, but the Casselman River Bridge State Park, Route 40 East, Grantsville 21536, has a picnic area and a scenic spot to enjoy for a few minutes or a few hours. Yes, it is on the National Register of Historic Places. (301) 895–5453.

East of Casselman Bridge is ***Penn Alps,*** home to numerous crafters who work in log cabins that have been brought here from the surrounding countryside. The shops in ***Spruce Forest Artisan Village*** are open from 10:00 A.M. to 5:00 P.M. Monday through Saturday.

Calling All Yoders

There are more than 200 Yoders listed in the phone book in Maryland (and that doesn't include Yoders who have married and changed their names). A Yoder House is under construction at Spruce Forest, made of "Yoder Stones." In other words, it will be built with stones collected from the foundations of Old Yoder homesteads in the area and perhaps other stones of Yoder importance. A genealogy display will trace the family from 1340 to today. For more information about this nonprofit organization, write to Yoder House Project, 177 Casselman Road, Grantsville 21536.

Penn Alps is on Route 40 in Grantsville 21536. The artisan village phone number is (301) 895–3332; the Web site is www.spruceforest.org.

Garrett County has drawn even more artistic talent with the relocation of Mark and Laura Stutzman, who operate Eloqui illustration studio. You've seen Mark's work on numerous McDonald's packages *(Batman, Jurassic Park),* but he's best known for designing the Elvis Presley postage stamp for the "Legends in American Music" series. Look for activities sponsored by the Garrett Lakes Arts Festival, and you'll probably find both Mark and Laura in attendance.

About a mile east of Grantsville, still on the National Pike, is the ***Fuller-Baker Log House***. The privately owned house is representative of those constructed on the Allegheny frontier, except that it is large enough to have been a tavern. It is believed to be the only remaining log tavern on the National Pike between Cumberland and Wheeling. Maryland's first governor, Thomas Johnson, owned the property when the house was built in 1815, but it is named for two other longtime residents. The first was Henry Fuller, who came to the area in 1837 to work as a stonemason. The Bakers were also early settlers and owned the house at a later date. The house in now on the National Register of Historic Places.

About 20 miles east of Oakland is the ***Baltimore and Ohio Viaduct*** at Bloomington. It was opened in 1851 to connect the port of Baltimore with industrial Wheeling and the Ohio Valley. The multispan stone-and-concrete bridge carries the railroad across the North Branch of the Potomac River. A Confederate raiding party schemed to demolish the viaduct but was driven away by Union troops before the bridge could be blasted. Blasting holes drilled by Capt. John H. McNeill and his McNeill's Rangers are still visible on the bridge. The Baltimore and Ohio Viaduct is on Route 135, just west of the Garrett and Allegany county line.

For additional information contact Deep Creek Lake–Garrett County Promotion Council, 200 South Third Street, Oakland 21550, or call (301) 334–1948. The E-mail address is GCTourism@gcc.cc.md.us.

Allegany County

Outdoor enthusiasts enjoy Allegany County and Cumberland, the county seat. Within the county borders are Rocky Gap and Dan's Mountain State Parks, Green Ridge State Forest, and the C&O Canal National Historical Park, where people can hunt, boat, fish, camp, bike, hike, and explore history.

Cumberland is considered the ***mibster capital*** of the country. For some reason the marble players of this town far surpass the players from other towns. A recent world champion was a twelve-year-old from Cumberland. If it has been a while since you played, or if you have never tried your hand at it, visit ***Constitution Park.*** In addition to the Little League baseball field, picnic groves, swimming pool, wading pool, playground, railroad caboose, 1937 fire truck, army tank, horseshoe pits, and courts for basketball, tennis, shuffleboard, volleyball, and badminton, there are two game areas with three marble rings each. Games and tournaments are held regularly at the park; six national marble champions have played and practiced here on their way to victory.

Constitution Park is off Williams Street in the southeast area of Cumberland. From Maryland Avenue turn left on Williams Street to reach the park entrance. Call (301) 759–6440.

A brochure is available to help you walk through the ***Victorian Historic District of Cumberland***, beginning at the east bank of Will's Creek and

Pedestrian Crossing

The 317-foot, one-lane, wooden-plank bridge crossing the North Branch of the Potomac River, linking Green Spring, West Virginia, with Oldtown, Maryland (about 15 miles southeast of Cumberland), was one of the last privately owned toll bridges. The bridge, constructed in 1937, was closed in 1995 because of "the deteriorated structural condition" of the Maryland-side abutment and evidence of pier decay, according to Allegany County Public Works officials. Without the fifty-cent toll bridge, those who want to travel between the two areas face an additional 40-mile commute. The bridge remains open to pedestrians.

extending to the western property line of 630 Washington Street. The brochure highlights the architectural details and historical importance of about three dozen buildings. One of these is the History House Museum, which has eighteen rooms available for touring and features Victorian furniture, antiques, and displays pertaining to Allegany County's history. For more information about the historic district, call (301) 777–5905.

There is also a brochure available on the Fort Cumberland Walking Trail, which highlights the site of the 1755 fort with plaques on its history. The trail passes by George Washington's headquarters, a cabin that he used when he served at the fort as an aide to Gen. Edward Braddock during the French and Indian War. Another brochure, this one entitled *Walking Tour of Historic Downtown Cumberland,* highlights the architectural gems in the Downtown Pedestrian Mall area.

The ***Western Maryland Station Center,*** which was in service from 1913 until 1976, now houses the Allegany County Convention and Visitors Bureau, the Western Maryland Scenic Railroad, the Canal Place Authority, and the new C&O Canal National Historical Park Visitor Center. The center has an interpretive display in the station, where photographs, models, and artifacts are exhibited.

The ***C&O Canal National Historical Park Visitor Center*** features exhibits relating to the history of the canal in Cumberland. Entering the exhibit center through a likeness of the famous Paw Paw Tunnel, you'll discover displays about boatbuilding, the importance of the coal industry to the canal operations, and Cumberland as a transportation center. Cumberland, known as the gateway to the West and home of the "Narrows," was the beginning point of the National Road and a major railroading center in addition to serving as the western terminus of the C&O Canal. The Visitor Center, 13 Canal Street, Room 304, Cumberland 21502, is open daily from 9:00 A.M. to 5:00 P.M. (301) 722–8226.

The ***Transportation and Industrial Museum,*** 13 Canal Street, Cumberland 21502 is open Tuesday through Sunday from 10:00 A.M. to noon and 2:00 to 4:00 P.M. The telephone number is (301) 777–5905.

The ***Allegany Arts Council,*** located on the downtown Cumberland Mall, has twenty-four arts organizations actively involved in choral singing, theater, cinema, photography, crafts, instrumental music, and visual arts. A gallery exhibits works that are for sale. It's open from 10:00 A.M. to 4:00 P.M. Tuesday through Friday, and from 11:00 A.M. to 4:00 P.M. on Saturday, or by appointment. It is located at 74 Baltimore Street, Cumberland 21502. (301) 777–2787; www.alleganyartscouncil.org.

The Allegany County Convention and Visitor's Bureau is open May through October from 9:00 A.M. to 5:00 P.M. daily; November through April from 9:00 A.M. to 5:00 P.M. Monday through Friday, and 10:00 A.M. to 4:00 P.M. on weekends. Call (301) 777–5132.

The romance of early twentieth-century steam railroading is with us once more on the ***Western Maryland Scenic Railroad,*** where passengers take a 16-mile ride combining mountaintop scenery and rich transportation history. The Western Maryland features a locomotive built in 1916 by the Baldwin Locomotive Works for the Lake Superior & Ishpeming Railroad, based in Michigan. It is a Consolidation 2-8-0 used from 1916 to 1956 for switching and freight hauling in Michigan's Upper Peninsula. It was on display at the Illinois Railroad Museum from 1971 until it was purchased by the WMSR in 1992.

As the train steams its way up the 2.8 percent grade on the westward trip from Cumberland to Frostburg, it travels along old Western Maryland Railway and Cumberland and Pennsylvania Railway rights-of-way. Riders view many memorable sights, including the famous Cumberland Narrows (a natural 1,000-foot breach in Will's Mountain known as the "Gateway to the West"), an iron truss bridge, Bone Cave, and Helmstetter's Horseshoe Curve.

Other interesting sights along the way include the 1,000-foot Brush Mountain Tunnel, the Allegheny Front, Victorian architecture, the C&O Canal, Buck's Horse Farm, and the frontier town of Mt. Savage (where America's first iron rails were produced). At the Frostburg terminus you can get a close-up view of the engineer and fireman in blue-and-white overalls and the locomotive turntable, which reverses the engine for the return journey.

At the other end, in Frostburg, is the Old Depot Center complex, which now features a restaurant and the ***Thrasher Carriage Collection***. This collection offers more than fifty examples of early nineteenth- and twentieth-century horse-drawn vehicles. Built by the finest manufacturers, the vehicles include a Vanderbilt family sleigh and the formal coach used by Theodore Roosevelt at his inauguration. The museum is open 11:00 A.M. to 3:00 P.M. Tuesday through Sunday May through September, daily during October, and weekends only in November and December. Call (301) 689–3380; www.cumberland.md.wm/thrasher.

The rail trip takes about three hours, including a ninety-minute layover in Frostburg. A special dining car has been dedicated as the Gov. William Donald Schaefer Special for the governor who was credited with inspiring state, local, and private development of the scenic railroad.

The train runs on a seasonal schedule, so call for days and times. There's an expanded schedule in October for fall foliage viewing. Ticket prices for the year 2000 were $17.50 and $19.50 for adults, $16.00 and $19.00 for seniors age sixty and older, and $11.00 and $12.00 for children age two and younger. Group rates are available. Prices may vary in October.

Charter trips and special events such as dinner trips or trips featuring murder mysteries, dinner theater, or dancing are scheduled periodically. Private parties for weddings, birthdays, business meetings, school outings, and other events also may be booked. Write to Western Maryland Scenic Railroad, Western Maryland Station, 13 Canal Street, Cumberland 21502, or call (800) TRAIN–50 or (301) 759–4400. Visit the WMSR on the Internet at www.wmsr.com.

One of the sights you will see on the railroad excursion, or on a drive through Mt. Savage, is the ***Mt. Savage Castle.*** This National Historic Landmark in stone, built in 1842, is a replica of the Craig Castle in Scotland. At the height of its grandeur, the castle was owned by industrialist Andrew Ramsay, a Scot who was renowned for his production of ceramic glazed brick, which can be found throughout the building.

The castle's unique rooms, carriage house, and terraced gardens have been restored to their former elegance and furnished with antiques. The castle is currently operated as a bed-and-breakfast with six elegantly furnished sleeping rooms. Four rooms have private baths; two rooms share a large main bathroom. A full breakfast is provided for overnight guests, and tea is served at 4:00 P.M. Weather permitting, both are served in the outside courtyard or terraces. In keeping with the Scottish tradition, croquet and putting can be enjoyed on the grassed terrace. Tours, receptions, parties, conferences, and other special events may be booked at the castle. Privacy is assured by the 20-foot stone wall that surrounds the grounds. The address is 15925 Mt. Savage Road, The Castle, Mt. Savage 21545. Call (301) 264–4645.

The ***Mt. Savage Museum & Historical Park*** is an 1800s ironworks house built to house laborers. It's also where Cardinal Edward Mooney was born. Mooney (1882–1958) was the archbishop of Detroit from 1937 until 1946, when he was named a cardinal. There's no admission fee to the museum, located at the Mt. Savage Historical Park, and the hours vary, so call first. (301) 264–4175.

Just as the railroad and the canal played an important part in the area's development, the National Pike has a claim to fame. You can drive to the top of either side of the ***Cumberland Narrows*** for an unparalleled view, on a clear day, of Cumberland and the surrounding countryside.

Mt. Savage Castle

To reach the eastern wall of the Narrows, take Will's Mountain Road off Piedmont Avenue to the parking lot of Artmor Plastics, park, and walk about 2 blocks. To reach the western wall, take exit 41, the Sacred Heart Hospital exit, off I–68. Go through the traffic light and up the hill to Bishop Walsh Road, where you will turn right to the high school. Drive to the back of the school, where the road ends, and walk through the woods, past the water tower, to the edge—about a five-minute walk. This is not a prepared path and it is not handicapped accessible. The park is open from dawn to dusk. Call (301) 777–5132.

Westvaco Paper Company at Luke spreads over three counties and two states—Allegany and Garrett in Maryland and Mineral in West Virginia. The town is named for William Luke, who founded the paper company on this site in 1888. The company manufactures more than 1,200 tons of high-quality, coated, white printing papers each day. The products are used for such magazines as *Forbes, Town and Country, Good Housekeeping, Fortune,* and Disney and National Geographic Society publications.

A ninety-minute tour allows visitors to view the papermaking process from pulpwood to cooking to the finished rolls and sheets. Call (301) 359–3311 to arrange a tour. Located at 300 Pratt Street, Luke 21540, the company prefers about two weeks' notice.

When you are driving from the Oakland area of Garrett County to Luke, you will have several miles of a very steep downhill grade on Route 135 where trucks are cautioned to drive no more than 10 miles an hour. If you are caught behind one of these trucks, slip into low gear (in the car and in your mind) and spend a little time looking at the beautiful countryside—something you would not be able to do if you were rushing through at 55 miles an hour. That is why you are off the beaten path, isn't it?

The ***Lonaconing Iron Furnace*** was erected about 1836 by the George's Creek Coal and Iron Company and produced iron for the next twenty years. When the furnace was constructed, it was unique in several

Lonaconing Iron Furnace

respects. It was 50 feet high and 50 feet square at the base—a daring departure from contemporary furnaces, which were 30 feet high and 30 feet square. Moreover, it was the first furnace built in this country that successfully used coke fuel at a time when all furnaces were using the less-efficient charcoal.

The furnace was built against a hillside because it was fed from the top. The site was chosen because the necessary iron ore, coal, wood, clay, limestone, sandstone, and water were readily available, although transportation to the marketplace was not convenient. Castings made here included stoves, farming implements, and dowels for the C&O Canal lock walls.

Today the furnace is the backdrop for a pleasant town park in Lonaconing, where you can stop to lunch at the picnic tables or enjoy the play equipment. A sign notes the location of the former Central School, and a bronze plaque honors Robert Moses "Lefty" Grove, a native son who was elected into the Baseball Hall of Fame in 1947. Lauded as the greatest left-handed pitcher of all time, he played for the Philadelphia Athletics from 1925 to 1933 and the Boston Braves from 1934 to 1941.

The furnace is located on Route 36, 35 East Main Street, Lonaconing 21539. (301) 463–6233. The park is open daily from sunrise to sunset.

For additional information write to the Allegany County Convention and Visitors Bureau, Western Maryland Station Center, 13 Canal Street, Cumberland 21502, call (301) 777–5138, or visit www.mdmountainside.com.

Washington County

Washington County—the first county to be named after George Washington—was founded on September 6, 1776, just months after our country itself was born. In a Civil War battle fought at Sharpsburg, along Antietam Creek, more than 23,000 casualties were suffered.

Since 1989 an annual remembrance of the battle at ***Antietam*** has been held the first Saturday in December; it is signified by 23,100 luminarias, one every 10 feet along 4½ miles of roadway, in the fields, along Bloody Lane, and around some of the monuments erected on the battlefield. It takes 400 volunteers to set the lights, starting at 3:30 P.M. Some 3,000 cars drive through to look at the candles, starting around 5:30 P.M.; the candles burn about ten hours. The luminarias are paid for by corporate sponsors; the drive is free, but a donation is requested.

The idea for the candles came from the Rest Haven Cemetery, which had previously placed a luminaria at every grave site. Borrowing the idea, Hagerstown residents lit luminarias every night for the two weeks prior to Christmas. One night it was the north side of town, another it was the south side, and so it continued throughout the area. Band members of the high schools sold 81,000 lights in the neighborhoods.

The newest battle monument, the first to be erected since 1967 and probably the last ever, is a tribute to the ***Irish Brigade*** that fought on Bloody Lane. More than 500 men were slaughtered or wounded in this battle, but they had never been formally recognized.

The campaign to have this monument erected helped cause the creation of the Adopt-a-Monument National Battlefield program. Budget cuts have reduced the funding of preservation and rehabilitation programs for the 103 monuments, and more than half of them have major sculptural elements, statues, carved reliefs, and ornamental embellishments. Now people and groups can donate time, supplies, or money to support the park or a specific monument or marker. Contributions, small enough to buy a paintbrush or large enough to paint, repair, and seal a War Department tablet for about $250, are readily accepted.

For more information about the Adopt-a-Monument program, write to P.O. Box 158, Sharpsburg 21782, call (301) 432–5124, or visit www.nps.gov/anti. The Antietam National Battlefield at Sharpsburg is open daily from 8:30 A.M. to 5:00 P.M. except on major holidays.

Washington County parks rate with the best and include the ***C&O Canal National Historical Park,*** the Appalachian Trail (37 miles), Fort Frederick State Park, Washington Monument State Park, Pen Mar County Park, at least eight other county parks, and Hagerstown City Park.

For lodgings with a real twist, you'll want to visit ***Maple Tree Campground*** near Gathland State Park. The unusual feature of this campground is that you sleep in a tree house. Did you always want one when you were a kid, but you lived in the city, or the only adults around had sixteen thumbs? This is not quite as rustic as you might remember, but it is as close as most of us will ever get. Your tree house—on stilts about 7 feet off the ground—has a couple of bunks (bring a sleeping bag), a woodstove, a table with benches, and a filled wood bin. A communal bathhouse is nearby, you have twenty-six acres of woods to roam through and explore, and you're not far from the Appalachian Trail. You may bring your tent for "regular" camping.

When Phyllis Sorocko started this campground after retirement, she dreaded the idea of tearing up the land and trees for campsites and dumpsites and was thrilled with this compromise. Pets, on leash at all times, are welcome. Reservations are recommended. There are eight tree houses and four cabins. The charge is $32 a night for the first four people in a tree house, and $45 a night for the first four people in a cabin. Each additional person is $8.00. Tent sites are $8.00 per person per night. The campground is located on 20716 Townsend Road, Gapland 21779. Call (301) 432–5585; e-mail mapletreecamp@aol.com; or visit www.thetree housecamp.com.

Trivia

The **Washington Monument,** *in the state park of the same name, was the first monument honoring George Washington (as opposed to the first architectural monument dedicated in Washington's memory—that's in Baltimore). Built of local stone by the citizens of Boonsboro in 1827, there's a great view of the valley below after a short climb. The Appalachian Trail runs through the park. (301) 791–4767; www.dnr.state.md.us.*

The ***Washington County Museum of Fine Arts*** in Hagerstown is an outstanding museum overlooking the fifty-acre City Park Lake (home to numerous waterfowl). It was the idea and gift of Mr. and Mrs. William Henry Singer Jr., who had collected many possessions during their European travels and were looking for a beautiful place to house them. The cornerstone was laid on July 15, 1930, by Mrs. Singer's grandniece, Anna Spencer Brugh.

Trivia

The **War Correspondents Arch,** *Gathland State Park, South Mountain built in 1886 by George Alfred Townsend, famous Civil War author and war correspondent, was the first monument in the world erected to the memory of war correspondents. The park is open from 8:00 A.M. to sunset. (301) 791–4767.*

The museum was built of homewood brick with Indiana limestone trim. Two wings were added in 1949: the Memorial Gallery, in honor of Mr. Singer, who died in 1943, and the Concert Gallery, in honor of Mrs. Singer's love of music. Mrs. Singer was eighty-six when she died in Laren, Holland, in 1962.

Among the museum's collection are the works of Mr. Singer, who was a Postimpressionist painter of note. Many of his landscapes show the fishing villages, fjords, and snow-covered mountains of Norway, where the Singers lived. Also in the collection are old masters, twentieth-century sculpture and painting, and a variety of decorative arts from around the world. The emphasis, though, is on American art.

In addition to tours, the museum offers art classes (weaving, clay, acrylics, quilting, and more), lectures, films, and music recitals. A bimonthly calendar is available.

The museum, located on City Park Lake, is open Tuesday through Saturday from 10:00 A.M. to 5:00 P.M. and Sunday from 1:00 to 5:00 P.M. There is no admission fee, but a donation is requested. Call (301) 739–5727, (301) 739–5764 (TDD), or visit www.washcomuseum.org.

After you've finished the War explorations, travel between Boonsboro and Sharpsburg to find the ***Red Byrd Restaurant and Motel*** in Keedysville to disprove the statement that not only can airport restaurants be good (see the note about Nick's below), but motel restaurants can provide a tasty repast as well. Definitely try the pies, and the daily special, and even the crab cakes. Yes, crab cakes in the wilds of western Maryland. The Red Byrd is at 19409 Shepherds Town Pike (Route 34), Keedysville 21756; (301) 791–5915.

Trivia

Boonsboro is known for its Civil War museum, but those who really know it know to visit in August and September, when Boonsboro cantaloupes ripen. You can buy them from a roadside stand, particularly on Saturday and Sunday, but it's best to plan an outing and pick your own. Then you'll really enjoy the thin-skinned "Heart of Gold" variety with all its natural sweetness.

Three ***Hagerstown Post Office murals*** represent different aspects of the railway transportation of mail. The paintings were done by Frank Long of Berea, Kentucky, in 1938 as part of the Section of Fine Arts program—placing appropriate art in federal buildings. The first painting depicts mailbags being loaded onto a train. A central panel depicts a railway post office in operation, with postal clerks sorting letters on a train. The third panel, over the lockboxes, shows figures on the station platform watching an approaching train that will pick up the mail. Frank Long also painted post office murals in Louisville and Berea, Kentucky; Crawfordsville, Indiana; and Drumright, Oklahoma.

Hagerstown, the county seat of Washington County, is also the home of the *Hagers-Town Town and Country Almanack,* which has been printed since 1797. The weather forecasts generate the most interest, and people swear by them. In fact, a folk tale has it that the book called for snow on July 4, 1874, and that it did snow on that date. Research indicates that the almanac did not predict snow, and the minimum temperature for that day was said to have been in the high sixties—not too conducive to snow.

A favorite base of operations of mine is the ***Beaver Creek House Bed and Breakfast,*** just south of Hagerstown, operated by Don and Shirley Day. The house was built in 1905 and the rooms are filled with family antiques and memorabilia. The white-brick home with dark shutters is huge, yet warm and friendly, with a great wraparound porch where you can sit on a swing and watch the scenery not go anywhere. Particularly pleasing are sunrises over the Blue Ridge Mountains, should you be up that early. Guests in any of the five centrally air-conditioned guest rooms (each with private bath) may have breakfast on the screened porch, in the courtyard, or in the dining room, and share afternoon tea in the parlor.

The Beaver Creek House bed and breakfast is located at 20432 Beaver Creek Road, Hagerstown 21740. Call (301) 797–4764 or (888) 942–9966 or visit the Web site www.bbonline. com/md/beavercreek.

Trivia

The **Beaver Creek School,** *almost next door to the Beaver Creek B&B, is a century-old one-room schoolhouse and museum, with a hat shop, music shop, dressmakers' parlor, and toolshed, that's open on Sunday from 2:00 to 5:00 P.M. June through September. (301) 797–8782.*

Airplane and airport food doesn't exactly enjoy a stellar reputation, but you're sure to change your mind when you stop at ***Nick's Airport Inn*** on U.S. 11 at the airport. In fact, many people fly their private planes here just to enjoy the tasty offerings. Fresh seafood is brought in from Baltimore and the prices are more than reasonable. Even the crab cakes are worthwhile. Nick's is open weekdays from 11:00 A.M. to 2:00 P.M. and 5:00 to 10:00 P.M.; Saturday hours are 5:00 to 10:00 P.M. They're closed on Sunday. (301) 733–8560.

The ***Wilson Village Old General Store*** is a classic country store with a post office, loose "penny" candy, yard goods, and much more. You'll also see a one-room schoolhouse. The store is on Old Route 40, and it is open Monday through Saturday from 7:30 A.M. to 6:00 P.M. and Sunday from 9:00 A.M. to 5:00 P.M. The general store is at 14921 Rufus–Wilson Road, Clear Spring 21722. Call (301) 582–4718 for details.

On your way to Wilson Village from Hagerstown, you may stop by the ***Historic Wilson Bridge*** Picnic Area. It's located along Route 40 West, adjacent to Historic Wilson Bridge, which is the oldest, longest, and most graceful of the twenty-three stone-arch bridges in the county. The five-arch span was built in 1819 as an early extension of the National Pike to the Ohio Valley. The structure was erected by Pennsylvanian Silas Harry at a cost of $12,000. Its style represented a triumph for the justices of the Levy Court (until 1829, the body similar to a Board of County Commissioners), who insisted on an all-stone structure in the face of army engineers' arguments that a wooden bridge laid over stone piers would suffice.

The bridge is located about 200 feet north of the west end of the "new" bridge that crosses Conococheague Creek, 5 miles west of Hagerstown

Wilson Village Old General Store

on Route 40. This one-acre site offers picnic tables, parking, and canoe access to the Conococheague.

Of particular interest to sports fans is the ***Hagerstown Suns*** baseball team of the South Atlantic League, an affiliate of the Toronto Blue Jays. This Class-A team draws more than 160,000 fans a year. In previous years, loyalists have seen the likes of Jeff Ballard, Jim Palmer, Bill Ripken, and Craig Worthington, all of whom have gone on to be well known in the baseball world. Palmer was elected to the Baseball Hall of Fame in 1989, his first year of eligibility. For information call the Municipal Stadium at (301) 791–6266.

The Washington County tourism office has a number of interesting brochures, and the personnel there are delighted to help you. Those traveling with children, or those who are young at heart, will like visiting Crystal Grottoes caverns or going on the ghost walk at Fort Frederick at Halloween time.

Seven miles west of Hancock, near the border between Allegany and Washington Counties, is ***Sideling Hill***. Interstate 68 diverts traffic off a steep, tricky road that twists to a roundhouse curve at the top of Sideling Hill. The 4½-mile section of the road took twenty-eight months to complete and cost about $21 million. Workers blasted an incredible, breathtaking 360-foot-deep cut in the mountain, which revealed millions of years of geological history. A four-story, handicapped-accessible interpretive center, which is approachable from both sides of the highway, allows you to see all those layers and folds of multihued rocks that have been exposed by the cut and explains their history. From my perspective, the most curious thing about the area is that the rock layers are in a syncline, which would make me think it would be a valley, not a mountain, but the newer sedimentary layers are on top so a syncline it is. This is one of the best rock exposures in the northeast.

Trivia

On October 14, 1790, Col. Elie Williams and Gen. George Washington met at the springhouse in Williamsport (in Washington County) to discuss the possibility of the town being the new capital of the United States. The idea was dismissed because the Potomac River was not navigable by large ships.

If you can make only one side trip in Maryland, only a momentary detour, this is the one to make. A late-fall visit just may bring a surprise of a southern migration of ladybugs. In 1994 and 1995, there were so many millions of these critters that they obscured the windows and just about any other surface on which they could land. The numbers have decreased in the past year or two, but you'll still find an amazing number of ladybugs on their annual trek.

The interpretive center, at 3000 Sideling Hill, Hancock 21750, is open from 9:00 A.M. to 5:00 P.M. daily except New Year's Day, Easter, Thanksgiving, and Christmas. For information about Sideling Hill, call the center at (301) 678–5442.

For additional tourism information write to the Washington County C&VB, 16 Public Square, Hagerstown 21740; (301) 791–3246 or (800) 228–7829.

PLACES TO EAT IN WESTERN MARYLAND

CUMBERLAND

All Aboard Cafe,
Western Maryland Railway Station,
(301) 722–7331

Bourbon Street Cafe,
82 Baltimore Street,
(301) 722–1116

Cafe Tivoli,
30 North Centre Street,
(301) 777–2885

Geatz's Restaurant,
206 Paca Street,
(301) 724–2223

The Inn at Walnut Bottom,
120 Greene Street,
(301) 777–0003 or
(800) 286–9718,
www.iwbinfo.com

JB's Steak Cellar,
I–68, Exit 46,
(301) 722–6060,
www.edmasons.com

Mason's Barn,
I–68,
Exit 46,
(301) 722–6155,
www.edmasons.com

Oxford House Restaurant,
129 Baltimore Street,
(301) 777–7101

Uncle Tucker's Brew House,
I–68, Exit 46,
(301) 777–7005,
www.edmasons.com

When Pigs Fly,
18 Valley Street,
(301) 722–7447,
www.pigsonline.com

Flintstone
Lakeside Dining Room,
16701 Lakeview Road,
(301) 784–8444 or
(800) 724–0828,
www.rockygapresort.com

Signatures Bar & Grill,
16701 Lakeview Road,
(301) 784–8400 or
(800) 724–0828

Frostburg
Au Petit Paris,
86 East Main Street,
(301) 689–8946

Cafe 101,
101 East Main Street,
(301) 689–1243

Giuseppe's Italian
Restaurant,
11 Bowery Street,
(301) 689–2220

Princess Restaurant,
12 West Main Street,
(301) 689–1680

Grantsville
Penn Alps Restaurant,
125 Casselman Road,
(301) 895–5985

Hagerstown
Nick's Airport Inn,
18615 Terminal Drive,
(301) 733–8560.

Roccoco,
20 West Washington Street,
(301) 790–3331,
www.roccoco.com

Schmankerl Stube
Bavarian Restaurant,
58 South Potomac Street,
(301) 797–3354

Keedysville
Red Byrd Restaurant,
19409 Shepherdstown Pike,
(301) 791–5915

LaVale
Gehauf's Restaurant/
Henny's Lounge,
1268 National Highway,
(301) 729–1746

Penny's Diner,
12310 Winchester Road,
(301) 729–6700, ext. 450

McHenry
McClive's,
Route 219,
1375 Deep Creek Drive,
(301) 387–6172

Oakland
Four Seasons Dining
Room,
20160 Garrett Highway,
(301) 387–5503, ext. 2201

Trader's Cafe and
Coffeehouse,
21311 Garrett Highway,
(301) 387–9245 (cafe),
(301) 387–9246
(coffeehouse)

Places to Stay in Western Maryland

Boonsboro
Old South Mountain Inn,
6132 Old National Pike,
(301) 432–6155 or
(301) 371–5400

Cascade
Blue Bird on the Mountain,
14700 Eyler Avenue,
(301) 241–4161 or
(800) 362–9526,
www.bbonline.com/md/
bluebird

Clear Spring
Breezee Hill Farm,
12140 St. Paul Road,
(301) 842–2608

Cedar Crest Cottage,
12527 Rockdale Road,
(202) 686–5339 or
(877) 787–8425

Inn on Fairview Mountain,
Mulberry Street,
(301) 842–1277

Cumberland
Continental Motor Inn,
15001 National Highway,
(301) 689–8835 or
(800) 381–6565

Diplomat Motel,
17012 McMullen Highway,
(301) 729–2311

Holiday Inn,
100 South George Street,
(301) 724–8800 or
(877) 426–4672,
www.crownamerican
hotels.com

Inn at Walnut Bottom,
120 Greene Street,
(800) 286–9718 or
(301) 777–0003,
www.iwbinfo.com

Deer Park
Deer Park Inn
Bed and Breakfast,
65 Hotel Road,
(301) 334–2308,
www.deerparkinn.com

Flintstone
Rocky Gap Lodge and Golf Resort, 16701 Lake View Road, (800) 724–0828 or (301) 784–8400, www.rockygapresort.com

Friendsville
Deep Creek Cellars, 177 Frazee Ridge Road, (301) 746–4349

Heritage Museum and Genealogical Library, 261 Maple Street, (301) 746–4690

Frostburg
Charlie's Motel, 220 West Main Street, (301) 689–6557 or (888) 230–9053

Failinger's Hotel Gunter, 11 West Main Street, (301) 689–6511

Frostburg Inn, 147 East Main Street, (301) 689–3831

Grantsville
Casselman Valley Farm Bed and Breakfast, 215 Maple Grove Road, (301) 895–3419, www.bbonline.com/md/casselman

Elliott House Victorian Inn, 146 Casselman Road, (301) 895–4250 or (800) 272–4090, www.elliotthouse.com

Savage River Lodge, Savage River State Forest, (301) 689–3200, www.savageriverlodge.com

Walnut Ridge Bed and Breakfast, 92 Main Street, (301) 895–4248 or (888) 419–2568, www.walnutridge.net

Hagerstown
Beaver Creek House Bed and Breakfast, 20432 Beaver Creek Road, (301) 797–4764, www.bbonline.com/md/beavercreek

Dagmar Hotel, 50 Summit Avenue, (301) 733–4363 or (800) 447–6227

Bed and Breakfast at Lewrene Farm, 9738 Downsville Pike, (301) 582–1735, www.inns.com/midatl/mdhagers.htm

Sunday's Bed and Breakfast, 39 Broadway, (301) 797–4331 or (800) 221–4828, www.sundaysbnb.com

Winnie Price's Wingrove Manor Bed and Breakfast, 635 Oak Hill Avenue, (301) 733–6328 or (301) 797–7769

Keedysville
Antietam Overlook Bed and Breakfast, Porterstown Road, (301) 432–4200 or (800) 878–4241

LaVale
Braddock Best Western, 1268 National Highway, (301) 729–3300 or (800) 296–6006, www.bestwestern.com/braddockmotorinn

Oak Tree Inn, 12310 Winchester Road, (301) 729–6700

Little Orleans
Town Hill Hotel/Bed and Breakfast, Scenic Route 40, (301) 478–2794

McHenry
Lake Pointe Inn, 174 Lake Pointe Drive, (301) 387–0111 or (800) 523–5253

Panorama Motel, 921 Moser Road, (301) 387–5230 or (800) 700–9257

Point View Inn, 609 Deep Creek Drive, (301) 387–5555

Wisp Mountain Resort, 290 Marsh Hill Road, (301) 387–5581 or (800) 462–9477, www.wisp-resort.com

Mt. Savage
The Castle Bed and Breakfast, 15925 Mt. Savage Road, (301) 264–4645

Oakland
Carmel Cove Bed and Breakfast, Glendale Road, (301) 387–0067, www.carmelcoveinn.com

Haley Farm Bed and Breakfast, 16766 Garrett Highway, (301) 387–9050 or (888) 231–FARM, www.haleyfarm.com

Oak and Apple Bed and Breakfast, 208 North Second Street, (301) 334–9265, www.oakandapple.com

Red Run Lodge, 175 Red Run Road, (301) 387–2626

Streams & Dreams Retreat/ Fishing Lessons, 8214 Oakland-Sang Run Road, (301) 3–TROUT–1, www.streams-and-dreams.net

Will O' The Wisp, 20160 Garrett Highway, (301) 387–5503, ext. 2206, www.gcnet.net/wow

Wisp Resort Hotel, 209 Marsh Hill Road, (800) 462–9477 or (301) 387–4911, www.gcnet.net/wisp

SHARPSBURG
Clipp's Mill and Log Cabin, 110 East Chaplain Street, (202) 686–5339 or (877) 787–8425

Ground Squirrel Holler Bed and Breakfast, 6736 Sharpsburg Pike, (301) 432–8288

Inn at Antietam, 220 East Main Street, (301) 432–6601 or (877) 835–6011

Jacob Rohrbach Inn, 138 West Main Street, (301) 432–5079 or (877) 839–4242, www.jacobrohrbach.hypermart.net

SMITHSBURG
Blue Bear Bed and Breakfast, 13810 Frank's Run Road, (301) 824–2292 or (800) 381–2292

Quitey Quite Bed and Breakfast, 22052 Holiday Drive, (301) 824–2801

SWANTON
Savage River Inn Bed and Breakfast, 2221 Dry Run Road, (301) 245–4440, www.savageriverinn.com

OTHER ATTRACTIONS WORTH SEEING IN WESTERN MARYLAND

1810 Brew House, Cumberland, (301) 777–7005

Albert Powell Trout Hatchery, Hagerstown, (301) 791–4736

Allegany County Historical Society, Cumberland, (301) 777–8678

American Legion Military Museum, Hagerstown, (301) 733–7676

Appalachian Collection, Cumberland, (301) 784–5276

Backbone Mountain, Red House, (301) 387–4386

Barron's C&O Canal Museum, Sharpsburg, (301) 432–8726, www.fred.net/kathy/canal.html

Bell Tower Building, Cumberland, (301) 722–2820

Bietscheheof Farm, Grantsville, (301) 895–3742

Big Run State Park, Grantsville, (301) 895–5453

Boonsborough Museum of History, Boonsboro, (301) 432–6969

Broadford Recreation Area, Mountain Lake Park, (301) 334–9222

C&O Canal Boat Replica, Cumberland, (301) 729–3136

C&O Canal Museum & Visitors Center, Hancock, (301) 578–5463

C&O Canal Paw Paw Tunnel, Cumberland, (301) 722–8226

Clarysville Bridge,
Cumberland,
(301) 777–5132 or
(800) 508–4748,
www.mountainside.com

Crystal Grottoes Caverns,
Boonsboro,
(301) 432–6336

Cumberland City Hall
mural,
Cumberland,
(301) 722–2000

Cumberland Theatre,
Cumberland,
(301) 759–4990,
www.alleganyarts
council.org

Dan's Mountain State Park,
Lonaconing,
(301) 777–2139

Deep Creek Lake
State Park,
Swanton,
(301) 387–4111 or
(301) 387–5563

Emmanuel Episcopal
Church,
Cumberland,
(301) 777–3364

Engine 202 Steam
Locomotive & Caboose
Display,
Hagerstown,
(301) 739–8393

Evergreen Museum,
Mt. Savage,
(301) 264–4106

Fort Frederick State Park,
Big Pool,
(301) 842–2155

Friend Family Association
Museum & Library,
Friendsville,
(301) 746–5615

Frostburg Depot (c.1891),
Frostburg,
(301) 689–1221

Frostburg Museum,
Frostburg,
(301) 689–6853

Frostburg State
Planetarium,
Frostburg,
(301) 687–4270

Garrett State Forest,
Oakland,
(301) 334–2038

George Washington's Head-
quarters,
Cumberland,
(301) 722–2492

Greenbrier State Park,
Boonsboro,
(301) 791–4767

Green Ridge State Forest,
Flintstone,
(301) 478–3124

Hager House and Museum,
Hagerstown,
(301) 739–8393

Hagerstown City Park,
Hagerstown,
(301) 739–8577

Hagerstown Roundhouse
Museum,
Hagerstown,
(301) 739–4665 or
(301) 739–1998,
www.trainweb.com/
roundhouse/index.htm

Hagerstown Speedway,
Hagerstown,
(301) 582–0640

Herrington Manor State
Park,
Oakland,
(301) 334–9180

Heritage Museum and
Genealogical Library,
Friendsville,
(301) 746–4690

Log House Museum,
Clear Spring,
(301) 842–2553

Kennedy Farmhouse
(John Brown HQ),
Sharpsburg,
(301) 432–2666

Mansion House Arts
Center,
Hagerstown,
(301) 797–6813

Michael Cresap Museum,
Oldtown,
(301) 478–5154

Miller House,
Hagerstown,
(301) 797–8782

Muddy Creek Falls,
Oakland,
(301) 334–9180

New Germany State Park,
Grantsville,
(301) 895–5453

Potomac State Forest,
Oakland,
(301) 334–2038

Puzzley Run Folk
Life Center Inc.,
Grantsville,
(301) 895–3742

Rocky Gap Veterans Cemetery, Flintstone, (301) 777–2185

Rocky Gap State Park, Flintstone, (301) 777–2139 or (888) 432–CAMP, www.dnr.state.md.us

Rose Hill Cemetery, Hagerstown, (301) 739–3630

Savage River State Forest, Grantsville, (301) 895–5453, www.dnr.state.md.us

Simon Pearce Glassblowing, Mountain Lake Park, (301) 334–5277, www.simonpearce.com

South Mountain State Park, Boonsboro, (301) 791–4767

Stanton's Mill (1797), Grantsville, (301) 895–5211

Swallow Falls State Park, Oakland, (301) 334–9180, www.dnr.state.md.us

Washington County Planetarium, Hagerstown, (301) 766–2898 or (301) 791–4172

Washington Monument State Park, Boonsboro, (301) 432–8065

Western Maryland Station Center, Cumberland, (301) 724–4398 or (301) 777–5905

Wisp Ski and Golf Resort, McHenry, (301) 387–4911 or (800) 462–9477, www.gcnet.net/wisp

Calendar of Annual Events in Western Maryland

January

Kick and Glide Cross Country Ski Race, *Herrington Manor State Park, (301) 334-9180*

February

Cabin Fever Weekend, *Spruce Forest Artisan Village , (301) 895-3332*

Cherry Pie Hike, *Washington Monument State Park, (301) 791-4767, www.dnr.state.md.us*

March

British Brigade Garrison, *Fort Frederick State Park, (301) 842-2155, www.dnr.state.md.us*

Turning Sap into Syrup, *Herrington Manor State Park, (301) 334-9180, www.dnr.state.md.us*

April

Eighteenth-Century Market Fair and Rifle Frolic, *Fort Frederick State Park, (301) 842-2155, www.dnr.state.md.us*

Easter Egg Hunt, *Herrington Manor State Park, (301) 334-9180*

Maryland House and Garden Pilgrimage, *Statewide, (410) 821-6933, www.mhgp.org*

Maryland Archaeology Month, *Statewide, (410) 514-7661*

May

C&O Canal Fest, *Canal Place Cumberland, (301) 724-3655, www.canalplace.org*

French and Indian War Rendezvous, *Fort Frederick State Park, (301) 842-2155*

Grand Encampment, *Fort Frederick State Park, (301) 842-2155, www.dnr.state.md.us*

Halfway Park Days, *Martin L. Snook Park, Hagerstown, (301) 739-3219*

Music at Penn Alps, *Grantsville, (301) 895-3332*

Muzzleloader Shoot, *Fort Frederick State Park, (301) 842-2155, www.dnr.state.md.us*

National Pike Festival and Wagon Train, *various locations, (301) 797-8782*

New Germany State Park Open House, *Grantsville, (301) 895-5453, www.dnr.state.md.us*

Open House at Deep Creek Lake Discovery Center, *Swanton, (301) 387-4111 or (410) 387-7067, www.dnr.state.md.us*

Sharpsburg's Memorial Day Parade, *Town Square, (301) 432-8410*

Spring Fling, *Hagerstown Junior College, (301) 791-2346*

Train Meet, *Allegany Fair Grounds, (301) 777-5905*

June

George's Creek Days, *Lonaconing, (301) 463-2189*

Governor's Youth Fishing Derby Against Drugs, *Herrington Manor State Park, (301) 334-9180*

Grantsville Days, *Grantsville Park, (301) 334-1948*

Heritage Days Festival, *Cumberland, (301) 777-2787, www.alleganyartscouncil.org*

McHenry Highland Festival, *Garrett County Fairgrounds, McHenry, (301) 387-9300*

National Trails Day, *Swanton, (301) 387-5563, www.dnr.state.md.us*

Summer Splash, *Deep Creek Lake, (301) 387-4386, www.garrettchamber.com*

Calendar of Annual Events in Western Maryland (Cont'd)

Western Maryland Blues Fest, *Hagerstown, (301) 739–8577, ext.116, www.blues-fest.org*

YMCA Rocky Gap Triathlon, *Rocky Gap State Park, (301) 777–9622*

July

Accident's Fourth of July Homecoming, *Accident, (301) 746–6346*

Allegany County Fair and Agricultural Expo, *Allegany County Fairgrounds, (301) 777–0911*

Colonial Family Days, *Fort Frederick State Park,(301) 842–2155, www.dnr.state.md.us*

Deep Creek Lake Fireworks Celebration, *McHenry, (301) 387–4386, www.garrettchamber.com*

Fiddler's Contest, *Banjo Contest, Friendsville, (301) 746–8194*

Maryland Mountain Cruise, *Allegany County Fairgrounds, (814) 767–9521*

Maryland Symphony Orchestra Independence Celebration, *Sharpsburg, (301) 797–4000, www.mdsymphony.com*

Military Field Days, *Fort Frederick State Park, (301) 842–2155*

Rocky Gap Country Music Bluegrass Festival, *Allegany College, (888) ROCKYGAP*

Summerfest and Quilt Show, *Grantsville, (301) 895–3332*

August

Antique and Custom Auto Show, *Frostburg, (301) 689–5431*

Augustoberfest, *Hagerstown, (301) 739–8577, ext.116, www.augustoberfest.org*

Garrett County Agriculture Fair, *Garrett County Fairground, (301) 334–4715, ext.321*

Jonathan Hager Frontier Craft Days, *Hagerstown, (301) 739–8393*

Maryland State Chili Championship, *Ali Ghan Shrine picnic grounds, (301) 722–5970*

Mountain Bike Camp 'n' Ride, *Green Ridge State Forest, (301) 478–3124, www.dnr.state.md.us*

September

A Taste of Fall Fest, *Allegany County Fairgrounds, (301) 729–3321*

Apple Butter Boil, *Oakland, (301) 334–9180*

Battle of South Mountain, *Boonsboro, (301) 241–4707*

Boonesborough Days, *Shafer Park, (301) 432–5889*

Canal Apple Festival, *Hancock, (301) 678–6555*

Cumberland Wine and Music Festival, *Rocky Gap State Park, (301) 722–1760, www.cumberlandwinefest.com*

Governor's Invitational Firelock Match, *Fort Frederick State Park, (301) 842–2155*

Muskets in Maryland, *Fort Frederick State Park, (301) 842–2155, www.dnr.state.md.us*

Outdoor Concert in the Park, *Grantsville, (301) 895–3332*

Rails-With-Trails Bike Train, *Cumberland, (800) TRAIN–50*

Sharpsburg Heritage Festival, *Sharpsburg, (800) 228–STAY*

Calendar of Annual Events in Western Maryland (Cont'd)

South Mountain Recreation Area Living History, *Burkittsville, (301) 791–4767, www.dnr.state.md.us*

Western Maryland Brew Fest, *Deep Creek Lake, (301) 387–2182, www.deepcreekbrewing.com*

Western Maryland Rail Trail Exposition, *Big Pool/Hancock, (301) 842–2155, www.dnr.state.md.us*

Western Maryland Street Rod Round–Up, *Allegany County Fairgrounds, (301) 777–3456*

Woodmont Lodge Open House, *Hancock, (301) 842–2155, www.dnr.state.md.us*

October

Alsatia Mummers' Parade, *Hagerstown, (301) 733–0033*

Autumn Glory Festival, *Oakland, (301) 387–4386, www.garrettchamber.com*

Fall Color Hayride, *Herrington Manor State Park, (301) 334–9180, www.dnr.state.md.us*

Ghost Walk, *Fort Frederick State Park, (301) 842–2155, www.dnr.state.md.us*

Greater Gortner Airport Fly-in, *Oakland, (301) 334–3541*

Hagerstown American Indian Pow-Wow Festival, *Hagerstown, (800) 228–STAY or (252) 257–5383*

Maryland Official State Banjo Contest, *Oakland, (301) 387–4386*

Maryland Official State Fiddle Contest, *Oakland, (301) 387–4386, www.garrettchamber.com*

Maryland Railfest, *Western Maryland Station, (800) TRAIN–50*

November

Muzzleloader Shoot, *Fort Frederick State Park, (301) 842–2155, www.dnr.state.md.us*

Venice Christmas Arts and Craft Shows, *Hagerstown, (301) 739–6860*

Victorian Christmas at History House, *Cumberland, (301) 777–8678*

December

Antietam National Battlefield Memorial Illumination, *Sharpsburg, (301) 733–7373*

Christmas in the Village, *Grantsville, (301) 895–3332*

Christmas Faire, *Hagerstown, (301) 791–2346*

Christmas Model Train Open House, *Allegany Fairgrounds, (301) 777–5905*

Central Maryland

Perhaps nowhere in the state is there more diversity than in the area referred to as central Maryland. In the rolling foothills and picturesque landscapes of this region are horse farms and vineyards, the commercial center of Baltimore City, huge stone farmhouses and old mills, busy waterways surrounding the Chesapeake Bay and its tributaries, some of the oldest towns in the country, and modern, vibrant cities. This core of five counties and two major cities encompasses it all.

Sixteen million vehicles use the ***William Preston Lane Jr. Bridge*** (Chesapeake Bay Bridge) every year. Only 50,000 people walk across it, though, on Chesapeake Bay Bridge Walk Day. Once Maryland was a leading contender in the number of "kissing" or covered bridges; now there are only a few. See also Frederick and Prince George's Counties in the Greater Washington section for more bridges.

Countless people stop by Annapolis to see its waterfront, Ego Alley (where the expensive boats parade), and the United States Naval Academy. They watch the sailboats in the harbor—even in the winter, when there is a Frostbite series of sailboat races—or the Naval Academy's noon meal formation, when the brigade of midshipmen assembles in front of Bancroft Hall for inspection. I chatted with Robert F. Sumrall, who re-creates scale models of the ships that have plied the bay.

Whenever anyone talks about Chesapeake Bay, blue crabs and oysters are sure to be discussed. I include an old inn that is relatively new, and a scenic waterside eatery for sightseeing while you dine.

Trivia

Edwin Booth's first theatrical performance was in the original Harford County Courthouse.

Trying to pick a starting point is tough, for several interstates lead into and out of this area of five counties and Baltimore City, including I–95 going north to Philadelphia and New York and south to Washington, D.C.; I–83 going north into Pennsylvania; I–70 going into the western part of the state; and I–97 heading south and then east into Annapolis.

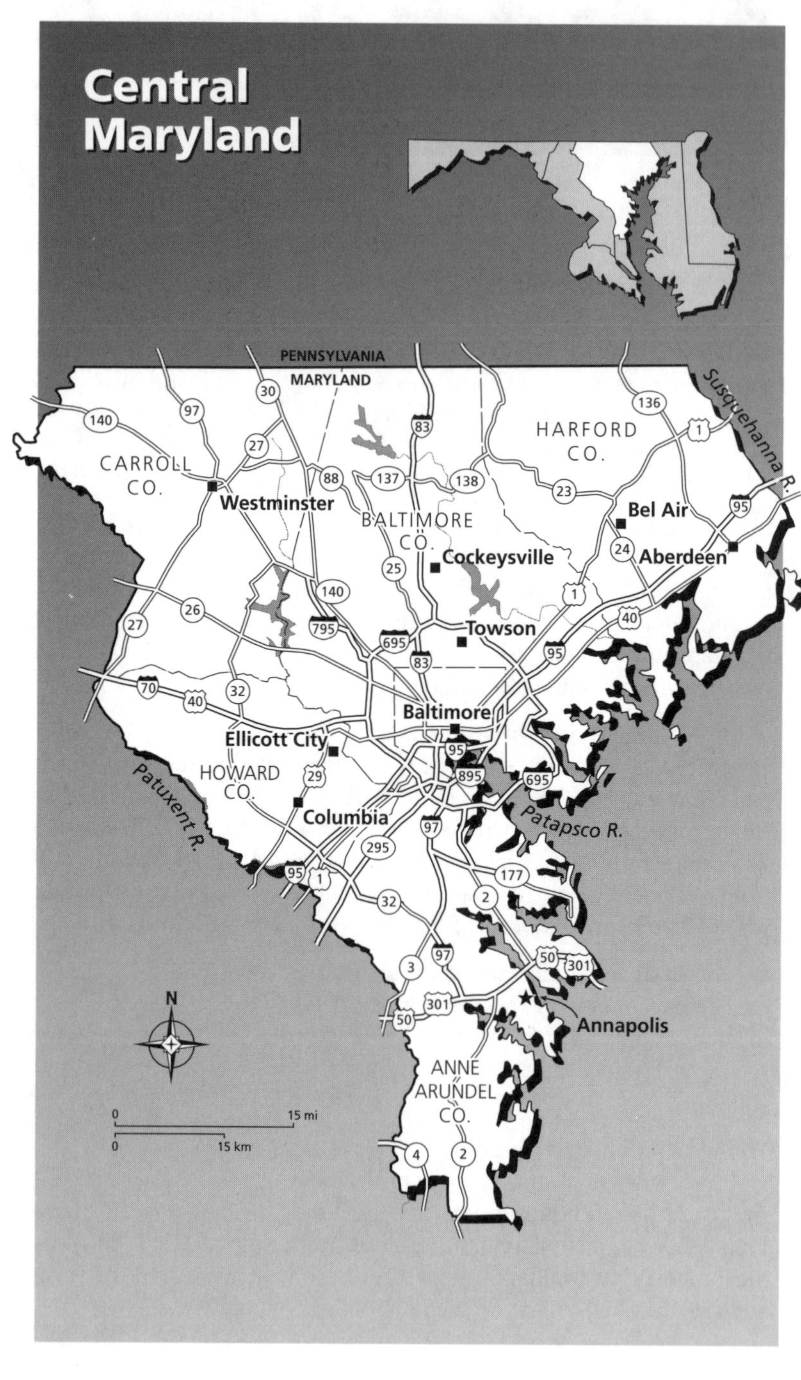
Central Maryland
PENNSYLVANIA
MARYLAND
CARROLL CO.
Westminster
BALTIMORE CO.
HARFORD CO.
Bel Air
Aberdeen
Cockeysville
Towson
Baltimore
Ellicott City
HOWARD CO.
Columbia
Patuxent R.
Patapsco R.
Susquehanna R.
Annapolis
ANNE ARUNDEL CO.
N
0
15 mi
0
15 km

Judy's Favorite Attractions in Central Maryland

Cider Mill Farm

Havre de Grace Decoy Museum

Oriole Park at Camden Yards tour

U.S. Naval Academy

Anne Arundel County

Perhaps the best place to start is at BWI, ***Baltimore-Washington International Airport,*** where millions of people pass through either going to or coming home from some place or picking up a passenger. It may be a scandalous thought, but you might actually want to arrive early or even stay a few minutes, for BWI has become a destination in itself. There's a beautiful observation gallery with information about flying and pieces of airplanes on display. The $6.4 million gallery has cutaway airplane sections (great to view if you or someone in your party has never flown or seen the workings of a plane), an interactive weather station (so you can see what a cold front is and how it affects weather, or check for the temperature in your destination city), and a 147-foot-wide observation window to watch airplanes refueling, taxiing, taking off, and landing. Plunk yourself in front of a computer screen, punch in your flight number, and the screen displays just where the plane is, how high, how fast it's flying, and when it's expected to land. Should you be an aviation history buff (or even just one or the other), then the story of Maryland aviation should satisfy your curiosity. A children's play area is in the lower of the two levels and is open twenty-four hours a day. The upper level with the gift shop, cafe, and interactive displays is open from 9:00 A.M. to 9:00 P.M. There is no admission charge.

Trivia

Across the Severn River from the Naval Academy in Annapolis is a memorial to Marylanders who served in World War II. Dedicated on July 23, 1998, the $2.7 million memorial is off Route 450, just below the Gov. Ritchie Overlook, with a commanding view of the Severn River, the Naval Academy, and Annapolis. A four-sided, open-air amphitheater is surrounded by a 100-foot-diameter ring of forty-eight 9-foot-tall gray granite slabs etched with the names of the 6,454 Marylanders killed during the war.

About fifty shops fill about 56,000 square feet of retail space throughout the airport. Some of the boutiques are a Smithsonian Shop, Starbucks, ASU Bags, Just Plane Crabs, 24-Hour Flower, Altitunes, the Museum Company, Tie Rack, Hudson News, the Body Shop, and more than a dozen eateries. BWI was one of the first major East Coast airports to establish a Web site for services, general information, and regional tourism information, which offers links to airline and other travel-service Web sites. The Web site, which has a terminal location map and travel tips is www.bwiairport.com.

A shuttle bus connects the airport to the nearby Amtrak station, and limousine (van and bus) service provides door-to-door transportation to and from the airport. Walking tours of the airport are provided through the marketing office for groups of twelve to thirty people, with a minimum age of nine. Usually groups include schoolchildren or civic organizations, VIP groups, or special-interest groups, such as firefighters or engineers, who receive a "behind-the-scenes" tour. Individuals who want an airport tour may call to see if a group tour is scheduled that they could join. The normal tour includes visits to and explanations of the baggage claim area, airline ticket counters, restaurants, gift shops, gate departure areas, the National Weather Service, and all the major concourses. Call at least a week to ten days ahead for group tours. Call (301) 261–1000 from the Washington, D.C., area or (410) 859–7026 from elsewhere.

BWI is home to the largest USO, for as many as a quarter-million military personnel and family members can use the facility annually. Why so many? Because about three fourths of the U.S. military personnel being sent to Europe or the Middle East travel through BWI. The $1.1-million, 5,000-square-foot USO International Gateway Center has a nursery, television lounge, sleeping room, computer room, and free coffee. The lounge is located in the lower level, near baggage claim number ten, and it's open from 9:00 A.M. to 10:00 P.M. daily.

About 3 miles from the airport is an incredible restaurant, one that receives my vote for the best crab cake in the entire state of Maryland! Others must agree because the ***G&M*** restaurant goes through about 500 pounds of crab meat a day! These crab cakes are about 8 ounces of backfin crab meat with almost no filler. That's large enough to take home half of it for another meal, yet you can order a crab cake platter, which has just about everything from soup to nuts, including two crab

America's First Radar

Among the items receiving grants from the Maryland Commission for Celebration 2000 for historic preservation is America's first radar, SCR-270. The SCR (Signal Corps Radar) 270 is considered to be the first operational radar in the United States, and was manufactured in Baltimore between 1941 and 1943. It allowed scientists to bounce the first radio signals off the moon. The only extant reconstructed SCR-270 radar is at the Historical Electronics Museum in Linthicum, and the $10,000 award will go toward restoring the historically significant artifact.

cakes. I've even taken a cooler full of them to Los Angeles to satisfy those ex-East Coast-pats living on the Left Coast. G&M has three eating areas, one with tablecloths, one in the bar where smoking is allowed, and one in the carryout area. A crab cake sandwich with a side of fries and cole slaw or potato salad is a little more than $10 as of this writing. G&M is open from 11:00 A.M. to 11:00 P.M. Monday through Saturday and until 10:30 P.M. on Sunday. 804 North Hammonds Ferry Road, Linthicum 21090; (410) 636–1777.

When airport construction was started on May 4, 1947, the airport site was known as Friendship, and many old homes and farms on the 3,200-acre tract were demolished. Only Rezin Howard Hammond's home was left standing, where it remains today at the edge of the airport. Originally known as Cedar Farm because of the cedar trees on the property, it was built in 1820 from bricks made of clay dug on the farm. It is now the ***Benson-Hammond House*** and is used by the Anne Arundel County Historical Society, whose purpose is to encourage appreciation among the general public of "the smaller centers of culture where so much of our heritage lies hidden." Within the house are a collection of dolls, a display of tokens known as picker checks (made of aluminum, fiberboard, and brass stamped into various shapes and used as currency by farmers, each of whom had his own set of checks with his initials), and a miniature replica of Angel's Store in Pasadena. The museum is open for tours on special occasions and Thursday through Saturday from 11:00 A.M. to 3:00 P.M. The suggested donation is $2.00 a person. The Browse and Buy Shoppe is also located at the house; it is open for the same Thursday hours and other times as volunteers are available.

Call the Benson-Hammond House, Aviation Boulevard and Andover Road, Linthicum 21090, at (410) 768–9518 for tours and additional information.

A second Browse and Buy Shoppe is located at Jones Station, at the corner of Old Annapolis and Jones Station Roads. This late nineteenth-century building was one of the "step-down transformer" power stations for one of the two railroads serving Annapolis. Hours at the Browse and Buy Shoppe are Tuesday through Saturday, 10:00 A.M. to 3:00 P.M.; call (410) 544–3370.

Should you be wandering this way on a Sunday afternoon and you'd like to wander about as far off the beaten path as you're likely to get in Anne Arundel County, head east on Route 100 to ***Hancock's Resolution*** near the end of Bayside Beach Road and the community of Bayside Beach.

Formerly a farm that encompassed more than 400 acres, this circa 1785 farmhouse and outbuildings have been restored to their nineteenth-century appearance. Because the house never had indoor plumbing or electricity, restoration was a fairly simple matter and the work was completed within a year. John Henry "Harry" Hancock was the last Hancock to live in the house, and was almost ninety when he died in 1962. His main concession to his advancing years was an oil heater when he could no longer chop wood for the fireplace. There's no definitive answer regarding the meaning of "Resolution," but the assumption is there had been some family disagreements about the property ownership and when it was finally resolved, the name was given.

Included in the $250,000 restoration of the ironstone (a local sandstone) farmhouse and property are plantings of typical crops including heirloom yellow cucumbers (little round vegetables), heirloom beans, Thomas Jefferson's red hibiscus, yellow tomatoes, flax, hops, the coralberry, strawberries, and the Anne Arundel County melon. Fruit orchards also may be planted.

Harry Hancock left no heirs, so the Annapolis Foundation acquired the property, and the county signed a twenty-five-year lease in 1989. James Morrison, president of the Friends of Hancock's Resolution, became interested in the restoration project in the late 1990s, and it has been through his efforts and the work of many other volunteers that you will be able to take a peek at life long ago. That's probably Morrison greeting you in his Sunday-go-to-meeting clothing when you visit.

Hancock's Resolution is open on Sunday from 1:00 to 4:00 P.M. April through October. Take Route 100 east to a left at Magothy Bridge Road. Turn right at Fort Smallwood Road, and then right on Bayside Beach Road for about 2½ miles. The address is Bayside Beach Road, Pasadena 21122. For more information, call (410) 255–4048.

Take Route 100 west to I–97 south, tool into historic Annapolis, and prepare yourself for a treat. Annapolis is full of authentic colonial architecture; Colonial Williamsburg in Virginia had to re-create what is already here. Annapolis is called a "museum without walls" because of the dozens of eighteenth-century buildings in the city, but Annapolitans are quick to point out that it is a living museum, not an artificial one. Annapolis is Old-World charm, the United States Naval Academy, sailboats and powerboats by the hundreds (212,435 boats were registered in Maryland in 1999), antiques shops, taverns, and, most of all, narrow, winding, hilly, and brick-paved streets that invite walking and exploring.

The ***Banneker-Douglass Museum*** is installed in a handsome Victorian-Gothic structure that was the Mount Moriah African Methodist Episcopal Church, the first African Methodist Episcopal Church of Annapolis, serving the community from 1874 until 1971. A storm damaged the building in 1897, so it was rebuilt with its present Gothic-Revival facade, including the splendid stained-glass rose window. The building is listed with the National Register of Historic Places, as a National Historic District, and in the National Register of Historic Districts.

The museum is named for Benjamin Banneker (mathematician, scientist, astronomer, and surveyor) and Frederick Douglass (writer, journalist, civil libertarian, abolitionist, and U.S. minister and consul general to Haiti), both of whom were born and lived in Maryland. Banneker was appointed to serve on a commission that surveyed and laid out the capital. He had such a phenomenal memory that he produced, in detail, Pierre L'Enfant's plans for the District of Columbia when L'Enfant left—with the plans—before the job was finished. There are rotating displays within the Hall of National Greatness, the Gallery of Black Maritime History, the Herbert M. Frisby Hall (Frisby was a Baltimore science educator, war correspondent for African-American newspapers, and explorer who made twenty-one trips to the Arctic region and was the second black explorer to reach the North Pole), and the reference library. The museum features African-American arts and crafts, lectures, and films, all to encourage a better understanding of the contributions of African-Americans to Maryland and the United States. Today's legacy is represented by such prominent African-American

Dem Bones, Dem Bones

In July 1989, some fifteen small, brittle bones, carefully wrapped in yellowed paper, were gently placed in a golden urn and laid to rest in a shady cemetery plot near St. Mary's Church in Annapolis. In mid-1987, the Reverend John Murray of St. Mary's had found these remains of St. Justin, who was beheaded at the age of twenty-six in the second century A.D. *According to Murray, it is not unusual for churches in Europe to have special tombs containing the relics of saints or martyrs, but few churches in the United States can claim such items because the country is so young. St. Justin's remains arrived in Baltimore in 1873 so the Reverend Joseph Wissel could protect them while Italy was in the middle of a political upheaval. Reverend Wissel and those who followed him displayed them prominently, but during the 1960s the church was renovated and the remains were placed in a box in a church safe. Call (410) 263–2396 for additional information.*

artists as Josephine Gross, Gerald Hawkes, Laurence Hurst, and Hughie Lee-Smith, whose works adorn the walls of the gallery.

The Banneker-Douglass Museum is located at 84 Franklin Street, Annapolis 21401. Hours are Tuesday through Friday 10:00 A.M. to 3:00 P.M., and Saturday noon to 4:00 P.M. There is no admission charge. Call (410) 974–2893.

There are many interesting things to see at the ***U.S. Naval Academy***. Start with a visit to the ***Armel-Leftwich Visitors Center*** (just inside and to the right of Gate 1 off King George Street), where you'll see a movie (*To Lead and To Serve*) and displays about life as a midshipman. You can then explore on your own or take a seventy-minute guided tour. The hours of operation vary according to the day and the season, but the noon tour departs at 11:45 to see the Noon Meal Formation. The center is open from 9:00 A.M. to 5:00 P.M. March through November, and 9:00 A.M. to 4:00 P.M. the rest of the year. It is closed Thanksgiving, Christmas, and New Year's Day. Call (410) 263–6933 or log on to www.usnavyonline.com for more information.

A short walk from the visitors center, along the seawall, is the foremast of the USS *Maine,* still misshapen from the mysterious explosion in Havana Harbor on February 15, 1898. The mast was recovered on October 6, 1910, and erected along the Academy Seawall at Trident Point on May 5, 1913.

At the site of the Noon Meal Formation is the Tecumseh Statue (in front of Bancroft Hall), a bronze replica of the wooden figurehead that graced the USS *Delaware*. It is frequently decorated by midshipmen as a symbol of victory and passed exams. Bancroft Hall Dormitory, 52 King George Street, Annapolis 21402, houses the *entire* 4,000-member brigade and (depending on who you consult) is either *the* largest dormitory in

Maynard-Burgess House

In May 2000, the Maryland Commission for Celebration 2000 awarded several "Save Maryland's Treasures" grants for historic preservation. One of the properties that received such a grant, to the tune of $22,500, is the Maynard-Burgess House in the historic district of Annapolis. This was the home of two successive African-American families from 1847 to 1900, and the structure shows the lives of free blacks in the 1800s. The funds will go toward the rehabilitation of the interior of the Maynard-Burgess House as a museum.

the world, or only one of the largest. Take a peek in the building, check out one of the model rooms, and delight in the murals and artworks that decorate the public areas.

One of the most fascinating exhibits in Annapolis is the display of model ships at the ***U.S. Naval Academy Museum*** on the ground floor of Preble Hall, housed in the Class of 1951 Gallery. My mind is totally boggled every time I visit this exhibit. In the collection are ship models from about the time the pilgrims landed in America to just after the War of 1812. The big (100-gun) ships took one person from four to six years to build, plus another year for the rigging. More likely than one person doing all the work, there would have been a master model maker supervising a crew of workers or apprentices, thus speeding up the process. You'll also want to see Bone Ships, which were crafted by prisoners of war on frigates from meat bones. They are intricate and accurate portrayals of the fighting ships of the times.

If you visit during the week, you may see Robert F. Sumrall, curator in charge of repairing and maintaining the fleet of 225 little ships, and others working on the collection. Due to age, heat, vibrations, and other forces of nature, the ships need periodic attention and repairs. Although patience is a virtue, enjoying what you do is even more important in this field.

Ship of State

Some people are just luckier than others, and Robert F. Sumrall has to be among the luckiest of the lucky, for his occupation is playing with model ships. Sumrall is the curator charged with repairing and maintaining the U.S. Naval Academy's fleet of 225 little ships, some of them more than 300 years old. Sumrall built his first model when he was six and went on to be a naval architect, author, historian, model builder, and one of the most highly regarded authorities on ship models and model construction. Sumrall has built models of significant and famous Maryland ships, including the Dolphin, *the* Pride of Baltimore, *the* J. T. Leonard *(a unique oyster dredger), and the skipjack* Minnie V. *Most of the work Sumrall does for the academy museum is in the realm of repair, maintenance, and restoration. He also has done an interpretive model of the* Arizona *wreck for the National Park Service memorial at Pearl Harbor, and he is doing another of the Japanese flagship* Akagi. *Private collections in Coronado, Virginia Beach, New York, and a gallery in Old Town Alexandria, hold his battleship* Wisconsin *and several destroyers.*

The main floor of the museum houses your typical 30,000-item collection of naval history, including class rings of all the graduating classes of the academy, silverware from naval vessels, flags, uniforms, medals, weapons, navigational instruments, documents, and the stories of several naval heros, including John Paul Jones. The Naval Academy Museum provides a valuable and convenient reference source for studying naval history. The good news here is the start of a massive fund-raising drive to modernize the exhibits and the exhibit area.

The museum, in Preble Hall, 118 Maryland Avenue, Annapolis 21402, is open Monday through Saturday from 9:00 A.M. to 5:00 P.M., and Sunday from 11:00 A.M. to 5:00 P.M. It is closed on Thanksgiving, Christmas, and New Year's Day. There is no admission charge. Call (410) 293–2108 or log on to www.nadn.navy. mil/museum for details.

Also on the ground floor is the ***U.S. Naval Institute and Bookstore*** for books and other naval-related items. The institute has 100,000 members and advances scientific and literary knowledge of the sea services. It publishes *Proceedings* and *Naval History* magazines, more than 400 books, and has a collection of more than 450,000 historic photographs. The store, at 118 Maryland Avenue, is open Monday through Saturday from 9:00 A.M. to 5:00 P.M., and Sunday from 11:00 A.M. to 5:00 P.M. (410) 268–6110 or (800) 233–8764.

The basement of the ***Naval Academy chapel*** is one of those "gee, I didn't know that" spots that I love to take visitors to, because that's where the crypt of Revolutionary War hero John Paul Jones is located. A little history and some personal effects complete this final resting place.

Upstairs the chapel is pretty awesome as well, with Tiffany studio–

Long Live the King

*One of my favorite hangouts over the years has been the **King of France Tavern** in the cellar of the Maryland Inn. Located on Church Circle, the inn was constructed by Thomas Hyde in 1772 and has operated continuously as an inn since the late eighteenth century. This triangular piece of land, called the "drummer's lot," was where the town drummer, or crier, told of the day's news in the early eighteenth century. For me, two centuries later, the King of France Tavern tells the news of today's best entertainers. Ethel Ennis, Charlie Byrd, Tim Eyermann, and others have filled its brick-walled room with delightful sounds and good times. The tavern is at 16 Church Circle, Annapolis 21401. Call (410) 263–2641 or (800) 847–8882.*

Aris T. Allen

As you drive around Annapolis, you may notice Aris T. Allen Boulevard (Route 665). Allen was president of his class at Howard University while in medical school there, becoming a physician and flight surgeon during the Korean conflict in the early 1950s. He served in the Maryland House of Delegates and then the state Senate, and was the first African-American chair of the state republican party. As a delegate to the republican national convention he served as the secretary of the convention, the person who calls the roll of states for voting. He also ran for lieutenant governor with former U.S. Senator J. Glenn Beall Jr. You can find a statue to Allen near the intersection of Forest Drive, Chinquapin Round Road, and Aris T. Allen Boulevard in Annapolis.

designed stained-glass windows behind the altar and elsewhere. Built on the highest point of ground at the academy (or "in the Yard"), the chapel cornerstone was laid in 1904 by Admiral Dewey. When you see television coverage of newly married couples leaving a chapel under raised swords, this is the chapel they're exiting. Call the United States Naval Academy Grounds at (410) 263–6933 or log on to www.usnavyonline.com for more information.

The skipjack is the symbol of the Chesapeake Bay waterman. These boats were developed in the 1890s, and they are the last surviving commercial sailing fleet in the United States. The oyster-dredging boats have become an endangered species, as their number has dwindled from roughly 1,500 a century ago to about eighty on the water in 1958. There are only three dozen in working condition now.

While at Annapolis Dock, stop by to see the ***Alex Haley statue,*** dedicated in December 1999. The life-size statue stands near the spot where the author's ancestor Kunte Kinte was brought ashore from a slave ship. Ed Dwight, a former astronaut, was the sculptor. You may also have seen his *Jazz: An American Art Form* series of seventy bronzes depicting famous jazz musicians; he is also responsible for creating the Black Patriots Memorial in Washington, D.C.

Another new statue, this one of former Maryland state comptroller ***Louis L. Goldstein,*** was installed between the Goldstein Treasury Building and the Income Tax Building in Annapolis in mid-2000. Goldstein died in 1998 at the age of eighty-five after six decades of public service, and was well-known for his "God bless y'all real good." Sculptor Jay Hall Carpenter, chosen from nearly two dozen artists who

Maritime Republic of Eastport

Across Spa Creek from downtown Annapolis is Eastport, originally home to the close-knit community of construction workers who built the Naval Academy. Lately it has become much more gentrified, but as of a singular moment in January 1998, the cohesion became palpable again. For that's when the Annapolis town fathers closed the Spa Creek bridge for three weeks for much needed repairs. That didn't totally isolate the residents of Eastport; they could get back and forth through a slightly more circuitous route, but they were concerned that "outsiders" would not take the effort to frequent the local businesses. A group of Eastporters decided it was time to promote their town, so they staged a mock secession from Annapolis and renamed their community the Maritime Republic of Eastport (a.k.a. MRE). They created T-shirts and sponsored a ½-mile race, and other festivities to make sure people remembered to find their way over there. Imagine their pleasure when business actually increased during the three-week period! Since then, they've been celebrating and reaffirming the anniversary of their secession, continuing the ½-mile race (started by a cannon and rifle shots), a parade, a dog show, and more. Look for future MRE festivities in late January.

submitted proposals, is best known for his twenty-two years at the Washington National Cathedral. Carpenter never met Goldstein, but he studied photographs and videos to capture the comptroller's movements, expressions, and gestures.

Annapolis has always been a vital area for commerce and trade, particularly when it comes to importing and exporting goods. But it played one of its most unusual commercial roles in 1862, when it became the major depot in the East for holding exchanged prisoners of war. Prisoners were held here until their back pay (earned during their incarceration) could be given to them. At first they were camped at St. John's College, but the eight small, wooden barracks were inadequate for groups as large as 6,000 men at one time. Two hundred fifty acres of farmland outside Annapolis were rented from Charles S. and Ann Rebecca Welch for $125 per month, and barracks and other buildings were constructed there. The forty-four barracks and all other buildings were sold at auction some time after 1865, when all the prisoners had been released. All that remains of this mustering place for Union prisoners, called Camp Parole, is the name of the town, Parole, on the western side of Annapolis.

Whether by land or sea, when you're near Annapolis you may as well take a drive over to ***Cantler's,*** noted for Jimmie Cantler, hospitality, crabs all year, and delicious food since the 1970s. The crab-cake and soft-shell crab sandwiches are superb. Cantler's at 458 Forest Beach Road, Annapolis 21401, can also be reached from the water. In either case, call (410) 757–1311 for directions.

An unofficial declaration of spring's arrival is the annual ***Chesapeake Bay Bridge Walk Day***, held on the first Sunday in May. The walk was first held in 1975 after a Towson, Maryland, scout leader who noticed that one span was closed for construction suggested one span could be closed for a daylong walk. An estimated 50,000 pedestrians, as well as people in wheelchairs and on crutches, cross the eastbound lanes of the bridge, and the only automobiles and trucks permitted are official vehicles and media trucks. Jogging, running, skateboarding, biking, and pets (except Seeing Eye dogs) are prohibited; an early morning race has been established for those who want to speed across the bridge instead of spending about ninety minutes walking and investigating various expansion joints, girder construction, architectural design, and engineering and assembly facets. Pedestrians normally are not allowed on the 4$^1/_3$-mile structure connecting the Annapolis area to the large spit of land known as the Eastern Shore. Blue waters lap innocuously about 185 feet below the twin spans of the bridge, also known as the William Preston Lane Jr. Memorial Bridge. Parking lots in Annapolis, at Anne Arundel Community College, and also on the Eastern Shore start filling up at 8:00 A.M. Buses start taking walkers to the east side at 9:00 A.M. There is no charge for parking, but there is a $1.00 charge for the bus. Call (410) 228–8405 or (877) BAYSPAN or visit www.mdta.state.md.us for information.

Capt. Salem Avery was a waterman of the 1860s, and to the delight of the members of the Shady Side Rural Heritage Society, his home on the banks of the West River became available to them to use as a museum. The ***Captain Salem Avery House*** opened its doors in 1989 as a museum to "protect, document, and illustrate the history and traditions" of Shady Side. The society members are particularly pleased that they were able to obtain some of the original Avery furniture from the owners of the house. The Captain Salem Avery House is located at 1418 East West Shady Side Road, Shady Side 20764. The house is open by appointment and on Sunday from 1:00 to 4:00 P.M., except during January and February, on Easter Sunday, and around Christmas. There is no admission fee. Call (410) 867–4486 for additional information.

For additional information about Anne Arundel County, write to the Annapolis and Anne Arundel County Conference and Visitors Bureau, 26 West Street, Annapolis 21401. Call (410) 280–0445 or log on to www.visit-annapolis.org.

Baltimore City

Now, zip on back to I–97 and head north to Baltimore. It's a slight left zig (off a right-hand ramp) to the beltway (I–695) to the west, and then a hop north onto the Baltimore–Washington Parkway (which becomes Russell Street), and there you are.

As you enter, on your left you'll see the Lee Electrical building, at 600 West Hamburg Street, near Camden Yards, and on it a Wyland whale painting, which Mayor Kurt L. Schmoke dedicated in 1993. The mural is of extinct Atlantic gray whales, and it's 260 feet long by 20 feet high. Wyland was born in 1956 in Detroit, and it's said he created his first painting, of dinosaurs, at the age of four. He first saw a whale a decade later, and began painting whales and dolphins in 1972. Wyland painted his first whale mural in 1981 in Laguna Beach, California.

Almost across the street is the Ravens football stadium, and not far away is ***Oriole Park at Camden Yards,*** where the Baltimore Orioles baseball team nests for home games. Sell-out games are commonplace, even if the O's aren't doing that well, and scalpers have been known to ask, and get, ten times face value for tickets, just so one can get into the park. The O's management has tried to solve that problem by having a scalp-free zone where people who have tickets to sell meet with people who want to buy tickets, with the stipulation that the sellers can't charge more than face value. The scalp-free zone is wonderful, and other teams should adopt this practice.

Arrive at the park early; in fact, make a reservation to take the approximately ninety-minute tour of the stadium. They're given weekday mornings except when there's a day game or other day event scheduled. As you take the tour, you'll hear that the warehouse, which houses the Orioles offices, souvenir shop, reception areas, and Camden Club, is the longest brick building east of the Mississippi (it's 51 feet wide). The tour guide may also tell you that the warehouse is longer than the Empire State Building is tall. The validity of that statement depends on whether you count antennas. At the very least, this is a long building. Should your guide not tell you, ask about the unbreakable windows and how many home-run balls have hit the building on the fly (to give you a clue, none in regulation play). As you walk around the stadium, you'll see the town homes or

Trivia

Port Discovery, which opened in Baltimore in December 1998, is one of the largest children's museums in the country. Aimed toward six- to twelve-year-olds, there's still plenty to keep the young-at-heart occupied. Port Discovery, Baltimore; (410) 727–8120.

Trivia

The Basilica of the Assumption in Baltimore was the first Roman Catholic cathedral built in the United States. It was founded in 1821, and Mass is still celebrated there daily.

row houses across the street that were part of an urban revitalization project. It's said they went for $1.00 a piece and were overpriced. The stipulation, of course, was the buyer had to renovate and was obligated to a residency requirement. You'll also see a party room, a sky suite, the press room, some of the 25 miles (length depending on your tour guide) of beer pipe for draft brews (so they don't have to schlep kegs around the stadium, clean up, have refrigeration for the kegs at each refreshment stand, and so on). The tour, as of 2000, costs $5.00 and is well worth it. 333 Camden Street, Baltimore 21201; (410) 685–9800.

Okay, so you've heard about the fantastic Walters Gallery and the incredible Baltimore Museum of Art. You've seen pictures of Harborplace, and you know you're going to go there for some eats and souvenir shopping. Good. There are a few other things you should see.

A spectacular way to start your Baltimore visit is at the ***Top of the World observation deck and museum***. On a clear day you will see an eye-opening, five-sided panoramic view of the city, its harbor, and beyond from the twenty-seventh floor of the tallest pentagonal building in the country, designed by I. M. Pei. Exhibits, films, and audiovisual material will familiarize you with Baltimore's past, present, and future. The World Trade Center is at 401 East Pratt Street, Baltimore 21202. Hours are Monday through Saturday from 10:00 A.M. to 5:00 P.M., and Sunday from noon to 5:00 P.M.; call about extended summer hours.

Fifteen Minutes of Warhol

The Baltimore Museum of Art has the second largest collection of Andy Warhol's work on permanent display, located in the $10 million wing that opened in October 1994. Included in the display are several pieces that had never been on permanent public exhibit, including Brillo Box, Del Monte Box, *and gold* Jackie. *The New Wing for Modern Art has an unusual design allowing the display of the large Warhol works. Instead of doors in the middle of each exhibit room, the "doors" are located at the corners, normally dead areas in an exhibit space. This also allows visitors a chance to look into the other three connecting galleries. An energy-saving cooling system creates big sheets of ice overnight when energy costs are low, which then are dropped into an underground pool during the day to sustain the seventy-degree temperature desired in the building.*

Trivia

The PSINet stadium, home to the NFL Baltimore Ravens, received its theatrical debut in 2000 as Nextel Stadium, the home field of the Washington Sentinels, in the movie The Replacements. *Those who've seen the film are sure to recognize the distinctive purple seating.*

Admission for adults is $3.00; for children fifteen and under and seniors, $2.00. (Children are admitted free if they're in strollers or carriages; there's a charge if they're walking.) Call (410) 837–8439 or visit www.bop.org.

Much of Baltimore revolves around the Inner Harbor, where the World Trade Center is. Here you'll find a carousel, the festival marketplace with its eateries and boutiques, paddle or pedal boats, the Science Center, the aquarium, and a submarine, the ***USS* Torsk.** The 311-foot black submarine (with a shark's-tooth grin at one end) sits by the aquarium. Under the command of Bafford E. Lewellen, the sub sank two small Japanese ships on August 14, 1945. The Japanese surrendered the next day, so the *Torsk* sank the last ships of World War II. Each year some 100,000 people tour the *Torsk* , located at Pier 3, East Pratt Street, Baltimore 21202. Call (410) 396–3854 or visit www.usstorsk.org.

In July 1999, the ***USS* Constellation** returned to Baltimore's Inner Harbor. When last in the harbor, her timbers were so rotten that the mast had to be removed, lest it fall through the bottom of the ship to the bottom of the harbor. Originally thought to have been built in 1797 and the sister ship of Boston's USS *Constitution,* after three years of restoration, she's known to be a sloop of war built in 1854, the last Navy ship powered solely by sail. A 36-gun frigate bearing the name *Constellation* was dismantled in 1853. A second ship was built a year later (but in Norfolk, not in Baltimore as the first ship had been). Nearly 12 feet longer than the first, the second *Constellation* is the one that's in the harbor now. It served in the Mediterranean in the mid-eighteenth century, as an antislavery patrol ship, as a supply ship for famine-stricken Ireland, and for a dozen years as a training ship for the U.S. Naval Academy. The Navy still honors the name, with its USS *Constellation* aircraft carrier.

If you saw the ship before its restoration, you may notice that the second gun deck, added to make it look more like the older frigate, has been removed, and her stern is rounded now, instead of squared off.

The *Constellation* is open for tours daily from 10:00 A.M. to 6:00 P.M. May through October and from 10:00 A.M. to 4:00 P.M. the rest of the year. It's closed on major holidays. Admission to the ship is $6.00 for adults, $4.50 for seniors sixty and older, and $3.50 for children fourteen and younger. The address is Pier 1, Inner Harbor, 301 Pratt Street,

Architectural Monument with a View

The Washington Monument and Museum in Baltimore, a 178-foot column, was the nation's first architectural monument (distinguishing it from the monument honoring George Washington that's in Boonsboro in western Maryland). It was designed by Robert Mills, architect of the Washington Monument in Washington, D.C. You reach the top via a 228-step spiral stairway, where you can get a four-window panoramic view of the city. I'm not sure what the difference is in that definition of "architectural monument" compared to the one in Washington State Park, for they both claim they were the first. The marble, a white, crystalline metalimestone, is Cockeysville marble, from a quarry near Texas, about 1½ miles north of Baltimore. This stone was also used for the first 152 feet of the Washington Monument in Washington, D.C. The admission is $1.00. (410) 396–7837.

Baltimore, 21202. Call (410) 539–1797 or (888) 225–8466, or log on to www. constellation.org.

If you would like an organized or specially designed personal tour of the city, call ***Baltimore Rent-A-Tour***. Ruth Fader started her business in the early 1970s when she realized no one was giving tours of Baltimore. Now her company conducts about 900 tours a year. Baltimore Rent-A-Tour specializes in the distinctive, such as African-American tours with highlights that include the Great Blacks in Wax Museum, the Civil War Museum, and the Eubie Blake Cultural Center. Another favorite tour is the early-bird insomniac tour, which always includes the Edgar Allan Poe grave site at Westminster Church, a poetry reading, and a sherry toast; the Baltimore Streetcar Museum for a ride on a century-old trolley; the Enoch Pratt Library for a poke among the books; and a nighttime view of the city from the Top of the World Trade Center. So, if you're in town with a convention, are part of a ski group, or belong to some other organization, check out Baltimore Rent-A-Tour, 3414 Philip Drive, Baltimore 21208; (410) 653–2998.You can also find them at www. Baltimorerent-a-tour.com.

For those who like the unusual, a visit to the ***American Dime Museum*** is essential. This is where you'll find a 40-inch-diameter ball of string, a two-faced calf, and shrunken heads, thanks to Dick Horne and James Taylor, cofounders of the museum. For years Taylor has published the magazine *Shocked and Amazed!,* a publication dedicated to sideshows and roadside museums. The admission price to the old sideshows, one thin dime, explains the name of the museum. There's an interesting story to each of the exhibit items; The huge ball of string replicates the one sold at auction when the dearly beloved Haussner's restaurant closed in 1999. In addition to such items as Fiji mermaids, shrunken heads, and unicorns, there's also a collection of reference books on sideshow history. The museum is open from noon to 3:00 P.M. Wednesday through Friday, 11:00 A.M. to 4:00 P.M. on weekends. Admission is $5.00 for adults and $3.00 for children six to twelve. It's located at 1808 Maryland Avenue, Baltimore 21201; (410) 230–0263, www.dimemuseum.com.

On May 28, 1989, the ***Maryland Vietnam Veterans Memorial,*** a circular-shaped version of the national Vietnam memorial, was dedicated to the memory of 1,046 Marylanders who were killed or became missing in action in the Vietnam conflict. The names and inscriptions are readable whether one is standing, in a wheelchair, or at a child's-eye level. The veterans' names are etched into granite, along with this inscription:

> MARYLANDERS, WHILE IN THIS PLACE, PAUSE TO RECALL OUR NATION'S IDEALS, ITS PROMISE, ITS ABUNDANCE, AND OUR CONTINUING RESPONSIBILITIES TOWARD THE SHARED FULFILLMENT OF OUR ASPIRATIONS. REMEMBER, TOO, THOSE WHOSE EXERTIONS AND SACRIFICES UNDERLIE THESE BLESSINGS. REMEMBER, INDEED, THE LIVING AND THE DEAD.

Funds were raised by Maryland veterans who called themselves "The Last Patrol." They marched across the state during sweltering August heat in 1986, from Oakland in western Maryland to Ocean City in the east, and another 200 miles from Point Lookout to Baltimore the next year. Architect Paul Spreiregan designed the monument that stands beside the Patapsco River in Middle Branch Park, off Route 2.

Maryland Vietnam Veterans Memorial

Lights, Camera, Action!

The NBC television series Homicide: Life on the Street *was shot primarily in the Fell's Point area of Baltimore, one of the stops on the water-taxi route. You can catch glimpses of buildings used in the series, from the police headquarters to the bar across the street. Barry Levinson, the show's producer, is a Baltimore native who attended Forest Park High School, and he has set many of his movies, including* Diner, Tin Man, *and* Liberty Heights, *in town and in the suburbs of his younger days. John Waters also is a product of the area and has shot a lot of his films here.* Hairspray *was set here. Divine, the female impersonator who starred in* Pink Flamingos, Mondo Trasho, *and* Polyester *and died on March 7, 1988, grew up at 1824 Edgewood Road in Loch Raven (no, his parents aren't living there anymore). Divine is buried in Prospect Hill Cemetery, York Road, Towson.*

Old Baltimore has long been known for its blocks and blocks of row houses, with their brightly scrubbed white-marble steps. Almost as historic, but not nearly as well known, are the ***painted screens*** for windows and doors that decorate the houses lining the streets of East Baltimore. It is said that William Oktavec painted the first screen on a hot summer day in 1913. Oktavec was a green grocer whose fresh produce was wilting in the heat, so he took it inside and painted groceries on the screens to show his customers what he had available.

When you understand that this area is all cement and brick, with very little greenery, no front yards, and few gardens or trees, you can appreciate the thoughts some had about providing a little colorful decoration. Another advantage of the painted screens is that windows and doors can be left open for the breezes, because the paint allows those who are inside to look out, but outsiders cannot see in.

People started painting on the screens pictures of red-roofed bungalows and ponds with ducks or swans swimming around in them. There are rainbows and religious scenes, but mostly the artwork reflects the memories of the inhabitants' home countries in Europe and scenes of a new life in America. The scenes depicted the single-family, country-cottage homes of the sort everyone dreamed of owning.

For the best screen viewing, start at the former Haussner's Restaurant at 3242 Eastern Avenue, and travel along both sides of Eastern Avenue. The Hatton Senior Center, at the corner of Fait and South Linwood Avenue, has screens in each of its twenty windows. This generally is a seasonal display, with the screens in place between May and October. Six or seven

Trivia

The oldest remaining commercial structure in the Fell's Point area of Baltimore is possibly the last surviving Colonial coffeehouse, built between 1770 and 1772. In May 2000 the Maryland Commission for Celebration 2000 awarded $22,500 to help restore the ***London Coffee House,*** *located at 854 South Bond Street.*

screen painters remain, but they are in their fifties or older. They still work away at it, saying, "Practice makes perfect, and perfect practice makes art."

You can have a screen painted for about $20 and up, even if you do not live in or visit Baltimore. Write the Painted Screen Society of Baltimore, Box 12122, Baltimore 21281.

Now, on to a few fascinating factory tours. The ***General Motors (Truck Group) Baltimore Assembly Plant*** turns out GMC Safaris and Chevrolet Astros at the rate of about forty an hour, sixteen hours a day, five days a week. In a cavernous room split by railroad tracks and boxcars, you can watch a flat piece of stamped sheet metal, instrument panel shells, heater controls, windshields, roofs, carpet (watching water nozzles cut carpet is really interesting), engines, and all the other components come together to form a van. It is a throbbing, pulsating, noisy, smelly operation, but big and little engineers love to watch it. The tour follows a 2½-mile-long assembly line and takes about two hours. Tours are offered weekdays at 9:00 A.M. and 6:30 P.M. They accept a minimum of ten and a maximum of twenty-five people and advise that no cameras are allowed, and *puh-lease,* no open-toed shoes, sandals, or high heels should be worn. Children must be ten or older, and safety glasses are provided.

Reservations with three weeks' notice are requested and can be made by calling Harry Chandler (410–631–2111) or by writing to General Motors Baltimore Assembly Plant, 2122 Broening Highway, Baltimore 21224. The plant is located near Sparrows Point. Take I–95 north to Fort McHenry Tunnel, turn right at Boston Street (the first exit after the tunnel), and right again on Broening Highway.

The ***Calvert Distilling Company, Seagram's America*** lets you follow the preparation of fine whiskey, vodka, and gin from distillation through the bottling process to quality control. The tour includes a view of the warehouses filled with the finished product and a sampling of one of the products. The ninety-minute tours are offered Memorial Day through Labor Day, on Friday only, at about 1:00 P.M. Wear sturdy shoes please. You should be twenty-one years of age or older, and a maximum of ten people

Trivia

Johns Hopkins Hospital in Baltimore was the site of the first use of silk sutures and the first use of rubber gloves to reduce the risk of surgical infection.

are allowed on the tour. Reservations are required, for they call in retirees to guide the tour. Call (410) 247–6019.

Public transportation around Baltimore City has become pretty convenient in the last few years. The trolley system is good and inexpensive. The subway system is also fine. There's also ***Ed Kane's Water Taxi,*** which makes seventeen stops around the harbor, going to almost every popular waterfront attraction, including Harborplace, the Maryland Science Center, the National Aquarium in Baltimore, the Baltimore Museum of Industry, Fell's Point, and Little Italy. Thus, you can park for the day and take the water taxi around to various spots you want to visit, not having to worry about finding parking places, having correct change, or fighting traffic. The blue-and-white water taxis, or water buses, run about every eight to eighteen minutes April through October and about every forty-five minutes the rest of the year. Operating hours are 11:00 A.M. to 11:00 P.M., Monday through Friday, and 10:00 A.M. to 11:00 P.M. on Saturday and Sunday, but call for seasonal hours. Adult fare is $5.00; the fare for children ten and under accompanied by an adult is $2.00. These prices cover unlimited use on the day of purchase. Call (800) 658–8947 or (410) 563–3901.

Trivia

The lyrics to the "Star-Spangled Banner," as penned by Francis Scott Key in 1814 after watching the Battle of Baltimore, is on display at the Maryland Historical Society in Baltimore. (410) 685–3750; www.mdhs.org.

Another option is the ***light-rail system,*** taking you from the suburbs to Oriole Park at Camden Yards and back again for less expense and aggravation than driving into the city and parking. It runs from Glen Burnie to Hunt Valley Mall, with stops in downtown Baltimore, including Camden Yards, and there are spurs to BWI Airport and Penn Station. It operates about every fifteen minutes from 6:00 A.M. to 11:00 P.M. Monday through Friday, every fifteen minutes from 8:00 A.M. to 11:00 P.M. on Saturday, and every thirty minutes from 11:00 A.M. to 7:00 P.M. on Sunday. Hours are extended or modified during the baseball season. Free parking is available at designated light-rail stops, and all light-rail trains are handicapped accessible. The cost is $1.35 per trip, $2.70 for a round-trip, or $3.00 for an all-day pass that's good on the subway, the bus system, and the light-rail. Call (410) 539–5000. For additional Baltimore information, write the Baltimore Area Convention and Visitors Center, 100 Light Street, 12th Floor, Baltimore 21202, call (888) BALTIMORE or (410) 659–3700, or log on to www.baltimore.org.

Trivia

The first umbrella factory in the United States was established in Baltimore in 1828. The umbrellas carried a very Madison Avenue–type slogan: BORN IN BALTIMORE—RAISED EVERYWHERE.

Baltimore County

Baltimore City is surrounded on the east, north, and northwest by Baltimore County, and the easiest way out of the city (barring rush-hour accidents) is to the north along I–83.

One of the things I like to do is check out ***post office murals***. No, they're not murals of post offices, but located in them, painted and installed in the late 1930s and early 1940s. Heading north and then a little to the east brings you to Towson and a set of murals at the Towson Post Office that caused a real ruckus.

Nicolai Cikovsky, a Russian-born, naturalized citizen, was an artist who lived in Washington, D.C. In 1939 he gave the postmaster, at the postal official's request, a series of panels depicting "Milestones in American Transportation." The populace took one look and cried foul. They declared the subject of the paintings was trite, derivative, and clichéd. They also were upset by inaccuracies, such as a wagon pulled by horses without reins, smokestack smoke going the wrong direction (ahead of the train), a train looking like a model railroad engine rather than a real locomotive, and a gun holster worn backward. This was the work of a painter who had studied at several distinguished schools in Russia, taught in the United States at the Corcoran Gallery, and sold paintings to the Chicago Art Institute, the Whitney Museum of American Art, and numerous other celebrated galleries across the country. The residents thought the paintings looked like bad "B" movie posters, at best. They wanted murals that reflected the life and history of Towson, and they wanted the artist to visit the area; often artists only went to see the location where their paintings would hang. The upshot is that the errors were corrected, and the murals stayed. They can still be found at 101 West Chesapeake Avenue, Towson—no longer the main post office, but the finance office.

Oops

Many of the WPA murals that supposedly depicted area activities were more figments of imagination or expressions of scenes from other parts of the country or world than a reflection of local reality. The Prince George's County mural in Upper Marlboro, Maryland, for example shows tobacco that's not grown in Maryland, but in North Carolina. And it's shown being harvested the way it's done in North Carolina, not the way it's done in Maryland.

At Towson State University, in the Fine Arts Center, is the ***Asian Arts Center*** at the Roberts Gallery. The gallery is named in honor of Frank Roberts, who donated a large number of Asian artifacts and artworks to start this collection. Changing and permanent displays of Asian, African, and pre-Columbian works are featured. Concerts, films, lectures, and workshops are sponsored throughout the school year. The Asian Arts Center in the Fine Arts Building is open Monday through Friday 11:00 A.M. to 4:00 P.M. No admission is charged. Groups are welcome by appointment. Call (410) 830–2807 or visit saber.towson.cdu/tu/asianarts/collections.html.

If you saw Clint Eastwood's film *Absolute Power* then your visit to Maryvale will be a déjà vu moment for you; the castle at ***Maryvale Preparatory School*** was the setting where the dastardly deed was done. The stone manor, set on 150 acres, was constructed in 1917 and modeled after Warwick Castle in England. Its Gothic arched windows, a great hall with European oak-paneled walls, diamond-paneled beveled-glass doors opening onto the terrace, boxwood gardens, stone towers, and incredible staircase are available for rent for your special event. As the school says, it fulfills "every girl's fantasy of the perfect storybook wedding." Maryvale, open by appointment only, is at 11300 Falls Road, Brooklandville, 21093 (just north of the I–695 and I–83 intersection). Call (410) 252–3528 or visit www.maryvale.com.

Southerners have known the joys of ***Krispy Kreme doughnuts*** for more than sixty-one years. A few years ago, sophisticated New Yorkers became devout fans. Then, on November 3, 1998, KK came to Baltimore, disrupting traffic and not meeting the demand for donuts, even though the 3,000-square-foot store is capable of making 270 dozen doughnuts per hour, or 6,480 dozen doughnuts per day. By far, the company's most famous and best-selling product is the glazed, yeast-raised doughnut known for generations as the "Krispy Kreme Original Glazed." If you've never seen a doughnut being made, then you should definitely pop on over to KK to watch the old-fashioned doughnut machine. When the glowing, red-hot HOT DOUGHNUTS NOW light is on, the doughnuts are literally coming out hot *now,* and that's when you should eat them. Krispy Kreme locations include 8010 Belair Road, Belair (410–377–8660), 4940 Campbell Boulevard, Baltimore (410–931–9053), 6604 Ritchie Highway, Glen Burnie (410–760–9356), and 2129 York Road, Timonium (410–308–3576).

One of the remaining covered bridges in Maryland connects Harford and Baltimore Counties and crosses over Gunpowder Falls. The ***Jericho Covered Bridge*** was constructed in 1864 and measures 88 feet, with a

Trivia

The Glenn L. Martin Aviation Museum in Middle River was the first museum dedicated to Maryland's aviation history. Opened on June 11, 1993, the museum is named in honor of the aviation pioneer and the tremendous contribution he made to Maryland's aviation history. Among the exhibits are a restored Martin RB-57A jet bomber, "the Intruder," modeled after the British Canberra. For more information about the museum, located at Martin State Airport, northeast of Baltimore, call (410) 682–6122.

14⅔-foot roadway. Steel beams, steel stringers, steel crosstie rods, and bottom chord were installed later for reinforcement, and today it remains in good condition. To reach the bridge, take Route 152 from exit 74 off I–95, turn left onto Jerusalem Road, and proceed to Jericho Road.

Ashland Furnace is one of the six relatively easy-to-reach furnaces in Maryland (the others are Catoctin Furnace, Lonaconing Iron Furnace, Antietam, and Principio in Cecil County; and Nassawango in Worcester County). Said to have been named for the Kentucky home of Henry Clay, Ashland's three furnaces, engine room, and casting house were kept functioning from around 1844 to 1893. Originally there were also large storage buildings for raw materials and a village with a school, church, store, and about five dozen houses. The ore was mined in Phoenix, Glencoe, Riderwood, Texas, Oregon Ridge, and other parts of what is now north-central Baltimore County.

Now the area is mined by a developer, and the Strutt Group has incorporated about a dozen of the old village's buildings. The office and mid-nineteenth century store, the school, several houses, and a group of dwellings called Stone Row have been renovated and assimilated into the industrial site. The old Ashland Presbyterian Church, near the gates of the new community, is still an active place of worship. Ashland Furnace is on Paper Mill Road east of York Road, just north of Cockeysville.

West of Ashland Furnance is the ***Oregon Ridge Park and Nature Center,*** a great place to take a break after hours of driving and seeing regular tourist attractions. Within its 836 acres are a number of marked trails of varying length and difficulty, downhill and cross-country skiing areas, a greenhouse, an archaeological research site, an outdoor stage, and a launching site for hang gliders. Starting in the nature center, you can see how a honeybee hive works, look at local flowers and plants in the greenhouse, or check on such live animals as fish, frogs, mice, salamanders, snakes, and Stubby, the pet opossum, all native to the park.

A huge tree exhibit reveals the various parts of the forest ecosystem, from the worms and moles living among the roots and underbrush to the owls and hawks perching in its highest limbs. The area's history is depicted by artifacts retrieved from archaeological digs in the park.

These items were reclaimed from the digs by students in the Baltimore County public school system. Students also constructed a full-scale replica of an 1850s storage shed, set on its original foundation outside the nature center. The nature trails crisscross the park, so a hiker sees the natural interactions of birds, fields, ponds, streams, swamps, wildlife, and woods.

For those who like nature on the cultured side, summer concerts are presented here by the Baltimore Symphony. Oregon Ridge Park and Nature Center, Beaver Dam Road, is reached by the Shawan Road exit 20-B off I–83; go west 1 mile, turn left on Beaver Dam Road, bear right at the fork, and follow the signs. Oregon Ridge Nature Center is open from 9:00 A.M. to 6:00 P.M. Tuesday through Sunday. Call (410) 887–1815 for more information.

Southwest of Oregon Ridge is Owings Mills, and there you'll discover ***Wild Acres Trail,*** a mile-long wildlife habitat demonstration trail that was opened in 1989. It's part of the seventy-two-acre Gwynnbrook Wildlife Management Area, and the trail features twenty-three ways gardeners and wildlife watchers can help invite birds, butterflies, and other animals to their property. Trail maps are available for the self-guided tour, and the trail is open from dawn to dusk daily except on Wednesday. No pets are allowed. Included along the trail are a backyard pond and rock garden; a bee, butterfly, and hummingbird garden; nesting structures for birds and squirrels; bird feeders; and a variety of garden plants that produce fruit eaten by all sorts of animals. Other examples are shown for owners of large properties. More than 120 kinds of birds live in or visit the Gwynnbrook area, making bird-watching a marvelous recreational attraction. Photo opportunities are wondrous because of the wildflowers that bloom in the spring and fall.

From Owings Mills, head south to Catonsville, where you'll find ***post office murals*** done by Avery Johnson in 1942. Johnson painted five scenes of historic note, entitled *Incidents of History of Catonsville.* The murals start with Native Americans, go on to farmers rolling tobacco in hogsheads to market, and then depict the romance of Richard Caton and Mary "Holly" Carroll. Holly, the daughter of Declaration of Independence signer Charles Carroll, was only sixteen when Caton proposed. Her father refused because he said Caton had a reputation for not paying his debts. Caton prevailed, and they were married in 1788. Charles Carroll built a house for them, Castle Thunder, on Frederick Road, where the library is now; then he built a newer home in Green Spring Valley (that home still stands). The last panel shows Caton, Holly, and Charles Carroll with his plans for the town of Catonsville.

Several years ago the post office roof began to leak, and that did not bode well for the plaster walls or the paintings. The late Thomas Cockey, whose family history also goes back to the eighteenth century, decided the murals should be repaired. Federal officials balked at the $35,000 repair bill, but Cockey (as in the town of Cockeysville, also in Baltimore County) and the Historical Society prevailed. A plaque documenting the story depicted in the panels has been installed by the society.

For additional tourism information contact the Baltimore County Conference and Visitors Bureau, 118 Shawar Road, Hint Valley Mall, Baltimore 21030; (410) 329–1001 or (877) 782–9636; www.visitbacomd.com.

Carroll County

West of Baltimore County, out U.S. Route 30 or 140, you're getting into horse country with some beautiful scenery to go along with your history. The county was named for Charles Carroll, an American Revolutionary War leader and Maryland signer of the Declaration of Independence.

Near Westminster, the county seat, is the ***Carroll County Farm Museum***. This complex has a general store that's reminiscent of the 1800s and sells items handcrafted by Farm Museum artisans, souvenirs, nickel candies, and much more. Among the activities scheduled on the grounds are a Civil War encampment (19th Georgia Regiment), a day honoring Older Americans, a fiddlers' convention, a day devoted to antique farm machinery, and a day to celebrate Maryland wines.

General admission is $3.00 for adults, $2.00 for those twelve to eighteen and sixty and over, and free for those under twelve. Group tours and rates are available. Higher admission prices apply for special events. The museum is open weekends May through October from noon to 5:00 P.M. and Tuesday through Friday in July and August from 10:00 A.M. to 4:00 P.M. It's located at 500 South Center Street, Westminster 21157. Call (800) 654–4645 or (410) 876–2667 or log on to www.car.lib.md.us/tourism/farmmus.htm.

Carroll County's streams, valleys, farms, woodlands, and villages provide an ideal backdrop for exploring off the highway, and the best way to do that is by bicycle. Bicycle tours have been designed by resident cyclists outlining ten of their favorite routes, ranging from short to long and easy to challenging. Each route is on a separate map with its own description of the tour. Brochures are available at the visitors center in Westminster.

Final Resting Place

In 1992 Frederick Hubbard Gwynne and his wife, Deborah, moved to a farm in rural Maryland. You may remember him as Fred Gwynne, the tall (6'5") and lanky actor who portrayed Herman Munster in TV's The Munsters *and as Gunther Toody in* Car 54, Where Are You? *He also played the part of Big Daddy in the 1974 Broadway revival of* Cat on a Hot Tin Roof, *among many other distinguished parts. His last films were* Fatal Attraction, Pet Sematary, *and* My Cousin Vinny. *He also wrote several children's books, including* A Little Pigeon Toad, A Chocolate Moose for Dinner, The King Who Rained, *and* Pondlarker. *Gwynne died of pancreatic cancer on July 2, 1993, just days short of his sixty-seventh birthday. He is buried at Sandymount Methodist Church in Sandyville, off Old Westminster Pike.*

For example, the Taneytown route, northwest of Westminster, is nearly 14 miles long, beginning at Taneytown Memorial Park. The moderately hilly ride takes you through rustic areas filled with deer and pheasants. The New Windsor tour, west of Westminster, travels for 8 miles through the rolling hills of Wakefield Valley. Attractions include Robert Strawbridge's Home (the birthplace of American Methodism) and the International Gift Shop at the New Windsor Service Center, 2650 Strawbridge Lane, New Windsor 21776.

According to local legend, you and I are not the only visitors to Carroll County. Several apparitions also frequent the countryside, and you may even meet a friendly one. The first of the ghosts of Carroll County is at the Shellman House on East Main Street in Westminster. A little girl in white, they say, delights at having visitors stop by the visitors center, located at the Historical Society of Carroll County, 210 East Main Street, Westminster 21157; (410) 848–6454; www.carr.org/hscc. Spirits, in addition to the liquid kind, are said to reside at Cockey's Tavern, 216 East Main Street; since the early 1800s this tavern has been the site of political rallies for Andrew Jackson, antitax meetings, fancy balls, and all-night debauchery. At Main and Court Streets, the ghosts of slaves supposedly return to the Carroll County auction block, where slave trading was done in pre–Revolutionary War times. Other specters have been reported at Ascension churchyard, the courthouse, the old Westminster jail, Western Maryland College (Levine Hall has a musical ghost), and Avondale—the home of Legh Master, the most celebrated of Carroll's ghosts—on Stone Chapel Road in Wakefield Valley. It is said that Master was a tyrant, a miser, a lecher, and a cad.

Two Confederate ghosts reportedly visit the last remaining building of Irving College on Grafton Street, and during a full moon, an Indian walks along a ridge in the tiny town of Lineboro. For those of you who choose to pursue these nocturnal visitors, talk with the Historical Society in general (through the Office of Promotion and Tourism) and Amos Davidson, a local historian, in particular.

Additional tourism information is available from the Carroll County Office of Tourism, 210 East Main Street, Westminster 21157; (410) 876–1399 or (800) 272–1932; www.carr.org/tourism.

Harford County

Head northeast of Baltimore City and east of Baltimore County, and you're probably taking I–95 to or from the Northeast corridor. Take a few minutes off that interstate, known as the Gateway to the Chesapeake Bay, and you'll find that Harford County goes from covered bridge to lighthouse.

Concord Point Light

Havre de Grace (pronounced as it is spelled, not with a French pronunciation) is the home of the ***Concord Point Light.*** Constructed in 1827, it is the oldest operating lighthouse on the East Coast. Following its decommissioning in 1975, it was vandalized and then, thank goodness, restored, and it is now in tip-top shape. You can climb the twenty-eight steps plus six steps on a ladder and see an impressive view of the Susquehanna River and Chesapeake Bay. The lighthouse is open on Saturday and Sunday afternoons from 1:00 to 5:00 P.M. April through October, or by appointment. It is located at the foot of Lafayette Street in Havre de Grace. The phone numbers are (410) 939–1340 and (410) 939–2016. From the lighthouse you can walk ½ mile via a prom-

Trivia

The town of Dublin, in Harford County, is named after Dublin, Ireland. In the eighteenth century it was a Scotch-Irish settlement.

enade (boardwalk) along the shore of the Chesapeake Bay to Tydings Park at Lafayette and Concord Streets.

Another interesting attraction is the ***Susquehanna Museum of Havre de Grace,*** where you can learn just about everything you need to know about the southern terminus of the Susquehanna and Tidewater Canal. There's a restored lockhouse and a pivot bridge. Admission is $2.00 per person. The museum is open from 1:00 to 5:00 P.M. Friday through Sunday May through October. The museum is located at the Lock House, 817 Conesto Street, Havre de Grace 21078; (410) 939–5780; www.erols.com/susqmuseum/index.html.

A self-guided tour brochure is available from Harford County Tourism in Bel Air; it highlights a sample of the 800 structures that contribute to the ***Havre de Grace Historic District.*** The buildings range in period from the 1780s through the Canal era (1830–50) and the Victorian era (1880–1910) to the contemporary.

Havre de Grace is the self-proclaimed decoy capital of the world, and the ***Havre de Grace Decoy Museum*** has complete collections of decoys by Madison Mitchell and Paul Gibson. An annual Decoy Festival is held about the first weekend of May at the museum and at the Havre de Grace Middle and High Schools. The Decoy Museum is open daily from 11:00 A.M. to 4:00 P.M., except major holidays. The address is 215 Giles Street, Havre de Grace 21078. Call (410) 939–3739.

About 10 blocks up the road, at Franklin Street and North Union Avenue, is the ***Susquehanna Trading Company.*** Owner Duane Henry has more than 2,500 old and new Chesapeake Bay decoys on display and locally handcrafted decoys for sale, starting at $9.95. He also features a large selection of waterfowl decorations, including miniature decoys; wildlife-decorated personal, household, and office accessories; limited-edition prints; and decoy lamps.

The Susquehanna Trading Company is open seven days a week from 10:00 A.M. to 5:00 P.M. at 320 North Union Avenue; (410) 939–4252.

Crossing the Susquehanna River north of Harve de Grace via Route 40 is the ***Thomas J. Hatem Memorial Bridge,*** between Harford and Cecil Counties (nice to know about when the bridge on I–95 is backed up). It opened in 1940 as the Susquehanna River Bridge and was renamed in 1986 to honor Hatem, a prominent Harford County resident who devoted his life to public and civic service. The bridge is 1½ miles long and rises 89 feet above the river, connecting the communities of Havre de Grace and Perryville. More than seven million vehicles use the bridge each year. The toll is $2.00 (northbound only) for passenger cars.

South of Havre de Grace is Aberdeen, once known primarily for its military base, the Aberdeen Proving Grounds. Driving through the grounds is like the reverse of a military parade, for here you drive past tanks and artillery, combat vehicles, and more, rather than them parading past you. It's a parade that's open every day of the year, not just on May 1, Veterans Day, or Memorial Day.

On the grounds of the base is the ***U.S. Army Ordnance Museum,*** with a comprehensive collection of small arms and just about everything else military you'd want to see that would be too small to fit in a parade or would not be suitable for exterior display.

The museum is open daily from 10:00 A.M. to 4:45 P.M.; it is closed on major holidays except Memorial Day, July 4, and Veterans Day/Armed Forces Day. There is no admission charge. Call (410) 279–3602 for additional information.

The other big gun from Aberdeen is Cal Ripken Jr., the Iron Man, the one who broke Gehrig's record of 2,130 consecutive games played. So if you can't get to Camden Yards, or if it's not baseball season, or when the day comes that Cal hangs up the cleats for the last time (except old timers' games), then head over to the ***Ripken Museum***. Hailed as a "repository of baseball and other Ripken family memorabilia," its mission is to "interpret and preserve the traditional values of Cal Ripken and to portray Cal's life and career as a symbol of American family values and the multifaceted meanings of pride, discipline and leadership." It also honors Cal Sr. and Billy. The museum is located at 8 Ripken Plaza.

The Ripken Museum opened on December 6, 1996, and in its first year of operation the museum welcomed more than 14,000 visitors. Charter membership, at $300, entitles one to a collectible charter club lapel pin, lifetime personal entry into the museum, subscription to the museum newsletter, and an invitation to special museum events. Oh, and your name will be included on the Charter Club plaque, permanently displayed in the museum.

The Ripken Museum is located in what was the former public meeting room of the Aberdeen City Hall building. It took more than a year and many hundreds of thousands of dollars to renovate this room into the showpiece it is today. In 1998 the museum took another bold step by purchasing City Hall from the city of Aberdeen. Architectural plans for the museum's expansion are underway, and a $3.5 million capital campaign will help pay for the expansion of the museum into the rest of the City Hall building and for the construction of a baseball field.

Museum hours vary seasonally, with summer (Memorial Day Monday through Labor Day) hours from 11:00 A.M. to 3:00 P.M., Monday through Saturday and noon to 3:00 P.M. on Sunday. In the fall it's open Thursday through Monday, noon to 3:00 P.M. It's closed on major holidays. Call for winter hours. Admission is $3.00 for adults, $2.00 for seniors (sixty-two and older), and $1.00 for students (six to eighteen). The museum is at 3 West Bel Air Avenue, Aberdeen 21001. Call (410) 273–2525 or visit www.ripkenmuseum.com.

Northwest of Aberdeen is Bel Air, the Harford county seat, and there you'll enjoy the pleasures of ***Liriodendron,*** a Palladian-style mansion with Greek columns, French doors, marble walls in the kitchen and bathroom, and thirteen fireplaces. Built as a palatial summer home in 1898 for Dr. Howard A. Kelly, one of the "Big Four" founders of Baltimore's Johns Hopkins Hospital and Medical School, the "Kelly Mansion" is now on the National Register of Historic Places. This historic house museum features changing exhibits and art displays as well as a permanent exhibit of memorabilia from the Kelly Collection.

It also serves as a cultural center for Harford County, with superb facilities for exhibitions, lectures, and concerts. Call (410) 838–3942 or (410) 879–4424 for a tour schedule. The address is Liriodendron, 502 West Gordon Street, Bel Air 21014; www.liriodendron.org.

For additional tourism information on Harford County, contact Discover Harford County Tourism Council Inc., 121 North Union Avenue, Suite B, Havre de Grace 21078; (410) 575–7278 or (800) 597–2649; harfordmd@ixim.com.

Howard County

South and west of Baltimore City, out I–70 or down I–95, is Howard County, a place offering tremendous contrasts in lifestyles, from Ellicott City, a former mill town, with its original stone buildings, antiques and specialty shops, historic sites, and B&O (Baltimore and Ohio) Railroad Station Museum, to Columbia, the planned village, with its Merriweather Post Pavilion, huge mall, and Columbia Information Center. As usual, I will cover some of the less visited and more countrified places.

Trivia

Ellicott Mills, in Howard County, was started in 1772 by three Ellicott brothers from Bucks County, Pennsylvania. By 1774, it was said to be the greatest gristmill in Colonial America, with seven mills in operation at its peak. Besides producing animal feed, flour, iron nails, oil, lumber, paper, wagons, and wool, the first commercial electricity in the county was produced in 1891 in a mill on Tiber Alley.

If you travel from Baltimore County to Howard County, just off Route 1, you can spot a bridge of note that is for trains rather than cars, known as the ***Thomas Viaduct*** (1833). Crossing the Patapsco River, eight elliptical arches support a 60-foot-high granite block structure, which allowed tall ships to pass under. Just as the Ellicott City Railroad Station has endured as a landmark to the growth of railroading in Maryland, so does the viaduct. When B&O Railroad officials began looking to expand the railroad south to Washington, D.C., they faced a monumental problem: how to cross the Patapsco River. They solved it with a monumental structure, the Thomas Viaduct. Named for the first president of the B&O Railroad, Philip Thomas, it was designed by Baltimorean Benjamin Latrobe, and it was the first curved, stone-arched bridge in America. Construction began July 4, 1832, and it was completed exactly three years later at a cost of a little more than $142,000. It still carries passenger and freight trains. The viaduct is off Levering Avenue at 6086 Old Lawyers Hill Road, Elkridge 21075. Picnic areas are in nearby Patapsco State Park, which is open from sunrise to sunset; (410) 796–3282.

Another bridge of interest, at Savage, is the ***Bollman Truss Bridge*** (1869). The red cast-iron, open railroad bridge is the only one of its type in the world. It is said to be the first bridge constructed of iron, as opposed to wood or stone. Restoration of the bridge took place in 1974, near Savage Mill (which is now filled with antiques shops and artists' studios), and there is a nice little park and hiking trails around the bridge. You can find the bridge off Route 1, at Savage, near Savage Mill.

Howard County is home to a few farms that are open for pick-your-own fruits and vegetables and lots of family fun.

Historic ***Cider Mill Farm*** (1916) has organic produce, herbs, pies, honey, and other country goods mid-September through November and mid-April through mid-May. During the apple season they offer guided tours of the cider-making process, including antique hand- and electric-press demonstrations in which children can participate and receive free cider samples. Tom Owens, the owner, says you can bring your own jug for fresh cider if you like. Weekend activities include face painting, marble and yo-yo presentations, apple butter making, scarecrow making, storytelling, pumpkin carving (bring your own tools and a blanket), and a teddy bear contest (bring your own bear). Remember to bring your camera. A schedule of contests and activities is available.

Cider Mill Farm is open daily 9:00 A.M. to 4:00 P.M. April through June, 10:00 A.M. to 6:00 P.M. September through Thanksgiving Day, and other times by appointment. It is located at 5012 Landing Road (off Montgomery Road, Route 103), Elkridge 21227; call (410) 788–9595 or 788–9596 or visit the farm's Web site: www.farmmd.com.

Trivia

In 1820 Amos Williams and his three brothers borrowed $20,000 from friend John Savage to start a textile-weaving business on the banks of the Little Patuxent River. With water flowing over a huge 30-foot water wheel, Savage Mill, named after their friend, was in use from 1822 through 1947. It is now a complex filled with artisans and antiques dealers. 8600 Foundry Street, Savage 20763; (301) 498–5751 or (410) 792–2820.

Larriland Farms has a pick-your-own season starting in late May or early June with strawberries and ending with a cut-your-own season for Christmas trees in December. In addition, the farm has succulent and delicious fruits and vegetables and beautiful flowers. The market is in a 125-year-old post-and-beam barn. Larriland Farms, owned and operated by the Moore family, also offers hayrides, evening campfires, and other programs that let city folk enjoy the pleasures of rural life. The farm is open May through August, Monday through Friday 8:00 A.M. to 8:00 P.M. and September through October, Monday through Friday 9:00 A.M. to 5:00 P.M. Weekend hours are Saturday 9:00 A.M. to 5:00 P.M. and Sunday 10:00 A.M. to 5:00 P.M. In December it's closed on Monday. The address is 2415 Woodbine Road, Woodbine 21797. Larriland Farms is 3 miles south of I–70 (exit 73) on Route 94, near Lisbon. The phone number is (410) 489–7034; in season you can call (410) 442–2605 or (301) 854–6110 for a recording of what fruits and vegetables are available. Their Web site is www.pickyourown.com.

Toby's the Dinner Theatre of Columbia celebrates the creative genius of Toby Orenstein and her dedication to fine theatrical productions. All the time she is working to entertain you, she is working to teach her "kids" the hows and whys of show business so they can go on to professional careers in entertainment if they wish.

The most interesting aspect of Toby's is the theater, which has performances in the round. You are never far from the action.

The productions may be an outstanding Broadway show from years gone by, such as *Funny Girl* or *Singin' in the Rain*, or an entirely new attraction, such as a musical version of *It's a Wonderful Life*, which was created at Toby's and offered during the 1989 holiday season. Other selections have included *The Pirates of Penzance, Sunday in the Park with George,* and *Ain't Misbehavin'.* In other words, it's good family entertainment.

Dinner at Toby's is an all-you-can-eat buffet that features prime roast beef, steamed shrimp, fresh salad and vegetables, and a dessert table.

Toby's is at 5900 Symphony Woods Road, Columbia 21044, 1/2 block east of Little Patuxent Parkway. The phone numbers are (410) 730–8311; (301) 596– 6161 (in Washington); (410) 995–1969 (in Baltimore); and (800) 88–TOBYS (in Maryland and surrounding states). On the Internet, go to www.tobysdinnertheatre.com.

For additional information on Howard County, write to Karen Justice, Executive Director, Howard County Tourism Council, 8267 Main Street, Ellicott City 21043; www.howardcountymdtour.com

Places to Eat in Central Maryland

Aberdeen

New Ideal Diner,
104 South Philadelphia Boulevard,
(410) 272–1880

Annapolis

49 West,
49 West Street,
(410) 626–9796

Buddy's Crabs and Ribs,
100 Main Street,
(410) 261–2500

Cantler's,
458 Forest Beach Road,
(410) 757–1311

Carrol's Creek Cafe,
410 Severn Avenue,
(410) 263–8102

Corinthian,
126 West Street,
(410) 263–7777

Pusser's Landing,
80 Compromise Street,
(410) 268–7555

Riordan's,
26 Market Street,
(410) 263–5449

Treaty of Paris,
16 Church Circle,
(410) 263–2641

Baltimore

Admiral's Cup,
1645 Thames Street,
(410) 522–6731

Attman's Delicatessen,
1019 Lombard Street,
(410) 463–2666

Burke's Cafe,
36 Light Street,
(410) 752–4189

Chick and Ruth's,
165 Main Street,
(410) 269–6737

Donna's Coffee Bar,
2 West Madison,
(410) 385–0180

Hampton's Restaurant,
Harbor Court Hotel,
550 Light Street,
(410) 234–0550

Max's,
300 West Pratt Street,
(410) 234–8100

Obrycki's Crab house,
1727 East Pratt Street,
(410) 732–6399

Phillips Harborplace,
Light Street Pavilion,
(410) 685–6600

Ruth's Chris Steak House,
600 Water Street,
(410) 783–0033

Sabatino's,
901 Fawn Street,
(410) 727–9414

Vaccarro's,
222 Albemarle Street,
(410) 685–4905

Chesapeake City

Bayard House,
11 Bohemia Avenue,
(410) 885–5040

Bohemia Cafe,
401 Second Street,
(410) 885–3066

Columbia
Kings Contrivance,
10150 Minstrel Way,
(410) 995–0500

Toby's Dinner Theatre of Columbia,
South Entrance Road,
(410) 730–8311 or
(301) 596–6161 or
(800) 88–TOBYS

Edgewater
Adam's Ribs,
169 Mayo Road,
(410) 798–6000

Edgewater Restaurant,
148 Mayo Road,
(410) 956–3202

Hayman's Crab House,
3105 Solomons Island Road,
(410) 956–2023

Ellicott City
The Trolly Stop,
6 Oella Avenue,
(410) 465–8646

Galesville
Inn at Pirates Cove,
4817 Riverside Drive,
(410) 867–2300 or
(301) 261–5050

Steamboat Landing,
4851 Riverside Drive,
(410) 867–7200

Topside Inn,
1004 Main Street at Galesville Road,
(410) 867–1321

West River Market and Deli,
1000 Main Street,
(410) 867–4844

Havre de Grace
McGregor's,
331 St. John Street,
(800) 300–6319 or
(410) 939–3000

Price's,
654 Water Street,
(410) 939–2782

Sawyer's Chat N' Chew Bar and Restaurant,
142 North Washington Street,
(410) 939–0018

Tidewater Grille,
300 Franklin Street,
(410) 939–3313

Linthicum Heights
G&M,
804 North Hammonds Ferry Road,
(410) 636–1777

North East
Woody's Crab House,
29 South Main Street,
(410) 287–3541

Westminster
Barristers Cafe,
55 North Court Street,
(410) 848–2233

Baugher's,
289 West Main Street,
(410) 848–7413

Bradley's Fox Briar Inn,
4115 Littlestown Pike,
(410) 848–2316

Bullock's Airport Inn,
1205 North Business Parkway,
(410) 857–4417

Chameleon,
32 West Main Street,
(410) 751–2422

Harry's Main Street Restaurant,
65 West Main Street,
(410) 848–7080

Hoffman's Hand Made Ice Cream,
934 Washington Road,
(410) 857–0824

Restaurant 1899 at the Westminster Inn,
5 South Center Street,
(410) 876–2893

Timonium
Timonium Dinner Theatre,
9603 Deereco Road,
(410) 560–1113

Towson
F. Scott Black Dinner Theatre,
100 East Chesapeake Avenue,
(410) 321–6595

Places to Stay in Central Maryland

Annapolis
55 East Bed and Breakfast,
55 East Street,
(410) 296–0202,
www.bbchannel.com/bbc/p601464.asp

Amanda's B&B Reservation Service,
1428 Park Avenue,
(800) 899–7533 or
(410) 225–0001

Annapolis Inn,
144 Prince George Street,
(410) 295–5200 or
(877) 295–5200,
www.annapolisinn.com

Annapolis Marriott Waterfront Hotel,
80 Compromise Street,
(410) 268–7555 or
(800) 336–0072,
www.annapolismarriott.com

Chesapeake Bay Lighthouse Bed and Breakfast,
1423 Sharps Point Road,
(410) 757–0248

Ark and Dove B&B,
149 Prince George Street,
(410) 268–6277

Barn on Howard's Cove,
500 Wilson Road,
(410) 571–9511,
www.bnbweb.com/howards-cove.html

Blue Heron Bed and Breakfast Inn,
172 Green Street,
(410) 263–9171 or
(888) 999–1839

Charles Inn B&B,
74 Charles Street,
(410) 268–1451

Chez Amis,
85 East Street,
(410) 263–6631,
www.chezamis.com

Coggeshall House,
198 King George Street,
(410) 263–5068

Eastport House,
101 Severn Avenue,
(410) 295–9710,
www.eastporthouse.com

Flag House Inn B&B,
24 Randall Street,
(410) 280–2721 or
(800) 437–4825,
www.flaghouseinn.com

Gatehouse B&B,
249 Hanover Street,
(410) 280–0024,
www.bbchannel.com

Georgian House B&B,
170 Duke of Gloucester Street,
(410) 263–5618 or
(800) 557–2068,
www.georgianhouse.com

Gibson's Lodgings,
110 Prince George Street,
(410) 268–5555,
www.avmcyber.com/gibson

Harbor View Inn,
1 St. Mary's Street,
(410) 626–9802,
www.harborviewinnofannapolis.com

Historic Inns of Annapolis,
58 State Circle,
(410) 263–2641 or
(800) 847–8882,
www.annapolisinns.com

Inn at Spa Creek,
417 Severn Avenue,
(410) 263–8866,
www.innatspacreek.com

Jonas Green House,
124 Charles Street,
(410) 263–5892,
www.bbhost.com/jghouse

Loews Annapolis Hotel,
126 West Street,
(410) 263–7777,
www.loewsannapolis.com

Maryland Inn,
16 Church Circle,
(410) 263–2641

State House Inn,
25 State Circle,
(410) 990–0024,
www.statehouseinn.com

William Page Inn,
8 Martin Street,
(410) 626–1506 or
(800) 364–4160,
www.williampageinn.com

BALTIMORE

Admiral Fell Inn,
888 South Broadway,
(410) 522–7377 or
(800) 292–INNS,
www.admiralfell.com

Baltimore Hilton and Towers,
20 West Baltimore Street,
(410) 539–8400 or
(800) 333–3333

Celie's Waterfront B&B,
1714 Thames Street,
(410) 522–2323 or
(800) 432–0184,
www.bbonline.com/md/celies

Harbor Court Hotel,
550 Light Street,
(410) 234–0550 or
(800) 824–0076,
www.harborcourt.com

Hyatt Regency-Baltimore, 300 Light Street, (410) 528–1234 or (800) 233–1234, www.hyatt.com

Marriott Inner Harbor, 110 South Eutaw Street, (410) 962–0202, www.marriott.com

Mr. Mole Bed and Breakfast, 1601 Bolton Street, (410) 728–1179

Sheraton Inner Harbor Hotel, 300 South Charles Street, (410) 962–8300, www.ittsheraton.com

Chesapeake City
Blue Max Inn, 300 Bohemia Street, (410) 885–2781

Inn at the Canal, 104 Bohemia Street, (410) 885–5995

Clarksville
Just-A-Mere B&B, 5073 Ten Oaks Road, (410) 531–3426

Columbia
Columbia Hilton Inn, 5485 Twin Knolls Road, (800) 235–0653 or (410) 997–1060

Peralynna Manor at Rose Hill, 10605 Clarksville Pike, (410) 715–4600 or (877) 737–2596, www.rent.net

Edgewater
Quiet Creek B&B, 3932 Cove Road, (410) 956–8459

Elkridge
Belmont Manor House and Conference Center, 6555 Belmont Woods Road, (410) 796–4300

Ellicott City
Turf Valley Resort and Conference Center, 2700 Turf Valley Road, (410) 465–1500 or (888) TEE–TURF, www..turfvalley.com

Essex
Bauernschmidt Manor B&B, 2316 Bauernschmidt Drive, (410) 687–2223

Friendship
Herrington Harbour Marina Resort, 7161 Lake Shore Drive, (410) 741–5100

Galesville
Inn at Pirates Cove, 4817 Riverside Drive, (410) 867–2300 or (301) 261–5050

Topside Inn, 1004 Main Street and Galesville Road, (410) 867–1321

Havre de Grace
Currier House, 800 South Market Street, (410) 939–7886 or (800) 827–2889, www.currier-bb.com

La Cle D'Or Guest House, 226 North Union Avenue, (410) 939–6562 or (888) 484–4837

Spencer-Silver Mansion, 200 South Union Avenue, (410) 939–1485 or (800) 780–1485, www.virtualcities.com/ons/md/c/mdc6501.htm

Vandiver Inn, 301 South Union Avenue, (410) 939–5200 or (800) 245–1655, www.vandiverinn.com

Highland
Inn at Paternal Gift Farm, 13555 Route 108, (301) 854–3353

Linwood
Wood's Gain Bed and Breakfast, 421 McKinstry's Mill Road, (410) 775–0308, www.woodsgainbnb.com

Middleburg
Bowling Brook Country Inn, 6000 Middleburg Road, (410) 876–2893

New Windsor
New Windsor Conference Center, 500 Main Street, (410) 876–2263, ext. 700 or (800) 766–1553, www.brethern.org/genbd/nwcc

Yellow Turtle Inn, 111 Springdale Avenue, (410) 635–3000

Stevenson
Gramercy B&B,
1400 Greenspring Valley Road,
(410) 486–2405 or
(800) 553–3404,
www.gramercymansion.com

Taneytown
Glenburn Bed and Breakfast,
3515 Renamed Road,
(410) 751–1187

Antrim 1844 Country Inn,
30 Trevanion Road,
(410) 876–0237 or
(800) 858–1844,
www.antrim1844.com

Westminster
Boston Inn,
533 Baltimore Boulevard,
(410) 848–9095 or
(800) 634–0846,
www.boston-inn.com

Westminster Inn,
5 South Center Street,
(410) 876–2893,
www.westminsterinn.com

Winchester Country Inn,
111 Stoner Avenue,
(410) 876–7373 or
(800) 887–3950

Other Attractions Worth Seeing in Central Maryland

African Art Museum of Maryland,
Columbia,
(410) 730–7105,
www.africanartmuseum.org

All Hallows Episcopal Church,
Davidsonville,
(410) 798–0808

American Visionary Art Museum,
Baltimore,
(410) 244–1900,
www.avam.org

B&O Railroad Museum,
Baltimore,
(410) 727–2490,
www.borail.org

Babe Ruth Birthplace and Orioles Museum,
Baltimore,
(410) 777–1539 or
(800) 435–BABE

Ballestone Manor House,
Essex,
(410) 887–0218

Baltimore and Annapolis Trail,
Severna Park,
(410) 222–6244

Baltimore County Historical Society Inc.,
Cockeysville,
(410) 666–1876,
www.bcplonline.org/branchpgs/bchs/bchshome.html

Baltimore American Indian Center/Museum,
Baltimore,
(410) 675–3535

Baltimore City Hall,
Baltimore,
(410) 837–5424

Baltimore Civil War Museum,
Baltimore,
(410) 385–5188,
www.civilwarinbaltimore.org

Baltimore Equitable Insurance Fire Museum,
Baltimore,
(410) 727–1794 or
(800) 272–1794,
www.1794insurance.com

Baltimore International College,
Baltimore,
(410) 752–4710,
www.bic.edu

Baltimore Maritime Museum,
Baltimore,
(410) 396–3453

Baltimore Museum of Art,
Baltimore,
(410) 396–7100,
www.artbma.org

Baltimore Museum of Industry,
Baltimore,
(410) 727–4808

Baltimore Public Works Museum,
Baltimore,
(410) 396–5565

Baltimore Streetcar Museum,
Baltimore,
(410) 547–0264,
www.baltimoremd.com/streetcar

Baltimore Zoo,
Baltimore,
(410) 396–7102,
www.baltimorezoo.org

Barge House Museum,
Eastport (Annapolis),
(410) 268–1802

Basignani Winery,
Sparks,
(410) 472–0703

Battle Acre Monument,
Dundalk,
(410) 583–7313

Bear Branch Nature Center,
Westminster,
(410) 848–2517

Boordy Vineyards,
Hydes,
(410) 592–5015,
www.bordy.com

Cab Calloway Jazz Institute,
Baltimore,
(410) 383–5522

Carroll County Arts
Council,
Westminster,
(410) 848–7272,
www.carr.org.arts

Cascade Lake,
Hampstead,
(410) 374–9111,
www.cascadelake.com

Catonsville Historical
Society,
Catonsville,
(410) 744–3034

Center Stage,
Baltimore,
(410) 332–0033,
www.centerstage.org

Charles Carroll House of
Annapolis,
Annapolis,
(410) 269–1737

Chase-Lloyd House,
Annapolis,
(410) 263–2723

Chesapeake Children's
Museum,
Annapolis,
(410) 266–0677

City Fire Museum,
Baltimore,
(410) 727–2414

Columbia Association Arts
Center,
Columbia,
(410) 730–0075

Contemporary Museum,
Baltimore,
(410) 783–5720,
www.contemporary.org

Cylburn Arboretum,
Baltimore,
(410) 367–2217

Cygnus Wine Cellars,
Manchester,
(410) 374–6395

Edgar Allan Poe House,
Baltimore,
(410) 396–7932

Ellicott City B&O
Railroad Museum,
Ellicott City,
(410) 461–1945,
www.ref.osc.edu/gkoma

Enoch Pratt Free Library,
Baltimore,
(410) 396–5430

Esther Pringley Rice
Gallery,
Westminster,
(410) 857–2599

Eubie Blake National
Museum and Cultural
Center,
Baltimore,
(410) 625–3113,
www.eubieblake.org

Evergreen House,
Baltimore,
(410) 516–0341,
www.jhu.edu/!evrgreen

Fire Museum of Maryland,
Lutherville,
(410) 321–7500,
members.home.net/fireman

Fort McHenry,
Baltimore,
(410) 962–4290, ext. 224,
www.nps.gov/fomc

Ft. George G. Meade
Museum,
Fort Meade,
(301) 677–6966

Government House,
Annapolis,
(410) 974–3531

Great Blacks in Wax
Museum,
Baltimore,
(410) 563–3404 or
(410) 522–9547,
www.gbiw.org

Gunpowder Falls State Park,
(410) 592–2897,
www.dnr.state.md.us

Hammond-Harwood
House,
Annapolis,
(410) 263–4683

Hampton National Historic
Site,
Towson,
(410) 823–1309,
www.nps.gov/hamp

Hart-Miller Island State Park,
Glenarm,
(410) 592–2897

Hays House Museum,
Bel Air,
(410) 838–7691,
www.netqsi.com/~hshc/c

Helen Avalynne Tawes Garden,
Annapolis,
(410) 974–3717

Heritage Society of Essex and Middle River,
Essex,
(410) 574–6934

Historic Annapolis Foundation Museum Store,
Annapolis,
(410) 268–5576

Historic Oakland,
Columbia,
(410) 730–0075,
www.historic-oakland.com

Historical Electronics Museum,
Linthicum,
(410) 765–3803,
www.erols.com/aradarmus

Historic Waverly,
Marriottsville,
(410) 313–5400

Historical Society of Carroll County,
Westminster,
(410) 848–6494,
www.carr.org/hscc

Homewood House Museum,
Baltimore,
(410) 516–5589,
www.jhu.edu/news_info/to_do

Howard County Center for the Arts,
Ellicott City,
(410) 313–2787

Howard County Center of African-American Culture,
Columbia,
(410) 715–1921,
www.hccaac.org

Howard County Historical Society,
Ellicott City,
(410) 461–1050

Irvine Natural Science Center,
Stevenson,
(410) 484–2413,
www.explorenature.org

James E. Lewis Art Gallery,
Baltimore,
(443) 885–1159

Jewish Museum of Maryland,
Baltimore,
(410) 732–6400,
www.jhsm.org

Joseph Myerhoff Symphony Hall,
Baltimore,
(410) 783–8000 or
(800) 442–1198,
www.baltimoresymphony.org

Jug Bay Wetlands Sanctuary,
Lothian,
(410) 741–9330,
www.aacpl.lib.md.us/rp/parks/jugbay

Kunte Kinte Plaque,
Annapolis,
(410) 263–7940

Lacrosse Museum/Nation Hall of Fame Baltimore,
(410) 235–6882,
www.lacrosse.org

Ladew Topiary Gardens,
Jarrettsville,
(410) 557–9466

Leakin Park,
Franklinville,
(410) 448–0730,
users.erols.com/seyfritp

Lexington Market,
Baltimore,
(410) 685–6169,
www.lexingtonmarket.com

London Town House and Gardens,
Edgewater,
(410) 222–1919,
www.historiclondontown.com

Lyric Opera House,
Baltimore,
(410) 685–5086,
www.baltimoreopera.com/xlyric.html

Maritime Museum,
Annapolis,
(410) 268–5576

Market House,
Annapolis,
(410) 269–0941

Maryland Hall for the Creative Arts,
Annapolis,
(410) 263–5544, ext. 23,
www.mdhallarts.org

Maryland Historical Society,
Baltimore,
(410) 675–3750,
www.mdhs.org

Maryland Maritime Museum,
Baltimore,
(410) 675-6750

Maryland Science Center,
Baltimore,
(410) 586-5225,
www.mdsci.org

Maryland State Archives,
Annapolis,
(410) 974-3914,
www.mdsa.net

Maryland State Fair-grounds,
Timonium,
(410) 252-0200,
www.marylandstatefair.com

Maryland State House,
Annapolis,
(410) 974-3400

Maryland State Police Museum,
Pikesville,
(410) 486-3101,
www.inform.umd.edu/UMS+State/MDResources/MDSP/history.html

Merriweather Post Pavilion,
Columbia,
(301) 596-0660 or
(410) 730-2424

Morris A. Mechanic Theatre,
Baltimore,
(410) 625-4230,
www.themechanic.org

Morris Meadows Historic Preservation Museum,
Freeland,
(410) 329-6636

Mother Seton House,
Baltimore,
(410) 523-3443

Mount Clare Museum House,
Baltimore,
(410) 837-3262

Museum of Industry,
Baltimore,
(410) 727-4808,
www.thebmi.org

National Aquarium,
Baltimore,
(410) 576-3800,
www.awua.com

National Cryptologic Museum,
Fort Meade,
(301) 688-5436 or
(301) 688-5849,
www.nsa.gov:8080/museum

National Historic Seaport,
Baltimore,
(800) NHC-PORT

National Museum of Dentistry,
Baltimore,
(410) 706-0600,
www.dentalmuseum.umaryland.edu

National Shrine of the Basilica,
Baltimore,
(410) 727-3564

Nixon's Farm,
West Friendship,
(410) 442-2151

North Point State Park,
Fort Howard,
(410) 887-7529,
www.dnr.state.md.us

Oella-Benjamin Banneker Site,
Oella,
(410) 887-1087

Oella Mill,
Oella,
(410) 465-1313

Old Treasury Building,
Annapolis,
(410) 267-8149

Orchard Street Church,
Baltimore,
(410) 523-8150

Patapsco Female Institute,
Ellicott City,
(410) 465-8500

Patapsco Valley State Park,
Ellicott City,
(410) 461-5005,
www.dnr.state.md.us

Patuxent River State Park,
Ellicott City,
(301) 924-2127,
www.dnr.state.md.us

Peabody Conservatory of Music,
Baltimore,
(410) 659-8124

Pier Six Concert Pavilion,
Baltimore,
(410) 625-3100

Pimlico Race Course,
Baltimore,
(410) 542-9400,
www.marylandracing.com

Piney Run Park,
Sykesville,
(410) 795–3274,
www.carr.org/sykes/gatehouse.htm

Port Discovery,
Baltimore,
(410) 727–8120

Potters Guild of Baltimore,
Baltimore,
(410) 235–4884,
www.pottersguild.org

Pride of Baltimore II,
Baltimore,
(410) 539–1151,
www.pride2.org

PSINet Stadium,
Baltimore,
(410) 547–8100,
www.ravenszone.net

Quiet Waters Park,
Annapolis,
(410) 222–1777

Rash Field Ice Rink,
Baltimore,
(410) 752–8632

Rectory,
Baltimore,
(410) 685–2886,
www.preserveMD.org

Robert Long House,
Baltimore,
(410) 675–6750

Rocks State Park,
Jarrettsville,
(410) 557–7994,
www.dnr.state.md.us

Sandy Point State Park,
Sandy Point,
(410) 974–2149

Shiplap House Museum,
Annapolis,
(410) 267–7619

Shot Tower,
Baltimore,
(410) 837–5424

Smithsonian Environmental Research Center,
Edgewater,
(301) 261–4190,
www.serc.si.edu

Soldier's Delight National Environmental Area,
Owings Mills,
(410) 461–5005

SS *John W. Brown,*
Baltimore,
(410) 661–1550

St. Anne's Episcopal Church,
Annapolis,
(410) 267–9333

St. Frances Academy,
Baltimore,
(410) 539–5794,
www.sfacademy.org

St. Francis Xavier Church,
Baltimore,
(410) 727–3103,
www.Josephite.comparish/md/sfx

St. John's College,
Annapolis,
(410) 263–2371

St. Jude Shrine,
Baltimore,
(410) 685–6026,
www.stjudeshrine.org

St. Vincent de Paul Church,
Baltimore,
(410) 962–5078

Star-Spangled Banner Flag House and 1812 Museum,
Baltimore,
(410) 837–1793,
www.flaghouse.org

Steamship Historical Society of America,
Baltimore,
(410) 837–4334,
www.ubalt.edu/archives/ship.html

Steppingstone Museum,
Havre de Grace,
(410) 939–2299 or
(888) 419–1762

Stillridge Herb Farm,
Woodstock,
(410) 465–8348

Susquehanna State Park,
Havre de Grace,
(410) 557–7994,
www.dnr.state.md.us

Sykesville Gate House Museum of History,
Sykesville,
(410) 549–5150,
www.carr.org/sykes/gatehouse.htm

Thomas Isaac's Log Cabin,
Ellicott City,
(410) 750–7881,
www.rcf.usc.edu/~gkoma

Thomas Point Park,
Annapolis,
(410) 222–1969

Tobacco Prise House,
Annapolis,
(410) 267–7619

Union Mills Homestead and Grist Mill, Westminster, (410) 848–2288, www.ccpl.lib.md.us/tourism/un_mills.htm

Uniontown Historic District, Uniontown, (410) 848–7903

U.S. Ordnance Museum, Aberdeen, (410) 278–3602

Walters Art Gallery, Baltimore, (410) 547–9000, ext. 337, www.thewalters.org

Weber's Cider Mill Farm, Parkville, (410) 688–4488

Western Maryland Railway Historical Society Museum, Union Bridge, (410) 775–0150

Westminster Hall and Burying Ground, Baltimore, (410) 706–2072

William Paca House and Garden, Annapolis, (410) 263–5553

Woodhall Vineyards and Wine Cellar, Parkton, (410) 357–8644

Calendar of Annual Events in Central Maryland

January

Baltimore on Ice Winterfest, *Baltimore, (410) 837–4636 or (800) 282–6632*

Bass Expo, Saltwater Fishing and Fly Fishing Show, *Timonium, (410) 838–8687, www.fishingexpo.com*

Polar Bear Plunge, *Sandy Point State Park, (410) 974–2149, www.dnr.state.md.us*

Paper Americana Show, *Elkton, (410) 398–7735*

February

Chinese Lunar New Year Festival, *Baltimore, (410) 377–8143*

Party Music Feast, *Inner Harbor, (410) 484–5600 or (888) 375–0080, www.crabfeast.com*

March

Elkton Salutes St. Patrick, *Elkton, (410) 398–1528*

Jewish Cultural Festival, *Baltimore, (410) 685–3750*

Maple Sugarin' Festival, *Westminster, (410) 848–9040*

Maple Syrup Pancake Breakfast, *Cockeysville, (410) 887–1815*

Marlborough Hunt Races, *Davidsonville, (410) 798–5040*

Maryland Day Convocation, *Baltimore, (410) 617–5025*

St. Patrick's Parade, *Baltimore, (410) 837–0685*

St. Patrick's Day Bash, *Baltimore, (410) 685–3750*

April

Carroll Carvers Annual Festival of Carving, *Westminster, (410) 854–0067*

Celebration of Asian Culture, *Towson, (410) 830–2807*

Decoy, Wildlife Art, and Sportsman Festival, *Havre de Grace, (410) 939–3739*

Flower and Plant Market, *Union Mills, (410) 848–2288, www.carr.org/tourism/index.htm*

Gunpowder Falls Annual Earth Day, *Perry Hall, (410) 592–2897, www.dnr.state.md.us*

Calendar of Annual Events in Central Maryland (Cont'd)

Harborplace Street Performers Auditions, *Baltimore, (800) HARBOR–1*

Maryland Orchid Society's Orchid Show, *Owings Mills, (410) 256–5503*

Maryland Archaeology Month, *statewide, (410) 514–7661*

Maryland House and Garden Pilgrimage, *various locations, (410) 821–6933, www.mhgp.org*

Maryland Hunt Cup Celebration, *Worthington Valley, (410) 685–3750*

Maryland Hunt Cup Steeplechase Race, *Glyndon, (410) 429–4231*

Maryland Sheep and Wool Festival, *West Friendship, (410) 531–3647, www.sheepandwoolfestival.org*

My Lady's Manor Steeplechase Races, *Monkton, (410) 557–9466*

Rites of Spring, *Timonium, (410) 554–2662*

Savage Mill Woodworking Show, *Savage, (301) 490–0187*

Spring Fair, *West Friendship, (301) 791–2346*

Springtime at the Mill, *Ellicott City, (410) 661–5633*

Symposium on Archaeology, *Crownsville, (410) 514–7661, www.smcm.edu/asm*

Taste of Southern Maryland, *Rose Haven, (410) 741–5101*

Towson Gardens Day, *Towson, (410) 825–2211*

Upper Bay Skipjack Invitational Races and Earth Day Festival, *Havre de Grace, (410) 939–3303*

Welcome the Skipjacks Bull and Oyster Roast, *Havre de Grace, (800) 406–0766*

May

A Cappella Singing Festival, *Towson, (410) 488–6824*

Annapolis Waterfront Arts Festival, *Annapolis, (410) 268–8828*

Annual Flower and Plant Market, *Union Mills, (410) 848–2288*

Art Blooms in Maryland, *Annapolis, (410) 974–3531*

Blue Angels Demonstration, *Annapolis, (410) 268–7600*

Chesapeake Bay Blues Festival, *Sandy Point State Park, (301) 794–5720, www.bayblues.org*

Chesapeake Bay Bridge Walk, *Annapolis, (877) BAYSPAN, www.mdta.state.md.us*

Civil War Encampment at Steppingstone Museum, *Havre de Grace, (410) 939–2299*

Colonial Highland Gather, *Fair Hill, (410) 392–4690, www.fairhillscottishgames.org*

Cylburn Market Day, *Baltimore, (410) 367–2217*

Dublin Country Fair, *Dublin, (410) 457–5167*

Delaware Valley Quilt Show, *North East, (302) 368–8626, www.dca.net//ladybugsquilt*

East Coast Rally, *Aberdeen Proving Ground, (410) 638–3059, www.apg.army.mil*

Flower and Jazz Festival, *Westminster, (800) 272–1933*

Greyhound Pets of America/MD Reunion Day, *Hunt Valley, (800) 600–8607*

Herb Festival, *Sykesville, (410) 795–3274*

Calendar of Annual Events in Central Maryland (Cont'd)

Howard County Jewish Festival, *Columbia, (410) 730–4976*

International Children's Spring Festival, *Lutherville, (410) 321–8555*

Ladew Plant Sale, *Monkton, (410) 557–9466*

Living American Flag Program, *Baltimore, (410) 563–3524, www.ubalt.edu/flagday*

Memorial Day Street Fest and Parade, *Elkton, (410) 398–8144*

Memorial Day, *Timonium, (410) 666–0490*

Plant, Home, and Craft Mart, *Taneytown, (410) 751–1100 www.ci.taneytown.md.us*

Preakness Celebration, *Baltimore, (410) 542–9400 or (410) 837–3030, www.preaknesscelebration.com*

Preakness Celebration Parade, *Baltimore, (888) BALTIMORE or (410) 837–4636, www.bop.org*

Preakness Crab Derby, *Baltimore, (410) 685–6169, www.lexingtonmarket.com*

Preakness Race, *Baltimore, (410) 542–9400*

Reservoir Hill Garden Tour, *Baltimore, (410) 669–2843*

Springfest, *Baltimore, (410) 727–3939*

Towsontown Spring Festival, *Towson, (410) 825–1144*

June

Annapolis Jazzfest, *Annapolis, (410) 349–1111*

Charles Village Parade, Garden Walk, and Festival, *Baltimore, (410) 662–7777*

CitySand, *Baltimore, (800) HARBOR-1, www.harborplace.com*

Cylburn Solstice Celebration, *Baltimore, (410) 367–2217*

Darlington Herb Festival and Garden Party, *Darlington, (410) 836–3409*

Farm Museum Fiddlers' Convention, *Westminster, (410) 876–2667*

Father's Day Party Music Crab Feast, *Baltimore, (410) 484–5600*

Gay, Lesbian, Bisexual and Transgender Pride Festival, *Baltimore, (410) 837–5445*

Gospel Music Crab Feast, *Baltimore, (410) 484–5600, www.crabfeast.com*

Howard County Jewish Festival, *Columbia, (410) 730–4976*

Juneteenth, *Baltimore, (410) 467–2724*

Latino Festival, *Baltimore City, (410) 783–5404, www.eblo.org*

Maritime Festival, *Havre de Grace, (410) 939–4800*

Maryland Rose Society Show, *Owings Mills, (410) 367–2217 or (410) 374–1070*

National Marriage Day, *Elkton, (410) 398–1640*

National Pause for the Pledge of Allegiance, *Baltimore, (410) 453–3524, www.ubalt.edu/flagday*

North East Flag Day Ceremony, *North East, (410) 287–5801*

North Bay Deer Creek Fiddlers' Convention, *Westminster, (410) 876–2667,*

Party Music Crab Feast, *Baltimore, (410) 484–5600 or (888) 375–0080, www.crabfeast.com*

Quilts by the Bay, *Annapolis, (410) 757–6859*

Scottish Festival, *Havre de Grace, (410) 939–2299*

Calendar of Annual Events in Central Maryland (Cont'd)

South County Festival, *Tracy's Landing, (410) 867–3129*

St. Nicholas Greek Folk Festival, *Baltimore, (410) 633–7700*

Strawberry Festival, *Sykesville, (410) 795–0494*

Summer Fair, *West Friendship, (301) 791–2346*

USNA Flag Day, *Annapolis, (410) 263–6933,*

July

Baltimore Symphony Orchestra Fourth of July Celebration, *Hunt Valley, (410) 783–8000*

Baltimore's Fourth of July Celebration, *Baltimore, (410) 837–4636 or (888) BALTIMORE, www.bop.org*

Carroll County Farmers Market-Christmas in July, *Westminster, (410) 848–7748*

Catonsville's July Fourth Celebration, *Catonsville, (410) 744–7042*

Cecil County Fair, *Fair Hill, (410) 658–7350*

Common Ground on the Hill's "Tradition" Workshops, *Westminster (410) 857–2771, www.commongroundonthehill.com*

Fourth of July Fireworks Cruise, *Annapolis, (410) 268–7600*

Fourth of July Extravaganza and Fireworks, *Elkton, (410) 398–8144*

Gumbo Jam, *Annapolis, (202) 861–6825*

Harborplace's Birthday Celebration, *Baltimore, (800) HARBOR–1*

Harford County Farm Fair, *Bel Air, (410) 838–8663, www.farmfair.org*

Havre de Grace Independence Celebration, *Havre de Grace, (410) 939–4362*

Heritage Fair, *Dundalk, (410) 284–4022*

Howard County Pow-Wow, *Friendship, (919) 252–5383*

Ice Cream Festival, *Baltimore, (410) 685–6169, www.lexingtonmarket.com*

John Paul Jones Day, *Annapolis, (410) 263–6933*

Old-Fashioned July Fourth, *Westminster, (410) 876–2667*

Party Music Crab Feast, *Baltimore, (410) 484–5600 or (888) 375–0080, www.crabfeast.com*

Rotary Crab Feast, *Annapolis, (410) 841–2841, www.annapolisrotary.com*

Salute to Cecil County Veterans Fireworks, *North East, (410) 287–5801*

Towson Area Fourth of July Parade, *Towson, (410) 832–2190*

World's Greatest Crab Feast, Music Festival, and Fireworks, *Baltimore, (410) 484–5600*

August

Carroll County Farmers Market Peach Festival, *Westminster, (410) 848–7748*

Celebrate Taneytown Festival, *Taneytown, (410) 751–1100*

Dutch Picnic Festival, *Westminster, (410) 848–8923*

Havre de Grace Seafood Festival, *Havre de Grace, (410) 939–1525*

Howard County Fair, *West Friendship, (410) 442–1022*

Kunta Kinte Heritage Festival, *Annapolis, (410) 349–0338, www.kuntakinte.org*

Calendar of Annual Events in Central Maryland (Cont'd)

Maritime Maryland, *Annapolis, (410) 263–6933*

Maryland Renaissance Festival, *Crownsville, (410) 266–7304, www.rennfest.com*

Maryland State Fair, *Timonium, (410) 252–0200, ext. 226*

Old-Fashioned Corn Roast Festival, *Union Mills, (410) 848–2288, www.carr.org/carroll/tourism/un-mills.htn*

September

A-Maize-ing Place: A Mammoth Maze and Harvest Happening, *Columbia, (410) 313–7275*

Aberdeen Heritage Day, *Aberdeen, (410) 272–1600*

Anne Arundel County Fair, *Crownsville, (410) 923–3400*

Annual Duck Fair, *Havre de Grace, (410) 939–3739*

Baltimore Irish Festival, *Baltimore, (410) 837–0685, www.irishfestival.com*

Bel Air Festival for the Arts, *Bel Air, (410) 836–2395*

Big M All Ford and Mustang Fall Show, *Bel Air, (410) 357–5615*

Catonsville Arts and Crafts Festival, *Catonsville, (410) 244–1999*

Chesapeake Airshow, *Middle River, (410) 686–2233*

Children's Day at Ladew Topiary Gardens, *Monkton, (410) 557–9466*

Columbia Class Grand Prix, *Columbia, (410) 772–4450*

Cruisers Unlimited Car Club, *Edgemere, (410) 282–5296*

Defenders' Day Remembered, *Dundalk, (410) 284–2331*

Duck Fair, *Havre de Grace, (410) 939–3739*

Fall Festival, *Lisbon, (301) 854–5037, www.defhr.org*

Fall Festival, *Elkton, (410) 392–3253*

Fall Harvest Day, *Marriottsville, (410) 922–3044*

Fall Harvest Festival, *Havre de Grace, (410) 939–2299*

Honey Harvest Festival, *Westminster, (410) 848–9040*

Howard County Farm Heritage Days, *Woodstock, (410) 531–2569 or (410) 988–8165*

Jones Falls Valley Celebration, *Baltimore, (410) 261–3515, www.greaterhomewood.org*

Lake Elkhorn Festival, *Columbia, (410) 381–0202*

Maryland Seafood Festival, *Annapolis, (410) 268–7682, www.annapolischamber.com*

Maryland Steam Historical Society, *Arcadia, (410) 239–6949*

Maryland Wine Festival, *Westminster, (410) 876–2667*

Navy Way Days, *Annapolis, (410) 263–6933*

Parkville Towne Centre Fair, *Parkville, (410) 665–0100*

Patapsco Valley Barbershop Show, *Woodlawn, (410) 795–2175*

Reister's Towne Festival, *Reisterstown, (410) 356–0688*

Septemberfest, *Havre de Grace, (410) 939–3303*

Smallwood Festival, *Westminster, (410) 848–8254*

Star-Spangled Banner Weekend, *Baltimore, (410) 986–4290, ext. 222*

Calendar of Annual Events in Central Maryland (Cont'd)

Union Bridge Fall Fest, *Union Bridge, (410) 775–2711, www.carr.org/~unionbr*

Westminster Fallfest, *Westminster, (800) 272–1933*

October

Autumn Wellness Festival, *Elkton, (410) 398–5566*

Baltimore Bird Fanciers Annual Bird Show, *Parkville, (410) 239–1928 or (410) 256–9326*

Blacksmith Days, *Westminster, (410) 876–2667*

Blessing of Baltimore's Work Boats, *Baltimore, (800) HARBOR–1*

Celtic Highlands Gathering, *Westminster, (410) 876–2667*

Chocolate Festival, *Baltimore, (410) 685–6169, www.lexingtonmarket.com*

Clandestine Tales and Tours by Candlelight, *Annapolis, (410) 269–1737*

Darlington Apple Festival, *Darlington, (410) 457–4189*

Elkton Halloween Parade, *Elkton, (410) 398–1640*

Fair Hill International Festival in the Country, *(410) 755–6065, www.fairhillinternational.com*

Fall Harvest Days, *Mechanicsville, (410) 461–5005, www.dnr.state.md.us/publiclands*

Fall Harvest Days, *Westminster, (410) 876–2667*

Fell's Point Fun Festival, *Baltimore City, (410) 675–6756*

Friendship Farm Heritage Show, *Friendship, (410) 257–7133, www.gbgm-umc.org/friendshipumc-md*

Great Chesapeake Bay Schooner Race, *Baltimore, (757) 393–2224, www.southernbranch.com/schoonerrace*

Halloween Party, *North East, (410) 287–2658*

Harvest Happening, *Glenwood, (410) 313–7275*

Harvest Hoe-down, *Chase, (410) 592–2897*

Harvest of Quilts, *Bel Air, (410) 879–7924*

Mt. Airy Fall Festival, *Mount Airy, (301) 829–2112*

Old Bay Crab Soup Stakes, *Baltimore, (800) HARBOR–1*

Patapsco Valley Barbershop Show, *Columbia, (410) 788–4595, www.heartofmaryland.org*

Pumpkin Appreciation Days, *Jarrettsville, (410) 557–7994, www.dnr.state.d.us*

Scarecrow Madness, *Annapolis, (301) 970–2510*

Ship of Ghouls, *Baltimore, (800) HARBOR–1*

United States Sailboat Show, *Annapolis, (410) 268–8828*

United States Powerboat Show, *Annapolis, (410) 268–8828*

Zoo-Booo!, *Baltimore, (410) 366–LION*

November

Annapolis by Candlelight, *Annapolis, (410) 267–7619*

Art Festival, *Annapolis, (410) 268–0474*

Baltimore's Thanksgiving Day Parade, *Baltimore, (410) 837–4636 or (888) BALTIMORE, www.bop.org*

Elkton's Holiday Light-up, *Elkton, (410) 398–1640*

Calendar of Annual Events in Central Maryland (Cont'd)

Family Holiday Hands-on Workshop, *Annapolis, (410) 269–1737*

Hauntings of Ellicott Mills Ghost Tours, *Ellicott City, (800) 288–8747, www.howardcountymdtour.com*

Holiday Train Garden, *Towson, (410) 321–1909*

Lights on the Bay, *Annapolis, (410) 260–3161*

Potters Guild of Baltimore Show, *Baltimore, (410) 235–4884*

Savage Mill Open House Weekend, *Savage, (800) 788–MILL*

Symphony Homes for the Holidays, *Baltimore, (410) 783–8023, www.baltimoresymphony.org*

Symphony of Lights, *Columbia, (410) 740–7666 or (410) 740–7645*

December

Annual Lighted Boat Parade, *Baltimore, (800) HARBOR–1*

Baltimore's New Year's Eve Extravaganza, *Baltimore, (888) BALTIMORE, www.bop.org*

Candlelight Pub Crawl, *Annapolis, (410) 263–5401*

Candlelight Tour of Historic Havre de Grace, *Havre de Grace, (410) 939–3947*

Christmas Cookie House Tour, *Baltimore, (410) 233–3168 or (410) 945–1497*

Dickens of a Tour, *Ellicott City, (800) 288–8747, www.howardcountymdtour.com*

Eastport Yacht Club's Lights Parade, *Annapolis, (410) 885–2415*

First Night Annapolis, *Annapolis, (410) 280–0700*

Frosty Follies, *Annapolis, (410) 956–0512*

Gallagher Fest, *Baltimore, (410) 783–8000*

Governor's Holiday Open House, *Annapolis, (410) 974–3531*

Holiday Pops Concert, *Baltimore, (410) 296–0748, www.baltimorejuniorleague.org*

Holiday Tour, *Westminster, (410) 876–2667*

Kwanzaa Celebration and New Years Celebration, *Baltimore, (410) 484–5600 or (888) 375–0080, www.crabfeast.com*

Lighted Boat Parade, *Baltimore, (800) HARBOR–1, www.harborplace.com*

Merry Tuba Christmas, *Baltimore, (800) HARBOR–1*

Port Deposit's Susquehanna Festival of Lights, *Port Deposit, (410) 378–4223*

State House by Candlelight, *Annapolis, (410) 974–3400*

Street Cars of Desire, *Timonium, (410) 461–0687*

Waverly Candlelight Tour, *Marriottsville, (410) 313–5400 or (301) 596–6542*

Greater Washington

Prince George's, Montgomery, and Frederick Counties make up the Greater Washington area. Washington, D.C., is at the center of a huge suburban megalopolis formed by the blending of these three counties and northern Virginia. Although there are areas of dense population, and seemingly miles upon miles of row or town houses, there are also miles and miles of parkland, green spaces, and open spaces. Because so many people who live here come from other places, such as places where it never snows, traffic seems to get jammed as soon as the TV and radio weather forecasters think about snow. Forget about what happens when it actually does snow. If you should be here when it snows, tune in to a radio or TV station, and go for public transportation. Or find a nice fireplace and cuddle up with a good book.

As a native of this area, I have received a steady stream of visitors over the years who want to tour Washington. I take them to the subway station, and the Metro Rail takes them downtown to the many Smithsonian buildings, galleries, the zoo, or anything else they want to see. The Washington Metro is as clean and safe as any subway system around and at last count was the second busiest subway in the country.

Three lines run in Prince George's County: the Green, the Orange, and the Blue. Green Line stations are at Greenbelt, College Park, Prince George's Plaza, West Hyattsville, Branch Avenue, Suitland, and Naylor Road; Orange Line stations are at New Carrollton, Landover, and Cheverly; and Blue Line stations are at Addison Road and Capitol Heights.

There's one line with two branches running in Montgomery County: the Red Line, with stations at Shady Grove, Rockville, Twinbrook, White Flint, Grosvenor, Medical Center, Bethesda, and Friendship Heights going in toward Washington on the northwestern branch, and Takoma Park, Silver

Trivia

In the spring and the fall, the Mary Surratt Society sponsors a "Booth's Trail" tour that follows the path of John Wilkes Booth from Ford's Theatre in Washington, D.C., to Dr. Mudd's home, to the Garrett Farm in northern Virginia. These fascinating tours fill up very quickly, and reservations are essential. Call (301) 868–1121 for tour dates and information.

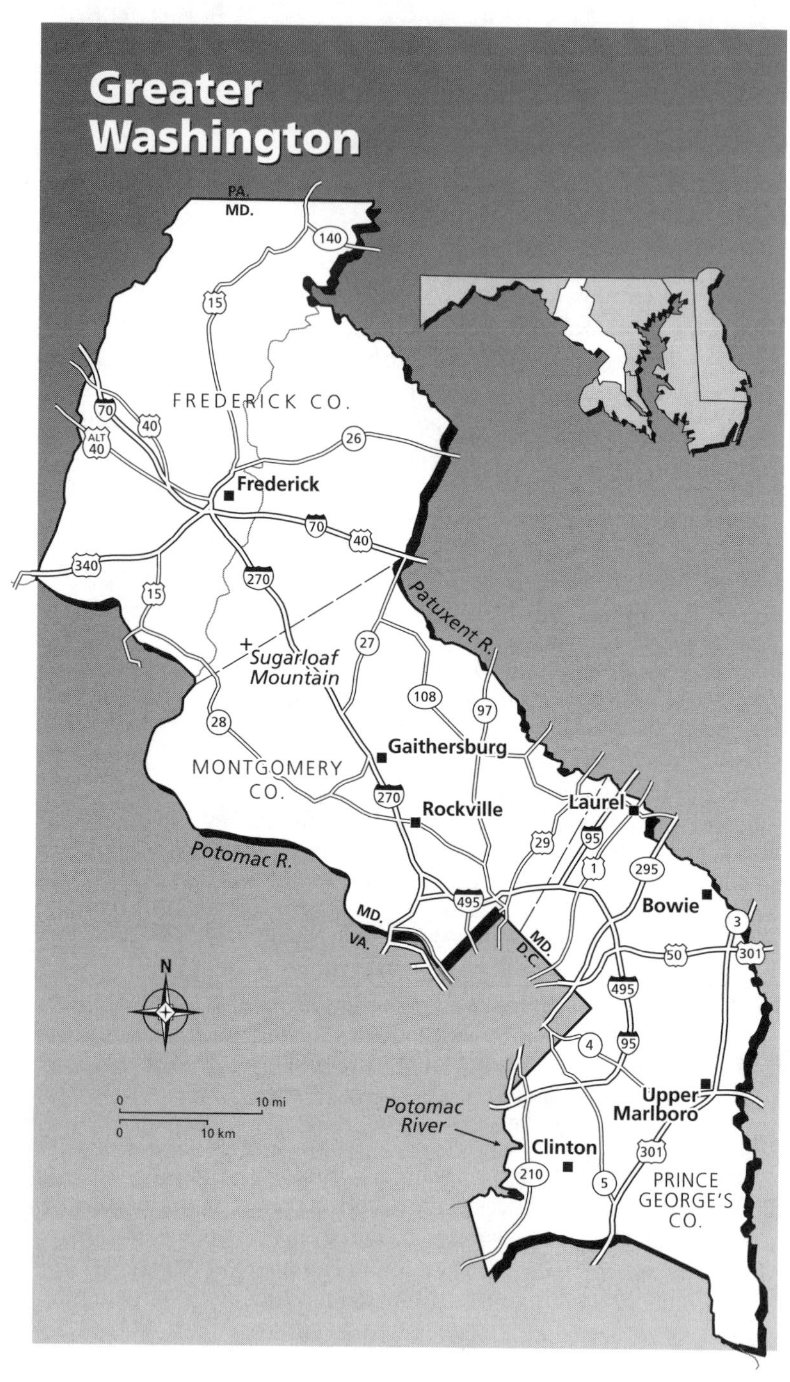

Greater Washington
PA.
MD.
140
15
FREDERICK CO.
70
40
ALT 40
26
Frederick
70
40
340
270
15
Patuxent R.
27
Sugarloaf Mountain
108
97
28
Gaithersburg
MONTGOMERY CO.
270
Rockville
Laurel
29
95
1
295
Potomac R.
495
Bowie
MD.
VA.
MD.
D.C.
3
50
301
495
N
4
95
0
10 mi
0
10 km
Upper Marlboro
Potomac River
Clinton
301
210
5
PRINCE GEORGE'S CO.

Spring, Forest Glen, Wheaton, and Glenmont coming out the more northerly route.

Trains run 5:30 A.M. to midnight Monday through Thursday, 5:30 A.M. to 2:00 A.M. on Friday, 8:00 A.M. to 2:00 A.M. on Saturday, and 10:00 A.M. to midnight on Sunday. Trains run about every five to fifteen minutes, depending on the time of day. Fares are based on time and distance, with rush hour (5:30 to 9:30 A.M. and 3:00 to 7:00 P.M., weekdays) costing more than off-peak times. For a bicycle permit, call (202) 962–1116. For general information about Metro Rail and Metro Bus (such as how to get from your door to your destination), call (202) 637–7000. This number is operational weekdays from 6:00 A.M. to 10:30 P.M. and weekends from 8:00 A.M. to 10:30 P.M.

Judy's Favorite Attractions in Greater Washington

- ***College Park Aviation Museum***
- ***Mount Olivet Cemetery***
- ***Patuxent Research Refuge***
- ***Roddy Road Covered Bridge***
- ***U.S. Department of Agriculture Research Center***
- ***White's Ferry***

Of course, this book is designed for people who are interested in seeing sights other than those along the subway routes. In the Greater Washington area you will find orchards, covered bridges, historic cemeteries, campgrounds, murals, a ferry, places to eat and to be entertained, old farm tools, and a museum dedicated to poultry, among other things.

Prince George's County

People hear more about Prince George's County in the news than they realize. A marriage is performed on the old wooden roller coaster at the Six Flags (formerly Adventure World) theme park outside Kettering; space flight information is reported from the Goddard Space Flight Center (and Museum) in Greenbelt, the hub of all NASA tracking

The Man of Steel

If you havent't been to the **Six Flags America** *amusement park recently and you have a passion for roller coasters, then you probably should schedule a return visit. Six Flags north of Upper Marlboro has added the Superman Ride of Steel, an ultra-fast, mega-coaster that soars 200 feet in the air (the tallest in the park—and what a view!) and races down the 1-mile track at 70 miles per hour. If you prefer your entertainment mild, not wild, look for the life-size cartoon characters, including Batman and Bugs Bunny. Six Flags America is located at 13710 Central Avenue, Upper Marlboro 20774. Call (301) 249–1501.*

Trivia

Andrews Air Force Base was named Andrews Field (formerly Camp Springs Army Base) on March 31, 1945, in memory of Lt. Gen. Frank Maxwell Andrews. During the early stages of World War II, Andrews was the Commander of all Air Forces in Europe, serving with Gen. Dwight D. Eisenhower. An outspoken proponent of air power, Andrews was born on February 3, 1884, in Nashville, Tennessee. He was killed in an aircraft accident in Iceland on May 3, 1943, and buried in Section 3 of Arlington National Cemetery.

activities; or the President or a visiting dignitary arrives at Andrews Air Force Base, the home base for Air Force One.

Of course, Prince George's County is rarely mentioned, but all of this commerce and history is taking place here on a day-to-day basis. Prince George's County is a place of "firsts" and "lasts."

Not far from Andrews, in the Clearwater Nature Center in Clinton, is the ***Suitland Bog,*** which technically is a fen. It's home to some interesting and rare plants (twenty species are on Maryland's rare, threatened, or endangered list), as well as the occasional carnivorous plant, such as the spatulate-leaved sundew and the Northern pitcher plant. The Suitland Bog is the last undisturbed Maryland coastal plain bog in Prince George's County. A short, winding wooden boardwalk cuts a shaded path through the area and signs are placed by the rarer plants. Call the Clearwater Nature Center for a guided tour reservation from May to September. The center is located at 11000 Thrift Road, Clinton 20735. Call (301) 297–4575.

Upper Marlboro is the county seat for Prince George's. Understanding that Prince George's County was and still is a very agrarian county, you will appreciate the work of W. Henry DuVall. A lifelong Prince Georgean, DuVall had the foresight to save tools from the nineteenth century, whether it was a scythe, can opener, carpenter's plane, or foot-operated dental drill. This was the beginning of the ***DuVall Tool Museum***. There is even a white building block that is blackened on one side, which apparently was obtained during a nineteenth-century architectural revision of the White House. The dark stains are said to be soot from the burning of the building during the War of 1812. DuVall's collection, which he started in the 1930s, had more than 1,200 items by the time he died in 1979.

The Maryland–National Capital Park and Planning Commission bought the agglomeration so that it would not be lost to the twentieth or twenty-first century. More tools are accepted, so if you have something tucked away in your attic or out in the garage someplace—particularly if it is unique to southern Maryland history—donate it here instead of to the dump. You can return to yesteryear by visiting

Crain Highway

Route 3, running between U.S. 50 and the Potomac River, is also known as Crain Highway, named after Robert Crain, a Charles County farmer and lawyer who persuaded the state to fund a highway so farmers could transport their crops from southern Maryland to northern cities. The highway had its official opening ceremonies in October 1927, with 20,000 people in attendance.

the museum, located in the Patuxent River Park, Sunday from 1:00 to 4:00 P.M. and by appointment. The address is 16000 Croom Airport Road, Upper Marlboro 20772. Call (301) 672–6074 or visit www.pgparks.com.

Just south of Upper Marlboro is the old-turned-to-new Prince George's Equestrian Center and the newer ***Show Place Arena***. Once a functional horse racetrack, it was closed and converted to fringe parking for county employees before it was reborn as an architectural masterpiece and the home of the annual county fair, concerts, and other special events. There are even a few days of horse racing now and then. You'll find the center and arena at 14900 Pennsylvania Avenue, Upper Marlboro 20772, at the intersection of Routes 301 and 4. Call (301) 952–7900 or visit www.showplacearena.com.

The City of Brotherly Love—in Suitland

Few of us can claim to be natives around this area, for people come and go with military assignments or as the "ins" of the government change, sometimes every two years. Although we may ask "where you from?" because we're fairly certain it isn't from here, we don't have a third-generation-or-more litmus test before accepting you. One of the reasons is all the great things you bring from wherever it was you were before. Such is the case with **LiLeons** *(pronounced Lillian's)* **Philadelphia Steaks and Hoagies.** *Those of you who really pine for a South Philly cheese steak, or those who've never had one, will be thrilled that the genuine article can be found in this Suitland eatery. And just so you won't miss the City of Brotherly Love too much (or maybe it will make your absence that much more severe) are banners for the '76ers, Flyers, and Eagles. LiLeons is at 3674 St. Barnabas Road, Suitland 20746. It's open from 11:00 A.M. to 11:00 P.M. Monday through Saturday. (301) 899–8233.*

To the west of Upper Marlboro is Largo, the home of the former USAirways Arena, formerly the Capital Centre and the USAir Arena (if McDonald's had bought it, would it be the McArena?). It's now the home of the FedEx field, where the Washington Redskins play.

Nearby you'll find the flagship restaurant ***BET Soundstage***, from BET Holdings Inc., the first and only cable network for the African-American community. This restaurant features a dynamic sensory experience through taped performances and a state-of-the-art multimedia display of video and music. Music celebrities, sports figures, artists, and business professionals provide a mix of the famous and the familiar among its clientele. A gift shop, filled with the latest BET-branded merchandise, including T-shirts, jackets, and caps, is on the premises. BET Soundstage is located near Lottsford Road and Route 202 at 9640 Lottsford Court, Upper Marlboro 20774. (301) 883–9500.

Trivia

On June 17, 1784, the first documented unmanned balloon flight in the United States took place in a field near the town of Bladensburg. Peter Carnes, the balloon owner, sent the manned balloon aloft a week later in Baltimore.

Northwest of Largo is Bladensburg and the ***Bladensburg Dueling Grounds,*** a small, wooded glen in the northeastern corner of Fort Lincoln Cemetery, adjacent to Colmar Manor. It was a court of last resort for nearly fifty years for offended gentlemen and politicians, who faced each other at ten paces with pistols and muskets. As noted on the historical marker placed by the Maryland–National Capital Park and Planning Commission, one of the most famous was that between Commodores Stephen Decatur and James Barron, which was settled here on March 22, 1820. Commodore Decatur, who had gained fame as the conqueror of the Barbary pirates, was fatally wounded by his antagonist.

Although Congress passed an antidueling law in 1839, duels continued here until just before the Civil War. The dueling grounds are in Anacostia River Park near the intersection of Bladensburg Road and 38th Avenue in Bladensburg. Also at Anacostia River Park is the Maryland–National Capital Park and Planning Commission Interpretive Center at the site of the old Bladensburg Marina.

At the junction of the Beltway (I–95, I–495) and John Hanson Highway (U.S. 50) is the New Carrollton Metro station, a MARC and AMTRAK railroad station, a first in intermodel transportation stops.

Several years ago the arts organizations of Prince George's and Montgomery Counties in Maryland, northern Virginia, and Washington, D.C., agreed to promote a ***MetroArts*** contest for public art to be displayed in subway stations throughout the system. It was very successful, and a number of artists had works displayed at several metro stations, such as New Carrollton, for a year. A second contest, this one with prize money totaling $100,000, has been held.

Trivia

The original events upon which the movie The Exorcist *was based took place in Mount Rainier, Maryland, starting on January 18, 1949, when weird noises were heard from the home at 3210 Bunker Hill Road. Father Albert Hughes came from nearby St. James Catholic Church to perform the exorcism, but four months later he still had not been successful. Okay, so Hollywood changed a few things, and the movie was set in the Georgetown area of Washington, D.C. The original home has been demolished.*

A 1998 permanent installation is now in place at the New Carrollton station. *Dawn and Dusk* was created by architect Ben Van Dusen and Kensington artist Heidi Lippman, and the Italian glass, marble, agate, and granite mosaic covers more than 2,000 square feet of the four stairway and elevator towers of the parking garage and the clock tower. Franz Mayer, a 150-year-old German company, and workers from the Mosaici Artisici of Spilimbergo, Italy, took Lippman's drawings and converted them into this colorful sight. Besides decorating these surfaces, the installation should save taxpayers money because it should protect the concrete surface from weather erosion.

The city of Bowie, east of New Carrollton, has several museums that let you explore the history of the area, and even some more modern electronic history. The ***Belair Mansion,*** circa 1745, is a five-part Georgian plantation house that was home to Samuel Ogle, Provincial Governor of Maryland. For several years it belonged to William Woodward, a noted horseman, and it was after his death in 1955 that suburban developer William Levitt bought the property and started building his Maryland version of a "Levittown." Objects on view range from paintings by Philippe Mercier (1689–1760) to a bronze statue of 1932's Triple Crown

Hoofbeats Heard on the Bridge

The newest **covered bridge** *in Maryland is in Bowie. There's nothing historic about this bridge, as far as its age goes, for it was built in 1988, but its use could be unique. It's located at the Bowie Race Course, which is now an equestrian center rather than a racetrack. The bridge is used to move horses from the stables to the track for their workouts, not for people or cars.*

winner Gallant Fox, who spent his yearling season at the Belair stables. Open Thursday through Sunday from 1:00 to 4:00 P.M. and for groups of ten or more by appointment, the mansion is located at 12207 Tulip Grove Drive, Bowie 20715. (301) 809-3088.

Also spending their yearling seasons at the Belair Stables were Nashua, the "Horse of the Year" in 1955, and Omaha, Gallant Fox's son. It's said that the first Thoroughbred horse, Selima, was stabled on the Belair Farm, making her the mother of all American Thoroughbred stock today. Until its closing in 1957, Belair was the oldest continually operating horse farm in the United States. Learn this and more at the ***Belair Stables Museum,*** open Sunday 1:00 to 4:00 P.M. May through October, 2835 Belair Drive, Bowie 20715. (301) 809–3088.

Genealogists will want to stop by the ***Prince George's Genealogical Library*** with its 4,000 volumes, periodicals, surname files, family group sheets, Bible records, and microfilms. The library, at 12219 Tulip Grove Drive, Bowie 20715, is open every Wednesday from 10:00 A.M. to dusk, except the first Wednesday of the month when it's open only until 1:00 P.M. It's also open on the last Saturday of the month from 1:00 to 5:00 P.M. Call (301) 262–2063 or e-mail pgcgs@juno.com.

The ***Bowie Railroad Station and Huntington Museum*** in "Old" Bowie is housed in buildings constructed in the early 1900s. This is the place to learn about railroading in this area, and watch today's trains zoom past on their way to New York, Boston, Washington, and across the country. Check out the old photographs and equipment from Bowie's bygone railroading days. The station is open Sunday noon to 4:00 P.M. April through October. It's located at 8614 Chestnut Avenue, Bowie 20715. Call (301) 809–3088.

There's no historical reason that the ***Radio and Television Museum*** is located in Bowie; it's just that the Radio History Society needed space and Bowie had it in the form of a rebuilt home that had been around from 1906 until a fire destroyed it in the mid-1980s. Inside the two-story structure are perhaps hundreds of pieces of radio and television history. Everyone of a certain age (there's no need to say what age that is) will recognize something in this collection, whether it's a crystal set (didn't every Boy Scout make one?) or a cathedral-shaped radio of the '30s and '40s. There are also several examples of Nipper, the RCA mascot. If you were around the D.C. area in the 1960s and 1970s, you may remember *The Joy Boys of Radio* on WRC. Ed Walker, one of the Joy Boys, has donated a number of items to this collection. Those who weren't around in those days may know his partner,

Willard Scott, from NBC's *Today* show. The museum, at 2608 Mitchellville Road, Bowie 20716, is open Saturday and Sunday from 1:00 to 4:00 P.M. (301) 390–1020.

None of these museums charge an admission fee, but contributions definitely are welcome.

Take U.S. 50 west, then head north around the Beltway, and you'll come to College Park, home of the University of Maryland and near there, the ***College Park Airport,*** where the first military training in a military-owned airplane took place in October 1909. The plane was designed by Orville and Wilbur Wright. College Park claims to be the "world's oldest continually operated airport," and today it is the only operating airport within the Capital Beltway. Pilots say they get a kick out of flying from the same airfield that the Wright Brothers used almost a century ago.

Budding aviators are sure to enjoy the 26,000-square-foot ***College Park Aviation Museum,*** which opened in 1998. Tours, movies, and special events are scheduled throughout the year, including an annual AirFair in September.

The museum is at 1965 Corporal Frank Scott Drive (named for the first civilian killed in an air accident), College park 20740. It's free and is open from 11:00 A.M. to 3:00 P.M. Wednesday through Friday and 11:00 A.M. to 5:00 P.M. Saturday and Sunday. Call (301) 864–6029.

Trivia

Mrs. Ralph H. Van Deman said, "Now I know why birds sing," after becoming the first woman in America to fly as a passenger in an airplane, when she went aloft with Wilbur Wright in College Park on October 27, 1909.

Just minutes from College Park is a planned city whose history starts in the 1930s. If you think planned cities are something new, then visit ***Greenbelt***. From its inception, Greenbelt had a sense of history about it. It has been chronicled, cataloged, dissected, scrutinized, and studied many times over in thorough detail. Although the town is now surrounded by town house communities for Washington commuters, you still can see the core of the town, its Art Deco architecture, and its attempts to retain its identity.

Greenbelt is one of three planned greenbelt towns that were to be satellite towns on the edge of larger urban cores (the other two are Greenhills, Ohio, and Greendale, Wisconsin, outside of Cincinnati and Milwaukee, respectively). The town was built around an inner core, allowing residents to walk everywhere they had to go on pedestrian paths so that people on foot would not have to intermingle with cars. The town was superorganized and highly democratic, and residents met to discuss everything. (In fact, at one point they met to declare a moratorium on meetings.)

For a more thorough explanation and visual interpretation, stop by the ***Greenbelt Museum*** on Sunday between 1:00 and 5:00 P.M. There's no admission charge. The museum is located at 10 B Crescent Road, Greenbelt 20768. Call (301) 474–1936 or visit www.otal.umd.edu/lvg/virtual-gb/gbtis.html. Greenbelt is at the northwest corner of the intersection of the Baltimore-Washington Parkway (I–295) and the Capital Beltway (I–495).

Head north up Baltimore-Washington Parkway (I–295) and you'll come to the outskirts of Laurel, the Montpelier Arts Center, and the Montpelier Mansion.

The ***Montpelier Arts Center*** is noted for its visual arts, serving as a home for eighteen professional resident artists. A rather full curriculum of visual arts classes is offered. The arts center is at 9401 Montpelier Drive, Laurel 20708. Call (301) 953–1993 or (301) 490–2329.

Next door is the ***Montpelier Mansion***, built in 1783 by Maj. Thomas Snowden, a significant landowner in Prince George's County. At one point the Montpelier site was about 10,000 acres of gently rolling parkland. Among the famed guests who stopped here were George and Martha Washington and Abigail Adams.

William Breckinridge Long, Undersecretary of State in the Franklin Roosevelt administration, and U.S. Ambassador to Italy from 1933 to 1936, was the twentieth-century owner, and his guests also were

Reading Is Fun-damental

Special library collections abound in Prince George's County. As the Belair Estate in Bowie claimed to be the "Cradle of American Racing," it seems entirely appropriate that the Bowie Library has the Selima Room, with its extensive collection of horse-racing records and materials. Selima was one of the original mares who started the bloodline that flows in almost every racehorse in this country. Other special collections in the Prince George's County library system include the Tugwell Room in the Green belt Library, the Sojourner Truth Room in the Oxon Hill branch, the Kerlan Room children's collection in the Hyattsville branch, and the Documents Library in the County Administration Building in Upper Marlboro, which appears to have every document pertaining to Prince George's County that was ever printed or penned.

notable, including Presidents Roosevelt and Wilson. Long's daughter, Christine Long Wilcox, donated the house in the late 1950s to the Maryland–National Capital Park and Planning Commission. The mansion and other buildings sit on about seventy-five acres of the original estate.

Many original Snowden pieces are still in the mansion, and other furnishings are period antiques. You may take a tour through almost a dozen rooms of the historic mansion most Sunday afternoons, between the hours of noon and 4:00 P.M. ($3.00 for adults, $2.00 for seniors fifty-five and older, and $1.00 for children five to fifteen).

And, if you wish, enjoy a lovely afternoon tea at the mansion, with a choice of teas and some delicious nibbles, usually on the second and fourth Friday of the month, at 2:00 or 4:00 P.M., for $15. Reservations and prepayment are required. Call (301) 498–8486 for reservations.

That phone number will get you to the Little Teapot at Montpelier, a gift shop that's open during the summer season from 10:00 A.M. to 6:00 P.M., Tuesday through Saturday, and from noon to 4:00 P.M. on Sunday. Call for winter hours.

Montpelier Mansion is located at 12826 Laurel Bowie Road, Laurel 20708. (301) 953–1993 or (301) 490–2329.

If you like murals as much as I do, you will be curious about Prince George's County's post office murals. The ***Laurel Post Office mural*** of the *Mail Coach at Laurel,* painted by Mitchell Jamieson in 1939, reportedly was taken down during a General Services Administration restoration of the building and has not been returned.

The Chesapeake Bay area is noted for its seafood, and one of the better places to enjoy it—on the half shell, in crab cakes, or as part of a seafood platter—is at the ***Bay 'n Surf*** restaurant. This has been an institution of fine food since Roxanne and Patrick Edelmann opened it in 1965. The community has grown up and changed around it, but Bay 'n Surf retains that friendly "Cheers" atmosphere. Of course, there are nonseafood options. Bay 'n Surf is located at 14411 Baltimore Avenue (U.S. Route 1), Laurel 20708. Call (301) 776–7021.

There is other wildlife occupying the minds of specialists in Prince George's County. Situated on 4,700 acres, the ***National Patuxent Wildlife Research Center, Patuxent Research Refuge*** specializes in research on endangered species, migratory birds, and environmental contaminants. Established in 1839 as America's first national wildlife experiment station, the center is charged with protecting and conserving the nation's wildlife and natural habitats through research and critical debate. Throughout the years, the center has been involved in history-making discoveries, including the detrimental effects of DDT. Rachel Carson did most of her research here for her book *Silent Spring.* Currently the center is working to save the endangered whooping crane, California condor, Mississippi sandhill crane, and masked bobwhite. It has successfully completed a program of repopulating America's proud symbol, the bald eagle.

Scientists from more than fifteen countries conduct research at the center on a regular basis. Patuxent is the largest wildlife research center in the world, and it is an exciting place to learn about global concerns, be a field researcher and travel through the five full-scale habitat areas, view acres of natural wildlife habitat, and see dramatic dioramas of wildlife. The center is open from 10:00 A.M. to 5:30 P.M. daily. A tram ride is available daily during summer months and on weekends in spring and fall. The cost is $2.00 for adults, $1.00 for children twelve and younger and seniors fifty-five and older. A gift shop offers a variety of environmental books, gifts, and educational materials.

If you have a really excellent memory, you may recall that the Center and the National Fund for the Patuxent Research Refuge were featured on a December 1989 *CBS Sunday Morning* with Charles Kuralt. A special committee of the Prince George's County Parks and Recreation Foundation Inc. facilitates a public/private partnership to raise funds on a national basis for the multimillion-dollar National Wildlife Visitor Center. The visitor center's mission is to "educate the public, especially students, about wildlife conservation from a global perspective." The research center is located off Powder Mill Road, 2 miles east of the Baltimore/ Washington Parkway, at 10901 Scarlet Tanager Loop, Laurel 20708-4027. Call (301) 479–5760 or (301) 479–0300 at least several days in advance to arrange a tour. On-line, visit www.prr.r5.fws.gov.

A little south of Laurel is Beltsville and the home of the ***U.S. Department of Agriculture Research Center,*** with a visitors center in the Log Lodge. Built by the Civilian Conservation Corps during the 1930s, it contains a Hall of Fame of agriculture scientists.

Approximately half of the 125 pounds of potatoes you eat each year are found in processed foods, a lot of which are instant potato flakes, developed in 1954 to use up a surplus of potatoes. Approximately 400 million pounds of potato flakes are produced each year in the United States. John F. Sullivan is honored for that invention and other works.

He's one of forty-four scientists honored for their contributions to our agricultural well-being. Herbert J. Dutton is enshrined for pioneering research leading to the establishment of soybean oil as the predominant edible vegetable oil in the world. And James H. Tumlinson III is celebrated for his research leading to the eradication of the boll weevil from the southeastern United States.

The visitors center, in Building 186 (East), is open weekdays from 8:00 A.M. to 4:30 P.M. Guided tours are available by appointment. Call (301) 504–9403 or log on to www.ars.usda.gov. The mailing address is United States Department of Agriculture, National Agriculture Library, Second Floor, 10301 Baltimore-Washington Boulevard, Beltsville 20705. There is no admission charge.

Travel down U.S. 1 into Hyattsville and you'll discover Eugene Kingman, a noted muralist, painter, and museum director who created the five panels in the ***Hyattsville Post Office*** in 1938, jointly entitled *Hyattsville Countryside.* Kingman was born in 1909, attended Yale University College of Fine Arts, and received an honorary Ph.D. from Creighton University. His work is in the Library of Congress collection and at the Philbrook in Tulsa, Oklahoma, among many other places. He also created murals in Wyoming, Rhode Island, and in the lobby of the New York Times Building in New York City.

The Hyattsville post office murals depict the working man in heroic proportions. They reflect the remains of the agricultural and pastoral quality of the Hyattsville lifestyle that still existed in 1937, when Kingman used such muralist techniques as stylized horses, foreshortening, and a decorative cornstalk border.

The Hyattsville Post Office is at 4325 Gallatin Street, Hyattsville 20781. Call (301) 669–8905.

For additional information about Prince George's County, from events to lodgings, contact Matt Neitzey and his staff at the Prince George's County Conference and Visitors Bureau Inc., 9200 Basil Court, Suite 101, Largo 20774. Call (301) 925–8300.

Montgomery County

West of Prince George's County and north and west of Washington, D.C., Montgomery County goes from really high-density suburbia at the south end to gorgeous open country with huge landed estates and farms in the middle and then into a mixture of town house developments set in the rolling countryside nearing the foothills of the Appalachian Mountains.

Trivia

Incidentally, the area, which is not incorporated, is called Silver Spring, not "springs," as in the Florida town.

Start at the D.C./Maryland border, where the unincorporated area known as Silver Spring is about to see a long-promised redevelopment. (I remember when the first department store opened out there and when the bus cost five cents, but you could never stand at a bus stop long enough to catch a bus, because a neighbor would drive by and give you a ride into town.)

Just blocks from the D.C./ Maryland line, just off Georgia Avenue, is the ***Silver Spring Acorn.*** It is easy to spot this little park, located near the spring from which the area received its name, with its gazebo shaped by pillars and a "hat" with the configuration of an acorn. Benches are provided for a lunch break or a moment of rest. Francis Preston Blair—a wealthy and prominent eighteenth-century landowner, power broker, newspaper owner, and member of President Jackson's Kitchen Cabinet—and his daughter were out riding one day when they found this spring. The sunlight reflecting off the sand or mica in the bottom made the minerals look like silver, and thus was born the name of his estate and the area, Silver Spring. In 1942 the park was acquired by a local citizens group, and it was restored in 1955. The Silver Spring Acorn is on Newell Road at the intersection of East-West Highway and Blair Mill Road, 1 block south of Georgia Avenue (across the street from the Canada Dry bottling plant).

Not far from the acorn is a ***post office mural*** painted in 1937 by Nicolai Cikovsky (of the Towson transportation mural incident); it's called *The*

MBHS Alums

The humongous building behind the noise-barrier walls along the outer loop of the Beltway (I–495) between the Colesville Road and University Boulevard exits is Montgomery Blair High School, home to approximately 2,500 students. It has all the bells and whistles one would like in a high school that saw its first students in September 1998. Its predecessor stands at Dale Drive and Wayne Avenue near downtown Silver Spring, maybe a mile away as the crow flies. That school opened in 1935, and I was graduated from there a few years later (quite a few, thank you). Among the other students attending Blair (go Blazers!) a few years before, after, and during my time there were Goldie Hawn, Ben Stein, Carl Bernstein, Sylvester Stallone, and former Baltimore Orioles pitcher Steve Barber.

Silver Spring Acorn

Old Tavern, reflecting life in the area during and after the antebellum period. The Old Post Office Building is at 8412 Georgia Avenue, Silver Spring 20901.

Continuing out Georgia Avenue, which parallels the railroad and subway tracks, you'll come to the intersection of Georgia and Colesville Road, and the Silver Spring subway station. A mural, 100 feet long and 8 feet high, was installed as part of the MetroArt I arts project (see also Prince George's County). Created by Sally Callmer of Bethesda, who previously was a miniaturist, the ***Penguin Rush Hour Mural*** was meant as a temporary installation but has become such an integral part of the community that the Montgomery County Department of Transportation has purchased the twenty-five panels as a permanent fixture.

In 1887 a resort hotel and retreat was built in the Forest Glen area of Silver Spring. Over the years, it also served as a finishing school for girls and a convalescent center for World War II soldiers. Known as the ***National Park Seminary,*** it has a number of exotic buildings in a variety of architectural styles. The building was neglected for years and has been a passion for preservationists. It recently received a $20,000 grant from the Maryland Commission for Celebration 2000 to help fund exterior restoration of the pagoda for a visitors center and museum. Tours are given every fourth Saturday of the month, from March to November. For more information, call Bonnie Rosenthal, Executive Director of the Save Our Seminary at Forest Glen, (301) 495–9079, or write to P.O. Box 8274, Silver Spring 20907.

Sometime soon there's going to be a Silver Theater again on Colesville Road in Silver Spring. Along with the new American Film Institute, it's part of the revitalization of "downtown" Silver Spring.

When the art deco–style Silver opened in October 1938, FDR was president. Within the early years, such movies as *Little Miss Broadway, Boys Town, Snow White and the Seven Dwarfs, The Wizard of Oz,* and *Gone with the Wind* were shown.

Trivia

The **Forest Glen metro station,** *which is nearly 200 feet below ground level, is the deepest in the system and maybe in the world.*

Once the nearly $8 million in restoration funds are spent, the theater is scheduled to look like it did when renowned theater architect John Eberson completed the project. His nautical theme includes porthole motifs and a metal tower. Other decorative touches included walnut, marble, and opaque Vitrolite glass. Two metal light sconces that look like large round flowers were found in the machine shop at the theater and are being reinstalled. Many of the interior doors, surfaced with Formica and inlaid with silver, were found in an Alexandria, Virginia, antiques shop, purchased by the DC Art Deco Society, and donated to the theater. Eberson constructed dozens of movie houses across the country during the '20s and '30s.

If you head north of Silver Spring on Route 29, you'll come to Burtonsville, and there, after a day of sightseeing, you can stop by the ***Burn Brae Dinner Theatre,*** the first dinner theater in the Washington area (opened in 1968). It has continued to provide outstanding entertainment. At times it presents a full-blown production with a huge cast, such as *Joseph and the Amazing Technicolor Dreamcoat* or *Evita*, and at other times it shows such small, intimate plays as *I Do! I Do!* There may even be a preshow tabletop magician or a weekly children's magic show. With each show there is a menu change, but a typical buffet might consist of seventeen items, including salad, fish, roast beef, honey-basted Virginia ham, pasta primavera, chicken, meatballs, hot vegetables, homemade bread and muffins, and desserts.

When Burn Brae opened in an unused dressing room of a community pool in 1968, little did Bernie Levin and John Kinnamon realize they were starting a terrific tradition. At one time the Washington area was the home of the largest number of dinner theaters in the country. Because there were so many of them, they fostered a group of performers who knew they would receive excellent training as well as be seen by the many talent scouts who came through this area.

Burn Brae Dinner Theatre is at 15029 Blackburn Road, Burtonsville 20866; call (301) 384–5800.

The city of Bethesda lies west of Silver Spring, and longtime area residents (anyone who's been here for more than fifteen years) can tell you about the awkward, sprawling image of the ***Bethesda Triangle*** intersection of Wisconsin Avenue, Old Georgetown Road, and East-West Highway. Personally, I remember it from when we used to hang out at the Hot Shoppes restaurant on Saturday after high school football games between archrivals Montgomery Blair and Bethesda Chevy Chase.

Known as the ***Bethesda Urban District,*** this area has nearly 200 restaurants, from traditional to trendy, from down-home to deluxe. There are more than fifty sculptures and murals tucked into little nooks and crannies or out in plain sight in the district. One of these is the **Pioneer Lady *statue,*** or Madonna of the Trail, symbolizing the importance of these roads even in their early days. Harry Truman dedicated the statue on April 19, 1929, in honor of the pioneer spirit and the National Pike, which connected the country from this spot on the East Coast to the town of Upland, California, on the West Coast. This was the last of twelve statues to be installed. The other statues were erected (chronologically) in Springfield, Ohio; Wheeling, West Virginia; Council Grove, Kansas; Lexington, Missouri; Lamar, Colorado; Albuquerque, New Mexico; Springerville, Arizona; Vandalia, Illinois; Richmond, Indiana; Washington, Pennsylvania; and Upland, California. The memorial (which faces east, whereas most of the other statues face west) is dedicated to the pioneer mothers of the covered-wagon days.

The engraving reads: OVER THIS HIGHWAY MARCHED THE ARMY OF MAJOR GENERAL EDWARD BRADDOCK, APRIL 14, 1755, ON ITS WAY TO FORT DUQUESNE, AND [THIS IS] THE FIRST MILITARY ROAD IN AMERICA, BEGINNING AT ROCK CREEK AND POTOMAC RIVER, GEORGETOWN, MARYLAND, LEADING OUR PIONEERS ACROSS THE CONTINENT TO THE PACIFIC.

The *Pioneer Lady* statue is located between the post office and the Hyatt Regency Hotel at the corner of Wisconsin Avenue, East-West Highway, and Old Georgetown Road in Bethesda. The statue was reinstalled in 1986, after years in storage due to subway and hotel construction.

For more information about the public art, contact the Bethesda Urban Partnership and request a copy of the *Discovery Trail* brochure, 7906 Woodmont Avenue, Bethesda 20814; (301) 215–6660; www.bethesda.org.

A few blocks from the Pioneer Lady statue is the ***Montgomery Farm Woman's Cooperative Market,*** which is open on Wednesday and Saturday throughout the year. This market was started during the Depression, with its first sale date set for February 4, 1932. A second sale was held on April 20, and it became so popular that the traditional Wednesday and Saturday selling days began.

You can stop by the market and find all manner of foods—including Pennsylvania Dutch double-baked ham and baked goods—and even some rocking chairs and other craft items, particularly during the winter. My favorite stall is the Marquez Farm Stand in the back left-hand corner as you walk in from Wisconsin Avenue, where Rick and Chun II Marquez, and sometimes their daughter, sell the most delectable pies, cakes, scones, Baltimore cheese breads, quiches, tarts, muffins, all-beef summer sausage, bratwurst, German salami, nitrite-free bacon, and the list goes on.

Montgomery Farm Woman's Cooperative Market

You can reach the Marquez family at (301) 530–9098. The Montgomery Farm Woman's Market, at 7155 Wisconsin Avenue, Bethesda 20814, is open Wednesday and Saturday 7:00 A.M. to 2:00 P.M.

Another view of the market is in the ***Bethesda Post Office mural*** painted by Robert Gates in 1939. This definitely represents a Montgomery County tradition, unlike the transportation scene painted in the Towson Post Office. The Bethesda mural was restored in 1967 with funds provided by the Montgomery Farm Woman's Cooperative Market. The post office is at 7400 Wisconsin Avenue, Bethesda 20814.

Take Old Georgetown Road west out of Bethesda, just outside the beltway, and you can stop by the ***Dennis and Phillip Ratner Museum.*** Phillip is a multimedia artist (sculpture, painting, etched glass, tapestry, drawing, and graphic arts) and native Washingtonian; his work is in the permanent collections of the Smithsonian Institution, the U.S. Supreme Court, the Library of Congress, the White House, and many other places. His cousin Dennis is the founder and chairman of the Hair Cuttery, the nation's largest privately owned salon chain with more than 800 salons internationally. His civic involvement includes raising funds for the Leukemia Society of America, the National Zoo, the Whiteman-Walker Clinic, the Institute for Advancement in Immunology and Aging, the United Jewish Appeal of Greater Washington, and other organizations.

The museum's collection includes examples of Phillip's sculptures, drawings, paintings, and graphics, and exhibits of the works of professional and student artists, from various institutions and from seminars in the museum. This facility is open to groups by appointment, with no

Panning for Gold

Minute quantities of gold have been found along the Potomac, near Great Falls, and in the Piedmont regions. If you'd like to try your hand at panning, or at least see where some gold has been mined, stop by the Chesapeake and Ohio (C&O) Canal Park and Great Falls Tavern Museum, near the intersection of MacArthur Boulevard and Great Falls Road. Park in the C&O Canal parking area and follow the unmarked trail to the Maryland Gold Mine, which was worked until the 1920s. No one has become rich with Maryland gold, but one can try. For more information about the history of gold finds in the state and rules and regulations about prospecting, write to the Maryland Geological Survey, 2300 St. Paul Street, Baltimore 21218.

admission fee charged. The Ratner Museum is located at 10001 Old Georgetown Road, Bethesda 20814. Call (301) 897–1518.

If you like nature or have children who have excess energy to burn (and how many children fit into that category?), be sure to visit the ***Cabin John Regional Park,*** part of the Maryland–National Capital Park and Planning Commission park system. (There's also Wheaton Regional, in Wheaton; Watkins Regional, in Kettering; and Cosca Regional, in Clinton.)

Cabin John covers more than 500 acres, with an ice skating rink (with Monday night curling, at least as of this writing), hiking trails, sports fields, indoor and outdoor tennis courts, picnic tables and pavilions, a nature center, and most important for the moment, an Action Playground. Designed by Heidi Sussman, this playground is an elaborate obstacle course covering more than a half acre of ground. There's a section for toddlers, one for preschoolers, one for older children, and places for parents to sit. Among the challenges are a 40-foot net tunnel, a 30-foot tire bridge, and a 50-foot tunnel slide. What's really nice about this playground is if you can lose your inhibitions for a few moments, you can enjoy the swings, slides, and challenges, too. Well, at least some of them. Sussman also designed the play area for Wheaton Regional Park. Cabin John is at 7400 Tuckerman Lane, Rockville 20854; (301) 299–4555.

Trivia

F. Scott and Zelda Fitzgerald, once residents of the area, are buried in the St. Mary's Church cemetery in Rockville, located at the corner of Viers Mill Road and Route 355 (Rockville Pike); (301) 762–0096.

The ***Rockville Post Office mural*** was done by New York artist Judson Smith in 1940 and is of *Sugar Loaf Mountain.* Supposedly, it was painted from the porch of an estate called Inverness, which was built in 1818 by Benjamin White. The view includes fields and farm buildings, and the mural hangs over the wall where the lock boxes used to be located. The Rockville Post Office is at 2 West Montgomery Avenue, Rockville 20850.

Northeast of Rockville is the little town with the theater that has the big reputation. The ***Olney Theatre Center*** opened in 1942 as a stop on the summer "straw hat" circuit, closed because of the war, and then reopened in 1946 with Helen Hayes starring in *Good Housekeeping.* Other luminaries who have graced its stage include Tallulah Bankhead, Gloria Swanson, and Bea Lillie. The late Reverend Gilbert Hartke, head of Catholic University's drama department, took over the management in 1953, providing exposure for his students as well as for Carol Channing, John McGiver, and Frances Sternhagen.

Also known as the State Summer Theatre of Maryland, Olney Theatre Center started a new tradition in 1989 with the annual production of *The Butterfingers Angel, Mary & Joseph, Herod the Nut,* and *The Slaughter of 12 Hit Carols in a Pear Tree*, a Christmas entertainment by noted playwright William Gibson. The theater also is known for the elected officials it attracts, particularly on opening night, both to see the outstanding presentations and to be seen. The Victorian farmhouse (circa 1880) next door is the Actors' Residence, where housing is provided for the cast in season. Actually, two casts stay there at one time, one for the show in production and one for the show in rehearsal. On opening night post-performance festivities take place here.

The mailing address for Olney Theatre is P.O. Box 550, 2001 Route 108, Olney 20832; (301) 924–3400 or www.olneytheatre.org.

When you tell someone you're going to ***Roy's Place,*** they think you're talking about that old cowboy movie star. But this Roy's Place is in Gaithersburg, northwest of Rockville, and it is far from fast food and fast eating. In fact, the menu tells you that if you are in a hurry, go someplace else. No, it is not fine dining. It is just sandwiches and more sandwiches—some of the weirdest sandwiches you've ever imagined. How would you like a sandwich with roast beef, fried oysters, and a side serving of tartar sauce? Would you prefer provolone cheese, anchovies, blue-cheese dressing, onions, and lettuce? Or would you like something else?

The menu features more than one hundred different sandwiches, or you can start at the front page with a salad selection and skip to the back page for a simple hamburger, if you do not feel like reading the equivalent of a novella before you eat. Roy's has been open since 1971, and several local and national celebrities have had sandwiches named after them. The decor is just as interesting and offbeat as the menu, with posters, old advertisements, and a sign by the skylight that says THIS WAY OUT.

Roy's Place is at 2 East Diamond Avenue, Gaithersburg 20877; call (301) 948–5548. Hours are Monday through Thursday 11:00 A.M. to 11:00 P.M., Friday and Saturday 11:00 A.M. to midnight, and Sunday noon to 11:00 P.M. Reservations are not accepted.

White's Ferry, well west of the Beltway, is the only remaining ferry system on the Potomac River, connecting White's Ferry, Maryland, to Leesburg, Virginia. It probably is more important these days than when it began operation in 1828, for it is the only river crossing between the American Legion Bridge on the Washington (or Capital) Beltway to the south and east, and the Point of Rocks bridge to the north and west. Regular commuters and tourists can easily tell when there is a major backup on the Beltway because these back-country roads become filled with drivers escaping the jam. The ferry *General Jubal Early* (named for a Confederate leader) runs the 1,000-foot crossing on a cable propelled by a diesel tug in about three minutes. It can hold fifteen cars and operates all year, weather and river conditions permitting, on a demand basis. A country store selling sundries and souvenirs is open on the Maryland side spring through fall. The ferry is off Route 107 at 24801 White's Ferry Road, Dickerson 20842. Call (301) 394–5200 for information.

Just up the ramp from White's Ferry landing is the ditch that was once the ***Chesapeake & Ohio Canal*** and is now the longest and thinnest National Historical Park in the country, narrowing to less than 50 feet at one point. There was a time when there were twenty trading posts along the 185-mile canal, which ran from Cumberland to Washington, D.C., roughly paralleling the Potomac River. In 1988 conservationists spent three months clearing away foliage and found the 150-foot foundation of a nineteenth-century depot and granary. From the Civil War until 1924, canal boats headed down to Washington, D.C., where they would tie up to a three-story wooden storage building called the Granary to load up with grain from area farms. In the sixty years since the canal closed, the Granary and canal have been neglected and overgrown by trees and shrubbery.

Other parts of the canal are alive and thriving, although hurricanes often wreak havoc upon the waterway. About four million people visit some part of the park, with May through October the busiest time. The 14 miles between Georgetown (in Washington, D.C.) and Great Falls sees the most visitors, so if you're looking for solitude in your nature walks, biking, or horseback riding expeditions, aim toward the upper areas. Primitive camping areas are located approximately every 5 miles, from Swain's Lock (mile 16) to Evitts Creek (mile 180), on a first-come, first-served basis, no permits needed (except for a group area at mile 12). Each site has a chemical toilet, pump water (May to November), picnic table, and fire ring with cooking grill.

The park is open from sunrise to sunset and there are six visitor centers; Georgetown, Great Falls Tavern, Brunswick, Williamsport, Hancock, and Cumberland. There's a $4.00-per-car entrance fee that's good for three days (an annual pass is $15.00) and $2.00 for cyclists and pedestrians at the Great Falls area of the canal. Golden Eagle and Golden Access passes are honored. Commercial vehicle fees are $25 for one to six people, $40 for seven to twenty-five people, and $100 for more than twenty-five people. Mule-drawn canal boat rides are available at Georgetown and Great Falls spring through fall. Besides the canal towpath, there are other hiking trails at Great Falls, including the Gold Mine, River, Woodland, Berma Road, Angler's Spur, and the appropriately named Billy Goat Trail. For information, contact the C&O Canal Headquarters, 16500 Shepherdstown Pike, Sharpsburg 21782; (301) 739–4200.

Trivia

Thurmont originally was called Mechanicstown because Jacob Weller, a mechanic of German descent, settled here with his family in 1751.

For additional Montgomery County tourism information, write to the Visitors Center Manager, Conference and Visitors Bureau of Montgomery County, MD Inc., 12900 Middlebrook Road, Suite 1400, Germantown 20874, call (301) 428–9702 or (800) 925–0880, or visit www.cvbmontco.com.

Frederick County

Abutting the northwest border of Montgomery County and going north to the Pennsylvania state line, with the Potomac River on its southern border, Frederick County is renowned in certain circles for the antiques shops in New Market and the city of Frederick. Steeped in history, the county also is home to the restored train depot and museum at Brunswick; the Barbara Fritchie and Roger B. Taney homes; wineries and orchards; the Catoctin Mountains (where Camp David, the presidential retreat, is located); the Grotto of Lourdes and the National Shrine of St. Elizabeth Ann Seton; the Lilypons Water Gardens; Gov. Thomas Johnson's Rose Hill Manor and Schifferstadt Architectural Museum; many churches and steeples; and, of course, that picturesque stopping point, Sugar Loaf Mountain.

A few words about ***churches in Frederick***. There are ten of note and one synagogue, and their histories and architectural styles date from the colonial, revolutionary, and Civil War eras. Tours are available during the year, and a brochure is available from the Frederick Tourism Council that details the history of each house of worship. A special event for all the houses of worship is the Candlelight Tour held in December; each is decorated for the holiday and hosts are on hand to greet visitors and answer questions. Special music and presentations are provided at various churches throughout the evening, and free parking is available. Hospitality rooms are located at a number of places, and the one at Trunk Hall in the Evangelical Lutheran Church is handicapped accessible.

Many prominent Marylanders now reside in ***Mount Olivet Cemetery***, including Francis Scott Key, Barbara Fritchie, and Gov. Thomas Johnson, along with veterans of the American Revolution, the Civil War (more than 800 Confederate soldiers), and World War II, as well as more than 25,000 other people. A statue of Key stands over 9 feet tall on a monument that is 16 feet high and 45 feet around; you can't miss the statue because it welcomes you at the main entrance. The United States flag standing by him flies twenty-four hours a day in honor of his writing the words to "The Star-Spangled Banner." Much of the money collected for the $25,000 monument was donated in dimes and dollars by people all over the country.

Little green-and-white signs direct you to the graves of Governor Johnson and Barbara Fritchie, which are across the road from each other. Johnson was a Revolutionary War patriot, born in Frederick County in 1732 (the same year as George Washington), and was a prominent member of the Continental Congress. He was the first governor of the state of Maryland and associate justice of the United States Supreme Court. Fritchie was made immortal by John Greenleaf Whittier's poem about her bravery against Gen. Stonewall Jackson, when she flew the Union flag and dared soldiers to "Shoot if you must, this old gray head, but spare your country's flag." A monument of Maryland granite with the Whittier poem on a bronze tablet was unveiled on September 9, 1914. The cemetery is considered one of the most beautiful and distinguished in this part of the country. Mount Olivet Cemetery, 515 South Market Street, Frederick 21701; (301) 661–1164.

Between Frederick and Thurmont is the old ***Catoctin Furnace***. For 125 years this was a prosperous iron-making community. Started by a group of men that included the future first governor of Maryland, Thomas Johnson, the stack went into blast in 1776 to produce pig iron, tools, and household items, including the popular ten-plate stove. Bombshells for 10-inch mortars were produced toward the end

Rosebud Salve

Those of you who've used Rosebud Salve, made by the Rosebud Perfume Co., will be delighted to know that its home offices are in an old three-story hotel in Woodsboro, north of Frederick. The company was started in 1892 by pharmacist George F. Smith and it's now run by two of his granddaughters and other family members. Items about the balm have appeared in Glamour, Allure, Woman's Day, *and* Self *within the past year or two, keeping sales at a brisk pace. Check in beauty salons and Walgreen's in the States, or in stores as far away as London. Rosebud Perfume Co., 528 Trail Avenue, Frederick 21701.*

of the Revolutionary War. By the mid-eighteenth century, the owner of the furnace had eighty houses for his workers, a sawmill, gristmill, company store, farms, ore railroad, three furnace stacks (including an anthracite coal stack), and more than 11,000 acres of land. By 1903 the furnace ceased to operate, although ore was taken out of this area until 1912.

For additional information write to the Catoctin Furnace Historical Society, Thurmont 21788, or call Cunningham Falls State Park, (301) 271–7574. The furnace, remaining houses in Catoctin Village, and Harriet Chapel can be seen along Route 806, on the east side of Route 15, about 12 miles north of Frederick.

There's just enough winter in Frederick County that covered bridges were desirable to assure safe passage over waterways. Bridges otherwise would have become frozen, slick, and impassable.

There are three covered bridges in Frederick County. The first is ***Loy's Station***. This 90-foot-long bridge, built between 1850 and 1860, crosses Owens Creek and is surrounded by a five-and-a-half-acre park. It's located on Old Frederick Road, off Route 77, about 3 miles from Thurmont. (301) 271–1843.

Roddy Road Covered Bridge (1856), near Thurmont, is considered the best looking of the state's remaining bridges by covered-bridge fans. It is a single span, about 40 feet long, with a 13⅔-foot roadway. It is a fine example of basic king-post truss design, though steel stringers were installed later. Surrounding the bridge, which crosses Owens Creek, is a seventy-acre natural area for picnicking and gentle afternoon outings. (301) 271–1843.

The ***Utica Covered Bridge***, at 101 feet, is the largest of the three. Built in 1850, it was moved in 1889 and has been structurally reinforced with concrete piers and steel-beam supports. The bridge crossed the Monocacy River until a summer flood in 1889 lifted the span from its abutments and placed it down on the river several yards away. Instead of replacing the still-intact bridge on its supports, it was dismantled, moved, and reassembled over Fishing Creek at Utica Mills. The bridge is located on Utica Road off Old Frederick Road, which is off Route 15. (301) 663–8687.

Fertile ground attracted many settlers, and you can still see and enjoy the fruits of many hard workers at a number of orchards.

Catoctin Mountain Orchard is known for its diversity and quality of all types of berries, soft fruits, apples, and vegetables. Cortland, Red and

Right off the Vine, Branch, or Bush

You can buy fresh fruits and vegetables or pick your own at some sixty or seventy farms and orchards in fourteen counties across the state, from Anne Arundel to Washington. Write to Marketing Resource and Development Group, Maryland Department of Agriculture, Annapolis 21401, for a copy of the current Pick Your Own and Direct Farm Markets in Maryland *brochure. Or stop by a library or county extension office to pick up a copy.*

Golden Delicious, Stayman, York, and Ida Red apples are available in autumn. You can pick your own blackberries, black raspberries, sour and sweet cherries, and strawberries, but call ahead for picking days and hours. Catoctin Mountain Orchard also offers preserved fruit and jam, packed in appealing, reusable containers.

The orchard is open 9:00 A.M. to 5:00 P.M. daily June through January, and Friday and Saturday January through March. The orchard is on Route 15, North Franklinville Road, and the mailing address is 15307 Kelbaugh Road; Thurmont 21788. Call (301) 271–2737.

Bell Hill Farm Market and Orchard is a hundred-acre farm, and the family-run fruit stand sits by a pre–Civil War home and stone springhouse. The McKissick family orchard features the traditional Red and Yellow Delicious and Stayman apples, as well as some older varieties, including Grimes Golden, York, Jonathan, and Winesap. In season you can buy peaches, plums, pears, nectarines, watermelons, cantaloupes, raspberries, corn, beans, cucumbers, potatoes, and other produce.

Bell Hill Farm is 1½ miles north of Thurmont on Route 15 and is open daily from 9:00 A.M. to 5:00 P.M. Call (301) 271–7264.

Pryor's Orchard has a modern storage facility housed in a rustic barn-type market, complete with racks of antlers and an antique cider press. Pryor's seventy-three-acre orchard is one of the oldest in the Thurmont area and a favorite of local canning enthusiasts. Pryor's is noted for its many varieties of peaches, summer and fall apples, and pears. You can pick your own blueberries and sour and sweet cherries.

The orchard is closed in the winter. It is ½ mile west of Thurmont on Pryor's Road (take a left off Route 77). Call (301) 271–2693.

Scenic View Orchard has a fine selection of produce, including peaches, plums, nectarines, pears, apples (and cider), melons, sweet corn, green beans, and other vegetables. It is open daily 10:00 A.M. to 6:00 P.M. July 15 through November 1. It's located 5 miles north of Thurmont on Route 550 at 16239 Sabillasville Road, Sabillasville 21780; (301) 271–2149.

Thurmont is not only the gateway to the mountains but also the gateway to ***Camp David,*** which was originally called High Catoctin and was one of three camps built by the Civilian Conservation Corps during the Depression. The other two camps, still in existence, are Misty Mount, used for group camping, and Greentop, used by the Baltimore League of the Handicapped since 1937. The camp buildings were constructed from local timber. High Catoctin was renamed Shangri La by Franklin Delano Roosevelt and then renamed Camp David by Dwight D. Eisenhower.

There are numerous campgrounds where you can spend a night or two, and Frederick is close enough to Washington and Baltimore to be used as a base, if you wish. One of the better-known private campgrounds is ***Crow's Nest Lodge Campground,*** owned and operated by Ned and Renna Haynes. It has 110 campsites located along Big Hunting Creek, a mountain trout stream that flows through the Catoctin Mountains. Each spacious campsite is designed to accommodate a large tent, tent trailer, or travel trailer. Most of the sites are shaded, and many have water and electricity. At the campground you can enjoy a spring-fed freshwater pond for swimming and wading, 10 miles of scenic foot trails that wind through the Catoctin Mountain Park, fishing, nature study, and a half dozen action sports. Pets are welcome, as long as they are on a leash at all times.

The address is Crow's Nest Lodge Campground, P.O. Box 145, Thurmont 21788. Call (301) 271–7632.

Old Mink Farm campground offers summer and winter escapes. You can rent a log cabin with fireplace, with either one or two bedrooms and

Footprints in the Park

Frederick County is considering a park to showcase Maryland's earliest dinosaur footprints, on a two-acre lot near Emmitsburg. That's where two-hundred-million-year-old footprints of three ancient reptiles were found, according to paleontologist Peter M. Kranz. The footprints are believed to be the tracks of atreipus, a 4-foot-long herbivore; coelophysis, a carnivore that was a little larger than the atreipus; and a prosauropod, a vegetarian that was ancestor of the brontosaurus and the Astrodon johnstoni, *Maryland's official state dinosaur. They're the only footprints in Maryland from the Triassic period.*

equipped kitchens, or log cabinettes with kitchenettes, or stay in the Coffee Hollow Lodge for extended family or management retreats. Reservations are required. Call (301) 271–7012 for additional information.

For additional tourism information, write to the Tourism Council of Frederick County, 19 East Church Street, Frederick 21701, or call (301) 663–8687 or (800) 999–3613. On-line, log on to www.visitfrederick.org or e-mail tourism@co.frederick.md.us

Places to Eat in Greater Washington

Bethesda
There are nearly 200 restaurants in and around the Bethesda Triangle (at the intersection of Old Georgetown Road, Wisconsin Avenue, and East-West Highway), catering to just about every taste you can imagine. Because of this competition, it's easy to find an excellent place to eat within your budget, from inexpensive to extremely pricey. Here are a few suggestions:

Bean Bag,
10400 Old Georgetown Road,
(301) 530–8090

Benihana,
7315 Wisconsin Avenue,
(301) 652–5391

O'Donnells,
8301 Wisconsin Avenue,
(301) 656–6200

Tastee Diner of Bethesda
7731 Woodmont Avenue,
(301) 652–3970

Uncle Jed's,
7525 Old Georgetown Road,
(301) 913–0026

Burtonsville
Burn Brae Dinner Theatre,
15029 Blackburn Road,
(301) 384–5800

Clinton
Wayfarer Restaurant,
7401 Surratts Road,
(301) 856–3343

College Park
94th Aero Squadron,
5240 Paint Branch Parkway,
(301) 699–9400

Comus
Comus Inn Restaurant,
23900 Old Hundred Road,
(301) 428–8593

Emmitsburg
Carriage House Inn,
200 North Seton Avenue,
(301) 447–2366,
www.amerimall.com/carriagehouseinn

Frederick
Di Francesco's,
26 North Market Street,
(301) 695–5499

Jennifer's,
207 West Patrick Street,
(301) 662–0373

Province,
129 North Market Street,
(301) 663–1441

Red Horse Restaurant,
996 West Patrick Street,
(301) 663–3030

Snow White Grill,
7 East Patrick Street,
(301) 662–9709

Tauraso's,
6 East Street,
(301) 663–6600

Gaithersburg
Roy's Place,
2 East Diamond Avenue,
(301) 948–5548

Largo
BET Soundstage,
9640 Lottsford Court,
(301) 883–9500

Laurel
Bay 'n Surf,
14411 Baltimore Avenue,
(301) 776–7021

New Market
Mealey's,
8 West Main Street,
(301) 865–5488

Potomac
Old Anglers Inn,
10801 MacArthur Boulevard,
(301) 365–2425

Suitland
LiLeons,
3674 St. Barnabas Road,
(301) 899–8233

Thurmont
Cozy Country Inn Restaurant and Village,
103 Frederick Road,
(301) 271–4301,
www.cozyvillage.com

Wheaton
Anchor Inn,
2509 University Boulevard West,
(301) 933–8111

Antonia's Trattoria,
11222 Grandview Avenue,
(301) 929–2503

El Pollo Ricco,
2541 Ennalls Avenue,
(301) 942–4419

Good Fortune,
2646 University Boulevard West,
(301) 929–8818

Lucia's,
2409 University Boulevard West,
(301) 949–2112

Places to Stay in Greater Washington

Most hotels and motels in the Greater Washington area belong to the major hotel chains, including Best Western, Days Inn, Doubletree, Econo Lodge, Holiday Inn, Marriott, Ramada Inn, Red Roof Inn, and Susse Chalet Inn. If, for some strange reason, you're bypassing all the wonderful things you can do and see in Maryland and you're headed toward the attractions of Washington, you'll probably be staying in Prince George's or Montgomery County, and you'll want one that's either on or near a subway line, or that provides shuttle service to a subway.

Bethesda
Lucy's Bed and Breakfast,
9203 Wadsworth Drive,
(301) 530–7256

Boyds
Pleasant Springs Farm,
16112 Barnesville Road,
(301) 972–3452,
www.pleasantspringsfarm.com

Brookville
Longwood Manor Bed and Breakfast,
2900 DuBarry Lane,
(301) 774–1002,
www.bbonline.com/md/longwood

Buckeystown
Catoctin Inn and Conference Center,
3619 Buckeystown Pike,
(301) 874–5555 or
(800) 730–5550,
www.catoctininn.com

Inn at Buckeystown,
3521 Buckeystown Pike
(301) 874–5755 or
(800) 272–1190,
www.virtualcities.com

Chevy Chase
Chevy Chase Bed and Breakfast,
6815 Connecticut Avenue,
(301) 656–5867

Derwood
Reynolds of Derwood,
16620 Bethayres Road,
(301) 963–2216,
www.reynolds-bed-breakfast.com

Frederick
Hill House Bed and Breakfast,
12 West Third Street,
(301) 682–4111

McCleery's Flat,
121 East Patrick Street,
(301) 620–2433 or
(800) 774–7926,
www.fwp.net/mccleerysflat

Middle Plantation Inn,
9549 Liberty Road,
(301) 898–7128,
www.mpinn.com

Morningside Inn,
7477 McKaig Road,
(301) 898–3920 or
(800) 898–1814,
www.bbonline.com/md/morningside

Spring Bank Inn,
7945 Worman's Mill Road,
(301) 694–0440 or
(800) 400–INNS,
www.bbonline.com/md/springbank

Turning Point Inn,
3406 Urbana Pike,
(301) 831–8232,
www.bbonline.com/md/turning-point

Tyler Spite Inn,
112 West Church Street,
(301) 831–4455

LARGO
Club Hotel by Doubletree,
9100 Basil Court,
(301) 773–0700 or
(800) 444–CLUB

MIDDLETOWN
Stone Manor,
5820 Carroll Boyer Road,
(301) 473–5454,
www.stonemanor.com

NEW CARROLLTON
Ramada Conference and Exhibition Center,
8500 Annapolis Road,
(301) 459–6700 or
(800) 436–0614

NEW MARKET
Strawberry Inn,
17 West Main Street,
(301) 865–3318

OLNEY
Thoroughbred Bed and Breakfast,
16410 Batchellors Forest Road,
(301) 774–7649

ROCKVILLE
Park Inn International,
11410 Rockville Pike,
(301) 881–5200 or
(800) 752–3800

Sleep Inn,
2 Research Court,
(301) 948–7406

SILVER SPRING
Little House at Wind Swept,
17000 Carwell Road,
(301) 384–3336 or
(800) 861–2434

Park Crest House Bed and Breakfast,
8101 Park Crest Drive,
(301) 588–2845,
www.bbhost.com/parkcrest

THURMONT
Cozy Country Inn Restaurant and Village,
103 Frederick Road,
(301) 271–4301,
www.cozyvillage.com

Cunningham Falls State Park,
Route 15,
(888) 432–CAMP

Rambler Inn,
U.S. Route 15 and MD Route 550,
(301) 271–2424

OTHER ATTRACTIONS WORTH SEEING IN GREATER WASHINGTON

Airmen Memorial Museum,
Suitland,
(301) 899–8386

Agricultural History Farm Park,
Derwood,
(301) 948–5053

Andrews Air Force Base,
Camp Springs,
(301) 981–1110,
www.andrews.af.mil

Antique Carousel,
Watkins Regional Park,
Kettering,
(301) 390–9224,
www.pgparks.com

Audubon Naturalist Society,
Chevy Chase,
(301) 652–9188,
www.audubonnaturalist.org

Baker Park,
Frederick,
(301) 663–8687

Barbara Fritchie House and Museum,
Frederick,
(301) 698–0630

Beall-Dawson House,
Rockville,
(301) 762–1492,
www.montgomeryhistory.org

Beatty Cramer Architectural Museum,
Ceresville,
(301) 298–2215

Belair Mansion and Stable Museums,
Bowie,
(301) 262–6200,
www.cityofbowie.org/parks.htm

Billingsley Manor,
Upper Marlboro,
(301) 627–0730,
www.pgparks.com

Black Hill Regional Park,
Boyds,
(301) 916–0220

Blue Blazes Whiskey Still,
Thurmont,
(301) 663–9388,
www.nps.gov/cato

Bowie Railroad Station and Huntington Museum,
Bowie,
(301) 809–3088

Boyds Negro School House,
Boyds,
(301) 972–0484

Brookside Gardens,
Wheaton Regional Park,
Wheaton,
(301) 946–9071,
www.clark.net/pub/mncppc/montgom/park/brookside/index.htm

Brookeville Academy,
Brookeville,
(301) 570–4465

Brunswick Railroad Museum,
Brunswick,
(301) 834–7100,
www.bhs.edu/brun/rrmus/rrmus.html

Butler's Orchard,
Germantown,
(301) 428–0444

C&O Canal National Historic Park,
Potomac,
(301) 299–3613,
www.fred.net/kathy/canal.html

Catoctin Mountain Park,
Thurmont,
(301) 663–9388,
www.nps.gov/cato

Catoctin Vineyards and Winery,
Brookeville,
(301) 774–2310

Catoctin Wildlife Preserve and Zoo,
Thurmont,
(301) 271–4922,
www.cwpzoo.com

Cedarville State Forest,
Brandywine,
(301) 888–1410 or
(800) 784–5380,
www.dnr.state.md.us

Clara Barton National Historic Site,
Glen Echo,
(301) 492–6245,
www.nps.gov/clba

Cultural Resources Center,
Suitland,
(301) 238–NMAI, ext. 6300

Cunningham Falls State Park,
Thurmont,
(301) 271–7574

Delaplaine Visual Arts Education Center,
Frederick,
(301) 698–0656

Darnall's Chance,
Upper Marlboro,
(301) 952–8010,
www.pgparks.com

Dorsey Chapel,
Glenn Dale,
(301) 464–5291

Elk Run Vineyards Inc.,
Mount Airy,
(410) 775–2513,
www.elkrun.com

Forest Glen Seminary,
Forest Glen,
(301) 495–9079

Fort Foote Park,
Oxon Hill,
(301) 763–4600

Fort Washington Park,
Fort Washington,
(301) 763–4600,
www.nps.gov/fowa

Frederick Brewing Company,
Frederick,
(301) 694–7899 or
(888) 258–7434,
www.fredbrew.com

Frederick Keys Baseball,
Frederick,
(301) 662–0013,
www.frederickkeys.com

Gaithersburg Heritage Alliance,
Gaithersburg,
(301) 869–1063

Gambrills State Park,
Frederick,
(301) 791–4767

George Meany Memorial Archives,
Silver Spring,
(301) 431–5451,
www.georgemeany.com

Glen Echo Park,
Glen Echo,
(301) 492–6282,
www.nps.gov/glec

Glen View Mansion,
Rockville,
(301) 309–3001

Greenbelt Park,
Greenbelt,
(301) 344–3948 or
(800) 365–2267,
www.nps.gov/gree

Gudelsky Gallery at the Maryland College of Art and Design,
Silver Spring,
(301) 649–4454

Hession Barracks,
Frederick,
(301) 663–8687

His Lordship's Kindness,
Clinton,
(301) 856–0358,
www.somd.lib.md.us.lordship

Historical Society of Frederick County,
Frederick,
(301) 663–1188,
www.fwp.net.hsfc

Huntington Railroad Museum,
Bowie,
(301) 805–4616 or
(301) 262–6200

John Poole House,
Poolesville,
(301) 972–8588

Lake Artemesia Natural Area Park,
College Park,
(301) 927–2163

Laurel's Historic Main Street,
Laurel,
(301) 725–7539,
www.laurelmainstreet.com

Laurel Museum,
Laurel,
(301) 725–7975,
www.laurelhistory.org

Laurel Park,
Laurel,
(301) 725–0400,
www.laurelpark.com

Legore Bridge,
Woodsboro,
(301) 663–8687

Lilypons Water Gardens,
Buckeystown,
(301) 874–5133 or
(800) 999–5459,
www.lilypons.com

Linganore Winecellars,
Mount Airy,
(410) 795–6432 or
(301) 831–5889,
www.linganore-wine.com

Locust Grove Nature Center,
Bethesda,
(301) 299–1990

Loew Vineyards,
Mount Airy,
(301) 831–5464

Marietta House Museum,
Glenn Dale,
(301) 464–5291

McCrillis Garden and Gallery,
Bethesda,
(301) 949–8230

Meadowside Nature Center,
Rockville,
(301) 924–4141

Merkle Wildlife Sanctuary/Visitor Center,
Upper Marlboro,
(301) 888–1410

Middletown Valley Historical Society,
Middletown,
(301) 371–7582

Monocacy National Battlefield,
Frederick,
(301) 662–3515,
www.nps.gov/mono

Montgomery County Agricultural Center/Fair,
Gaithersburg,
(301) 926–3100,
www.mcagfair.com

Montgomery County Historical Society,
Rockville,
(301) 762–1492,
www.montgomeryhistory.org

Mormon Temple Visitor Center,
Kensington,
(301) 587–0144

NASA/Goddard Visitor Center and Museum,
Greenbelt,
(301) 286–8981,
www.gsfc.nasa.gov

National Archives at College Park,
College Park,
(202) 501–5205,
www.nara.gov

National Capital Trolley Museum,
Silver Spring,
(301) 384–6088,
www.dctrolley.org

National Colonial Farm Museum,
Accokeek,
(301) 283–2113,
www.accokeek.org

National Library of Medicine,
Bethesda,
(301) 496–6308

National Oceanic and Atmospheric Administration,
Silver Spring,
(301) 713–2227

National Shrine Grotto of Lourdes,
Emmitsburg,
(301) 447–5318,
www.msmary.edu/grotto

National Shrine–
St. Elizabeth Ann Seton,
Emmitsburg,
(301) 447–6606,
www.msmary.org

National Museum of Civil
War Medicine,
Frederick,
(301) 695–1864,
www.civilwarmed.org

National Wildlife Visitor
Center,
Laurel,
(301) 497–5760,
www.prr.r5.fws.gov

Northampton Slave
Quarters Archaeological/
Historical Park,
Mitchellville,
(301) 218–9651,
www.pgparks.com

Noyes Children's Library,
Kensington,
(301) 929–5533

Olde Bowie Antiques Row,
Bowie,
(301) 464–1122

Oxon Hill Farm,
Oxon Hill,
(301) 839–1177

Oxon Hill Manor,
Oxon Hill,
(301) 839–7782

Patuxent River Park,
Upper Marlboro,
(301) 627–6074,
www.pgparks.com

Paul E. Garber Facility,
Suitland,
(202) 357–1400 or
(202) 357–1505 (TDD)

Peerless Rockville Historic
Preservation,
Rockville,
(301) 762–0096,
www.millkern.com/
peerless

Piscataway Park,
Accokeek,
(301) 283–2113,
www.nps.gov/pisc

Prince George's County
Trap and Skeet Center,
Glenn Dale,
(301) 577–7178

Prince George's Publick
Playhouse,
Cheverly,
(301) 277–1710,
www.pgparks.com

R. Brooke Taney and
F. Scott Key Museum,
Frederick,
(301) 663–8687

Riversdale (Calvert
Mansion),
Riverdale,
(301) 864–0420,
www.pgparks.com

Rock Creek Regional Park,
Rockville,
(301) 924–4141

Rosaryville State Park,
Upper Marlboro,
(301) 888–1410

Rosecroft Raceway,
Fort Washington,
(301) 457–4000,
www.rosecroft.com

Rose Hill Manor Museum,
Frederick,
(301) 694–1648 or
(800) 999–3613

Sandy Spring Museum,
Sandy Spring,
(301) 774–0022

Schifferstadt Architectural,
Frederick,
(301) 663–6225

Seneca Creek State Park,
Gaithersburg,
(301) 924–2127,
www.dnr.state.md

Seneca Schoolhouse
Museum,
Poolsville,
(301) 428–9702 or
(800) 925–0880

Six Flags America
(formerly Adventure
World),
Largo,
(301) 249–1500 or
(800) 491–4FUN,
www.sixflags.com

Stonestreet Museum of
19th-Century Medicine,
Rockville,
(301) 762–1492,
www.montgomery
history.org

Strathmore Hall Arts
Center,
North Bethesda,
(301) 530–0540,
www.strathmore.org

Sugarloaf's Mountain
Works,
Gaithersburg,
(301) 990–1400

(Mary) Surratt House
Museum,
Clinton,
(301) 868–1121,
www.surratt.org or
www.glue.umd.edu/
~clwspoon/surratt.html

Walkersville Southern Railroad, Walkersville, (301) 898–0899

War Correspondents Memorial, Burkittsville, (301) 791–4767

Washington Temple Visitors' Center, Kensington, (301) 587–0144, www.washingtonlds.org

Watkins Regional Park, Upper Marlboro, (301) 390–9258

Weinberg Center for the Arts, Frederick, (301) 228–2828, www.weinbergcenter.org

Weiner Judaic Museum, Rockville, (301) 881–0100

Woodend Mansion, Chevy Chase, (301) 652–8107

Calendar of Annual Events in Greater Washington

January

Winter/Spring Display Spring Has Sprung, *Wheaton, (301) 949–8230, www.clark.net/pub/mncppc/montgom/parks/brookside*

February

Cabin Fever Festival, *Frederick, (301) 898–5466, www.cabinfeverfestival.com*

East Coast Jazz Festival, *Rockville, (301) 933–1822, www.listen.to/eastcoastjazz*

March

Maple Syrup Demonstration and Mountain Heritage Festival, *Thurmont, (301) 271–7574, www.dnr.state.md.us*

Fruhlings Fest, *Frederick, (301) 663–8687*

Hearthside Sampler, *Frederick, (301) 663–8687*

Sugarloaf Craft Festival, *Gaithersburg, (301) 990–1400*

Quilt Show, *Bowie, (301) 249–6810, www.geocities.com/soho/gallery/8682*

April

Farm and Family Festival, *Frederick, (301) 694–1650*

John Wilkes Booth Escape Route Tour, *Clinton, (301) 868–1121*

Marching Through Time, *Glenn Dale, (301) 464–5291*

Maryland Archaeology Month, *statewide, (410) 514–7661*

Surratt Open House, Clinton, (301) 868–1121

May

Andrews Air Force Base Open House, *Camp Springs, (301) 568–5995*

Beyond the Garden Gates, *Frederick, (301) 694–2489 or (800) 999–3613, www.citoffrederick.com*

Bowie Heritage Day, *Bowie, (301) 805–5029, www.cityofbowie.org/comserv/museums.htm*

Colesville Strawberry Festival, *Colesville, (301) 384–3864*

Frederick Art and Craft Festival, *Frederick, (800) 277–5046, www.nationalcrafts.com*

Calendar of Annual Events in Greater Washington (Cont'd)

Grand Exposition, *Frederick, (301) 694–1100*

Hometown Holidays, *Rockville, (301) 309–3330*

Indoor Sculpture Show, *Wheaton, (301) 949–8230*

Landon Azalea Garden Festival, *Bethesda, (301) 320–3200*

Laurel Main Street Festival, *Laurel, (301) 483–0838*

Marlboro Day Festival, *Upper Marlboro, (301) 627–2828*

Montpelier Spring Festival, *Laurel, (301) 776–2805*

Rose Hill Days Festival, *Frederick, (301) 694–1648*

Sculpture Show, *Wheaton, (301) 949–8230, www.clark.net/pub/mnccp/montgom/parks/brookside/index.htm*

Spring Festival, *Derwood, (301) 924–4141*

Springfest, *Brandywine, (410) 535–0312*

Spring Garden Party, *Kensington, (301) 933–3750*

Summer Display, *Wheaton, (301) 949–8230*

Taste of Wheaton, *Wheaton, (301) 240–8122*

June

American Indian Inter-Tribal Pow Wow, *Frederick, (301) 869–9381*

Bowiefest, *Bowie, (301) 262–6200, ext. 3068*

Ethnic Heritage Festival, *Silver Spring, (301) 565–7300*

Frederick Festival of the Arts, *Frederick, (301) 694–9632, www.frederickarts.org*

Montpelier Summer Concert Series, *Laurel, (301) 776–2805*

Rose Hill Manor Quilt Show, *Frederick, (301) 694–1648 or (301) 694–1650*

Sandy Spring Museum Strawberry Festival, *Sandy Spring, (301) 774–0022*

Strawberry Festival, *Thurmont, (301) 271–4301*

Taste of Wheaton, *Wheaton, (240) 777–8122*

July

Bowie Fourth of July Celebration, *Bowie, (301) 262–6200, ext. 3009, www.cityofbowie.org*

Civil War Medicine Conference, *Frederick, (301) 695–1864, www.dcivilwarmed.org*

Farm Tour and Harvest Sale, *various locations, (301) 590–2823*

Frederick's Fourth of July, *Frederick, (800) 999–3613 or (301) 694–2489, www.cityoffrederick.com*

Montgomery General Hospital Women's Board Picnic and Bazaar, *(301) 774–4956*

Rockville Independence Day Celebration, *Rockville, (301) 309–3330*

August

Balloon Fest, *Frederick, (301) 694–1100*

Butler's Orchard Peach Festival, *Germantown, (301) 972–3299*

Montgomery County Agricultural Fair, *Gaithersburg, (301) 926–3100, www.mcagfair.com*

Peach Festival, *Thurmont, (301) 271–7373*

Wings of Fancy-Butterfly Show, *Wheaton, (301) 949–8230*

Calendar of Annual Events in Greater Washington (Cont'd)

September

Brunswick Railroad Days, *Frederick, (301) 834–7100*

Catoctin Colorfest, *Thurmont, (301) 271–4432*

Children's Day Harvest Celebration, *Wheaton, (301) 949–8230, www.clark.net/pub/mncppc/montgom/park/brookside/index.htm*

Damascus Community Fair, *Damascus, (301) 253–3807*

Fall Festival, *Frederick, (301) 694–1650*

Germantown Oktoberfest, *Germantown, (240) 777–6820*

Grand Parade, *Frederick, (301) 694–1100*

Great Frederick Fair, *Frederick, (301) 663–5895, www.thegreatfrederickfair.com*

Greeting of the Geese, *Upper Marlboro, (301) 888–1410*

Harvest Festival, *Derwood, (301) 924–4141*

Hispanic Festival, *Adelphi, (301) 445–4500, www.smart.net/~parksrec*

Irish Festival, *Gaithersburg, (301) 565–0654, ext. 15*

John Wilkes Booth Escape Route Tour, *Clinton, (301) 868–1121, www.surratt.org*

New Market Days, *New Market, (301) 831–6755, www.newmarketmd.com*

Old Bowie Antique and Craft Fall Fling Street Fest, *Bowie, (301) 262–3743, www.ahcweb.net/antiques*

Olde Towne Gaithersburg Day, *Gaithersburg, (301) 258–6310*

Pumpkin Festival, *Germantown, (301) 972–3299*

Riverfest, *Laurel, (301) 483–0838*

Shaker Forest Festival, *Gaithersburg, (724) 643–6627*

Washington Irish Festival, *Gaithersburg, (301) 565–0654, www.ncta.net*

October

Arts Expo, Bowie, *(301) 809–3009, www.cityofbowie.org*

Butler's Orchard Pumpkin Festival, *Germantown, (301) 972–3299*

Catoctin Colorfest, *Thurmont, (301) 271–4432*

Chrysanthemum Display, *Wheaton, (301) 949–8230*

Colonial Day, *Laurel, (301) 953–1376, www.pgparks.com*

Del-Mar-Va Depression Glass Club, *Lanham, (202) 342–9021, www.glassshow.com/Shows/DelMar*

Farm Museum Fall Festival, *Frederick, (301) 694–1650*

German Fest, *Thurmont, (301) 271–4301*

Greeting of the Geese, *Upper Marlboro, (301) 784–5380, www.dnr.state.md.us*

Harvest Festival, *Derwood, (301) 924–4141*

Hastings Fair, *Glenn Dale, (301) 464–5291, www.pgheritage.org*

In the Street, *Frederick, (800) 999–3613 or (301) 694–2489, www.cityoffrederick.com*

Maryland Mountain Festival, *Frederick, (301) 898–5466, www.maryland mountainfestival.com*

National Art and Craft Festival, *Gaithersburg, (800) 277–5046, www.nationalcrafts.com*

Calendar of Annual Events in Greater Washington (Cont'd)

Oktoberfest at Schifferstadt, *Frederick, (301) 663–3885*

Pumpkin Festival, *Germantown, (301) 972–3299*

Riverfest, Laurel, *(301) 483–0838*

Queen Anne Day Arts and Crafts Festival, *Upper Marlboro, (301) 249–9761, www.patuxent.net*

Taste of Bethesda, *Bethesda, (301) 215–6660, www.bethesda.org*

Trolley Museum Fall Open House, *Wheaton, (301) 384–6088*

Victorian Mums Show-Fall Display, *Wheaton, (301) 949–8230*

Vintage Jazz Wine Festival, *New Market, (410) 795–6432 or (301) 831–5889, www.lingamore-wine.com*

November

Fall Gaithersburg Craft Festival, *Gaithersburg, (301) 990–1400*

Festival of Lights, *Kensington, (301) 587–0144*

Gaithersburg Railroad and Transportation Show, *Gaithersburg, (703) 536–2954*

Garden of Lights, *Wheaton, (301) 962–1453, www.clark.net/pub/mncppc/montgom/park/brookside/index.htm*

Surratt Open House, *Clinton, (301) 868–1121, www.surratt.org*

Winter Lights, *Gaithersburg, (301) 924–2127, www.dnr.state.md.us*

December

Candlelight House Tour, *Frederick, (301) 694–2489, www.cityoffrederick.com*

Candlelight Tour of Belair Mansion, *Bowie, (301) 809–3088*

Candlelight Tour of Historic Houses of Worship, *Frederick, (301) 663–8687 or (800) 999–3613, www.visitfrederick.org*

Christmas Candlelight Tours, *Laurel, (301) 953–1376, www.pgparks.com*

Christmas in New Market, *New Market, (301) 865–5544, www.newmarketmd.com*

Christmas in the Country Church Tour, *various towns, (301) 695–2633, ext. 7240*

Festival of Lights, *Kensington, (301) 587–0144*

First Night Montgomery, *Gaithersburg, (240) 777–6820*

Holiday Magic, *Frederick, (301) 694–1650*

Museums by Candlelight, *Frederick, (301) 663–8687, www.visitfrederick.org*

Victorian Yuletide by Candlelight, *Clinton, (301) 868–1121, www.surratt.org*

Wild X-mas at Merkle, *Upper Marlboro, (301) 888–1410 or (800) 784–5380, www.dnr.state.md.us*

Winter Gaithersburg Craft Festival, *Gaithersburg, (301) 990–1400*

Southern Maryland

Although civilization (or at least suburban sprawl) has entered southern Maryland, parts of Charles, Calvert (pronounced "Cawlvert" or "Calvit" by the locals), and St. Mary's Counties probably have changed more because of avulsion and accretion than because of developmental encroachment since the first English colonists settled here in the mid-1600s.

As you drive down these roads, you will see signs of early settlements established by brave men and women who came seeking new lives, religious freedom, and adventure. Dozens of churches, some dating from the early eighteenth century, dot the historic landscape.

Water has made its influence felt, of course; there are many waterside communities, places to buy and eat fresh seafood, and aquatic research centers. In southern Maryland I looked for markets that keep a community alive, and I found several community craft centers and talented artisans. I hope you will take the time to enjoy the maritime influence and the fine and unusual dining surrounding, or perhaps surrounded by, this rich coastal area.

Bikers particularly enjoy the terrain of Southern Maryland, and a bicycle map has been created just for you, highlighting the sights through ten loops. The map is color-coded to indicate routes that are good (light traffic and/or road shoulders), fair (moderate traffic), caution (no shoulder, short sight distances, and/or bridges), special (historic or scenic sites along the route), and dangerous (extremely heavy traffic, intersections, and/or no shoulders). The loops range from 5.3 to 37 miles. Bike stores and points of interest are designated along the various routes, and rules of the road are included. Contact any of the tourism bureaus for a copy.

Calvert County

The ***Battle Creek Cypress Swamp Sanctuary*** is one of the northernmost stands of bald cypress trees in the country, and the only one on Maryland's western shore. Forget the images of cypress tress

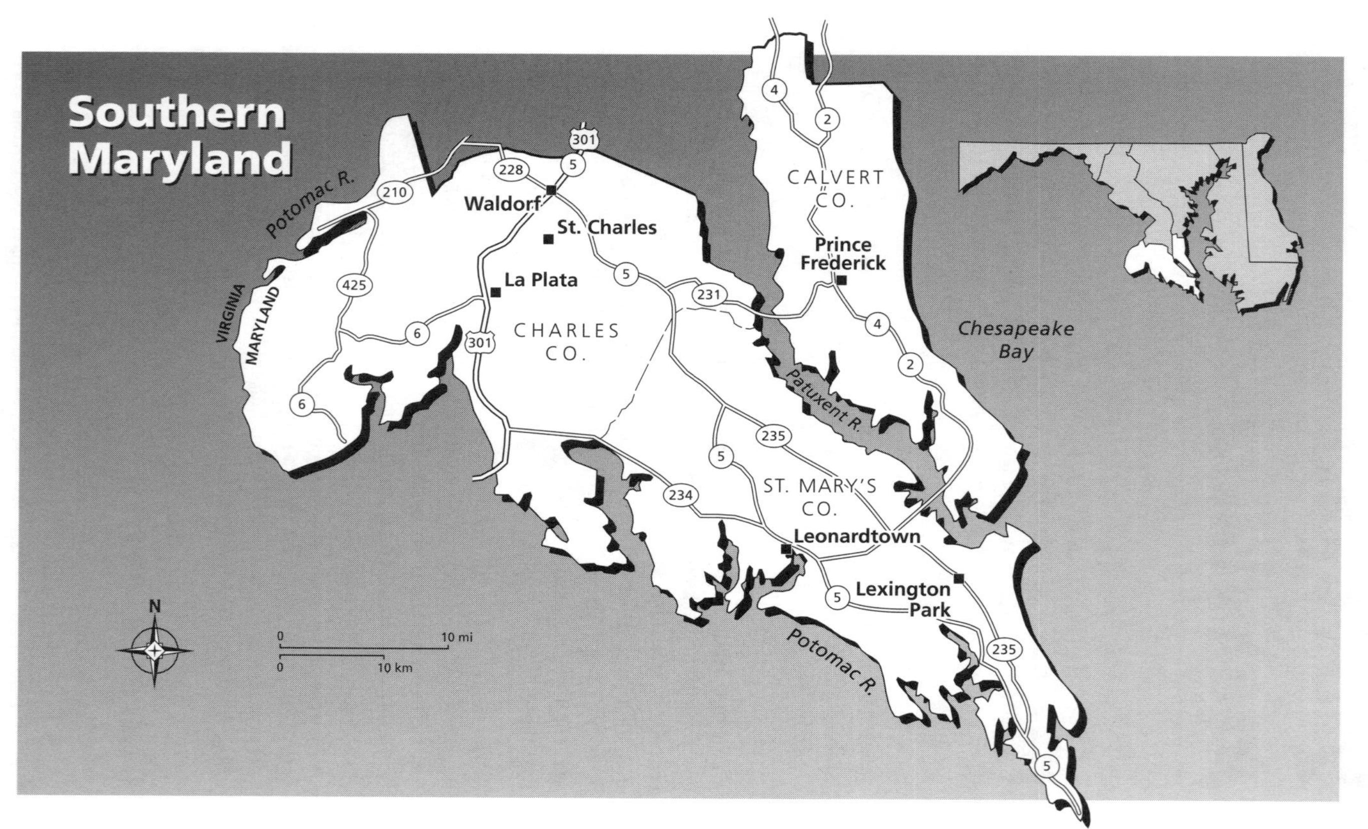
Southern Maryland
Potomac R.
Virginia
Maryland
210
228
301
5
Waldorf
St. Charles
La Plata
425
6
301
CHARLES CO.
231
CALVERT CO.
4
2
Prince Frederick
Chesapeake Bay
Patuxent R.
235
5
234
ST. MARY'S CO.
Leonardtown
Lexington Park
Potomac R.
N
0
10 mi
10 km

and the Old South, for there is neither Spanish moss hanging from these boughs nor Southern belles in hoop skirts. The cypress in this swamp are thought to be descendants of trees growing here some 5,000 to 15,000 years ago, shortly (relatively speaking) after the glaciers started receding. Some of the trees reach more than 100 feet in height and are 4 feet in diameter.

Judy's Favorite Attractions in Southern Maryland

Battle Creek Cypress Swamp Sanctuary

Calvert Marine Museum

Flag Ponds Nature Park

Historic St. Mary's City

Within this one-hundred-acre nature sanctuary is an interpretive center and a great place for nature photography in the spring (when violets, mayapples, and pink lady's slipper orchids are in bloom) and early summer when the blooms are most profuse. Bring fast film and a tripod, because the light is heavily filtered through the canopy. With its rich wetlands, look for such species as sweet gum, ash, southern arrowwood, and spicebush. You'll also see tulip tree, mountain laurel, and Virginia pine.

Just take the 1,700-foot boardwalk through the swamp to get real close to nature. However, you don't want to get too close to some of it. Those thick, fuzzy vines climbing the trees along the boardwalk through the swamp are poison ivy, and they are just as dangerous as their cousin with the three shiny leaves if you are allergic to it.

The sanctuary, the first Nature Conservancy preserve in Maryland, is at 2800 Grays Road off Sixes Road (Route 506), Port Republic 20676. Call (410) 535–5327 or visit www.calvertparks.org. It's open Tuesday through Saturday from 10:00 A.M. to 4:30 P.M. and Sunday from 1:00 to 5:00 P.M. April through September. It closes at 4:30 P.M. on Sunday the rest of the year. It is closed on Monday, and on Thanksgiving, Christmas, and New Year's Day.

If you want to hobnob and brush shoulders with the movers and shakers of Calvert County, you probably should find your way to ***Stoney's Seafood House*** at the Fox Run Shopping Center, 545 Solomons Island Road North in Prince Frederick. Sit down for a crab cake or oyster sandwich (you might hear that pronounced "arester," but no matter how you say it, they'll understand you). There's room for 225 people in three areas, including an infamous, somewhat private back room used frequently for deal-making. This is the second restaurant former custom-home builder Phillip Stone has opened; the first is a smaller seasonal variety located on Broomes Island. For more information and opening dates of the Broomes Island restaurant, call (410) 535–1888.

Francis and Ann Koenig donated the thirty-acre park known as ***Annmarie Garden*** to the people of Calvert County, but it's there for everyone to enjoy. Located at the headwaters of St. John Creek, the park was dedicated in October 1993. There's a range of sculpture and botanical treasures here, starting with the glazed ceramic gateposts, perhaps the largest and most complex hand-built enterprise ever attempted by a United States pottery studio. It consists of seven tons of ceramics in 630 pieces.

The first major permanent installation was a tribute to the oyster tonger, without whom we wouldn't have those succulent morsels. Maryland artist Antonio Tobias Mendez created the statue that was dedicated at Artsfest '94, an annual weeklong September event that combines the visual and performing arts. There's also a Gardenfest every spring, and a late-winter Garden in Lights. Among the flora attractions are more than 460 azaleas. Another special treat is the Surveyor's Map, a floating walkway that's more than 300 feet long, ending at a lookout within the tree canopy.

Annmarie Garden on St. John is open from 10:00 A.M. to 4:00 P.M. daily, and is located on Dowell Road, Prince Frederick 20678. Call (410) 326–4640.

Contained within the 327-acre park known as ***Flag Ponds Nature Park*** are wooded uplands, ponds, swamps, freshwater marshes, sandy beaches, and part of Chesapeake Bay. Here you can clearly see the difference between the uplands and the wetlands, between the Cliffs of Calvert and Chesapeake Bay. Wildlife abounds, including fox, muskrat, otter, turkey, whitetail deer, and pileated woodpecker. Special facilities include 3 miles of gentle hiking trails, rare plants such as the blue flag iris (from which the park derives its name), pond observation decks, picnic sites, a beach, a fishing pier, and a visitors center with wildlife exhibits.

One building remains from what was once a thriving "pound net" fishery that supplied trout, croaker, and herring to the bustling Baltimore markets during the first half of the twentieth century. April 1 through October 1 there is a daily vehicle charge of $4.00 for residents and $6.00 for nonresidents, or a seasonal pass for $15.00 and $20.00, respectively. November through March the charge is $3.00 for both residents and nonresidents.

Flag Ponds is open from 9:00 A.M. to 6:00 P.M. daily and 9:00 A.M. to 8:00 P.M. on weekends during the summer. From Labor Day through Memorial Day the park is open from 9:00 A.M. to 6:00 P.M. on weekends and closed during the week. It's located on North Solomons Island Road, Prince Frederick 20657. For additional information call (410) 586–1477 or visit www.calvertparks.org.

There are places called Hollywood and California in Maryland (both in St. Mary's County), and major motion pictures have been made in the state, but nothing equals ***Vera's White Sands*** restaurant. A summer pastime that should not be missed, Vera Freeman's restaurant is decorated with souvenirs from her worldwide travels. Imagine you are Lauren Bacall, Humphrey Bogart, or Peter Lorre, or even Bob Hope, Bing Crosby, or Hedy Lamarr on the road to someplace; you would feel right at home here. What are your decorative tastes? Would you like banana trees framing the flamingo-pink structure? Perhaps you would like beaded room dividers, carved elephants inlaid with ivory, giant clamshells, and leopard-skin bar stools to provide the atmosphere. Steam up the scene with a little romantic intrigue, and you do not have to travel far to find the wondrous.

In June, July, and August you may have your cocktails poolside. About 6:30 P.M. on Friday, Saturday, and Sunday evenings your attention will be diverted by live entertainment, and around 7:30 P.M. the J. Arthur Rank–style gong (from Hong Kong) will be sounded as Vera makes her entrance. Vera's is a place you will long remember.

The sunset view from the appropriately described picture windows is astounding, and the piano overlooks historic John's Creek, off the Patuxent River. The creek is wide, and the channel depth is 14 feet. The marina has boat docking facilities (water depth at dock is 12 feet), and a dockmaster is on the premises twenty-four hours a day, year-round.

Vera's White Sands is in Lusby on White Sands Drive. The restaurant is open Tuesday through Saturday 5:00 to 9:00 P.M. and Sunday 1:00 to 9:00 P.M. roughly between Memorial Day and Labor Day, and on weekends in the spring and fall. In other words, call before you make the drive. Reservations are suggested. (410) 586–1182.

Lusby is also where you'll find the geologically significant Calvert Cliffs. At ***Calvert Cliffs State Park*** you can seek your own fossils, formed more than fifteen million years ago, by taking a 2-mile hike to the beach (and hiking 2 miles back up, of course).

The fossils of more than 600 species have been identified from these cliffs, which were formed more than fifteen million years ago when the entire Southern Maryland area was covered by a warm, shallow sea. Sharks' teeth are the most common fossils found here. The park also has fishing, nature trails, picnic areas, playground equipment (including an accessible tire playground), youth group camping, and a variety of interpretative programs. Some 600 acres are open to hunting for

Trivia

Solomons was named for Issac Solomons who opened an oyster cannery here in 1867.

upland game, including deer (during season only, and hunters must register at the parking area), rabbits, squirrels, and turkeys (hunting permitted only during the spring gobbler season).

The park, at 1650 Calvert Cliffs Parkway, Lusby 20657, is open from sunrise to sunset. An admission of $3.00 per car is charged. Call (301) 872–5688 or log on to www.dnr.state.md.us/publiclands/sounterhn/calvertcliffs.html.

Continuing south on Route 2-4 will bring you to Solomons. A visitors center is open spring through late fall at 14175 Solomons Island Road South, Solomons 20688; (410) 326–6027. Across the street is the ***Calvert Marine Museum*** and ***Drum Point Lighthouse***; parking is behind the administration building.

The Calvert Marine Museum is proof that a museum can be fun, fascinating, and fact filled. This museum has grown from a seed planted by LeRoy "Pepper" Langley in 1970, and it is certainly worth a visit for a number of reasons. One reason is the Children's Discovery Room, where there is a pile of earth from Calvert Cliffs that you can dig in to find fossils. It can be difficult and time-consuming to search for fossils at outdoor sites, but not here. One shark's tooth per person, please. This room is more fun than a bushel of crabs that has just been dusted with seasoning.

Yet there is more, and you are on your own to enjoy, to be entertained, and to be educated. Even the more conventional exhibits about boating, the paleontology of Calvert Cliffs, and the estuarine biology of the Patuxent River and Chesapeake Bay are well handled.

Trivia

"Pepper" Langley is one of the prime treasures at the Calvert Marine Museum. Although he no longer spends a lot of time there on a daily basis, you can see him once in a while working on a model boat (or see his son, which is almost as good). "Pepper" received his name a very long time ago because of the fastball he used to pitch.

The museum's second treasure is the Drum Point Lighthouse, one of the old screw-pile, cottage-style lighthouses that used to protect the adventuresome watermen of the bay. The two-story, hexagon-shaped structure was built in 1883 to mark the entrance of the Patuxent River from the Chesapeake Bay. A crane and barge moved the stilted cottage to its current location in 1975.

Take a few minutes to walk through the lighthouse (watch your head when going up and down the steps) and mentally transport yourself to the time when people lived here and tended the light. It is romantic to think of the "good old days" when there were

Drum Point Lighthouse

lightkeepers, but most don't think this remote lifestyle is very attractive these days.

The third treasure is an old bugeye, the *William B. Tennison,* which takes people on cruises around the bay. This bugeye is a Chesapeake Bay sailing craft built in 1899 at Crabb Island by B. P. and R. L. Miles. Her hull is "chunk built," or made of nine logs, rather than by a plank-and-frame method of construction. Originally rigged for sailing, she was converted to power in 1907, and a new, larger cabin was added aft. The Maryland Commission for Celebration 2000 recently awarded a $10,000 grant to help repair the hull of the *Tennison,* one of the few vessels of this type left in the world.

You can cruise on the *Tennison* and see the Governor Johnson Bridge, the Solomons Island and Chesapeake Biological Laboratory, and the U.S. Naval Recreation Center at Point Patience. This allows you to view the inner harbor and Patuxent River as you can never see them from land. Capt. Donald Prescott runs the one-hour cruise at 2:00 P.M. Wednesday through Sunday (minimum of ten people required) between May 1 and October 1, or you can charter the boat for your own event. Fares begin at $5.00 per adult and $3.00 per child (five to twelve) per hour for the charter. Call (410) 326–2042 for additional information.

The Calvert Marine Museum is open daily 10:00 A.M. to 5:00 P.M. except New Year's Day, Thanksgiving, and Christmas. A wheelchair is available, but the lighthouse is not handicapped accessible. Admission is $5.00 for adults, $2.00 for children two to five, and $4.00 for seniors fifty-five and older. The Calvert Marine Museum is at 14150 Solomons Island Road, Solomons 20688. Call (410) 326–2042 or visit www.calvertmarinemuseum.com.

For more information about Solomons, call (410) 326–6027 or log on to sba.solomons.md.us.

For additional information about Calvert County, contact the Calvert County Department of Economic Development, Courthouse, 175 Main Street, Prince Frederick 20678; (410) 535–4583, (301) 855–1880, or (800) 331–9771.

Charles County

Most of the usual tourist attractions in Charles County are centered in La Plata and Port Tobacco (one of the oldest communities on the East Coast). On the eastern and western "ends" of the county, however, are two interesting views of early Charles County.

On the northeastern-most tip of Charles County is the town of Benedict, named for Benedict Leonard Calvert, the fourth Lord Baltimore. It was a flourishing town at least three times. The first was a period between 1817 and 1937, when steamboats carrying freight and passengers stopped here on their way to and from Baltimore and ports on the Rappahannock and Potomac Rivers. The second time was when slot machines were legal in the county and people came to gamble from as far north as New Jersey and New York. The third time was in 1988, when

British Invasion

Benedict is also notable as the landing site for 4,500 British troops in August 1814. Local historians say it is the only small town on United States soil that has been invaded by foreign troops, for these were the troops who marched on to the nation's capital. The British troops returned to Benedict with their wounded, and two of their soldiers were buried at Old Fields Chapel cemetery in Hughesville. During the Civil War, Camp Stanton was established here for recruiting and training African-American infantrymen to serve in the Union Army.

the Governor Thomas Johnson Bridge from Solomons Island to St. Mary's was temporarily closed. Ferries were put in service, but many people detoured to Benedict and used the Patuxent River Bridge.

Today this waterside town, the farthest inland port on the Patuxent River, has a post office (Dolores Buick is the postmaster) that is also a paperback lending library, a restaurant or two, and some "boatels" for storing boats.

Mount Carmel Monastery was the first convent for religious women in colonial America, founded on October 15, 1790. It was started by four Carmelite nuns, three of whom—Ann, Ann Theresa, and Susan Mathews—along with the Reverend Charles Neale were natives of Charles County. The group set up temporary quarters at Chandler's Hope, then owned by the Neale family.

Father Neale donated 860 acres to the Carmelites to build their monastery. Two of the original convent buildings have been restored and are open to visitors during the summer season. The other buildings are still used as an active convent.

If you are driving in from Route 301 on Mitchell Road, Mount Carmel Monastery is on the left about ½ mile past Charles County Community College at 4035A Mount Carmel Road, La Plata 20646. The monastery is open in the summer from 9:00 A.M. to 4:00 P.M. Mass is said daily at 7:15 A.M. and on Sunday at 8:00 A.M. Call (301) 934–1654 or log on to www.erols.com/carmel-of-port-tobacco.

Across from the monastery on Mitchell Road, on the community college property, is ***Friendship House***, one of the oldest homes in the county. This four-room hall-and-parlor-style house was built by William Dent in 1680 on Nanjemoy Creek. In 1968 it was dismantled by the Historical Society of Charles County and moved to its current location. Openings have been left in the structure so visitors can view the seventeenth-century construction techniques.

Friendship is open for tours and a ten- to fifteen-minute slide presentation from noon to 4:00 P.M. on Saturday and Sunday, May through September. Tours by appointment are available at other times. Call (301) 934–2251, extension 610, for information on Friendship House from the Southern Maryland Studies Center at Charles County Community College.

Pope's Creek is the best place to go for crabs and a view of the Potomac River. The 3-mile drive off Route 301 down Pope's Creek Road is also a little history lesson, for it was along this route that John Wilkes Booth found refuge after assassinating Abraham Lincoln. Two historical markers designate where he stopped along Pope's Creek Road for three

Trivia

On January 1, 1873, the first trains started running on the Pope's Creek Line of the Baltimore and Potomac Railroad. Although it was created so goods could be transported from Charles and Prince George's Counties to Baltimore and is used today to transport coal to the power plant on the Potomac, the line also allowed a "spur" to be run from Bowie to Washington, D.C., something that would otherwise have been prohibited because this new line provided competition to the Baltimore & Ohio line between the two cities.

days and where he crossed the Potomac into Virginia. (***Dr. Samuel A. Mudd***'s ***house,*** where Booth was treated, is farther north in the county on Route 232, south of Route 382 in Waldorf. It is open for tours from March to November, with a $3.00 admission charge for adults; call 301–934–8464.)

Down at Pope's Creek are the shells of oysters eaten over the centuries, first by Charles County Native Americans, then by settlers, and today by travelers. These shells cover some thirty acres to a depth of 15 feet in some places.

If you prefer eating crabs and oysters to looking at old shells, stop by Robertson's, Captain Billy's, or Pier 3 for some crabs served in a traditional style. The tables are covered with paper and piles of those tasty crabs; a pitcher of beer accompanies the feast. Here you can learn why Maryland is called the Land of Pleasant Living.

The old building on your right as you drive along Pope's Creek Road to the water is an old Rural Electrification Administration powerhouse with lovely arched windows reminiscent of the Palladian style.

The bridge across the Potomac, 3 miles downriver, is the Governor Harry W. Nice Bridge. It opened in 1940, replacing Laidlow's Ferry, and was the first crossing of the Potomac River south of the nation's capital. The 1938 groundbreaking was presided over by President Franklin D. Roosevelt. The bridge is 1⅔ miles long, rises 135 feet above the water, and carries nearly four million vehicles yearly. Passenger cars pay a 75-cent toll in either direction.

For additional tourism information write to the Charles County Office of Tourism, P.O. Box B, La Plata 20646; call (410) 934–0107, (301) 645–0558, or (800) SOME–FUN; or visit www.explorecharlescountymd.com.

St. Mary's County

There are some counties in Maryland that are off the beaten path even when you are on their most-traveled roads. St. Mary's is one of them. The county offers many different attractions that draw thousands of people each year, yet it remains primarily historic and underdeveloped. From the Naval Air Test and Evaluation Museum (connected with the Naval Air Station, Patuxent River), to the Old Jail Museum, to Point Lookout State Park with its terrific camping area and beaches, to the crafts at Cecil's Mill and Christmas Country Store, you can spend a good deal of time down here.

Historic St. Mary's City was the first proprietary colony in America and the first capital of Maryland. There are still numerous traces of colonial times in and around this area, including ***Sotterley Plantation,*** an eighteenth-century working plantation overlooking the Patuxent River.

The Sotterley tale is one of inspiration, for it has gone from America's most endangered historic site to its most promising. This plantation, the only remaining Tidewater plantation in Maryland open to the public with a number of visitor and educational programs, is older than Mount Vernon and Monticello. Over the years the property had decayed, and it was feared it would have to be shut down. However, John Hanson Briscoe, great-grandson of a Sotterley slaveholder, and Agnes Kane Callum, great-granddaughter of a Sotterley slave, spearheaded the campaign for funds and restoration, and with the help of people across the country and the foundation's trustees, Sotterley is returning to its former impressive self.

Sotterley's grounds are open Tuesday through Sunday from 10:00 A.M. to 4:00 P.M. The manor house, off Route 245 at 44300 Sotterly Lane, Hollywood 20636, is closed from October 31 to May 1, although special tours may be arranged. Admission is $2.00 per person Monday through Friday, and $7.00 for adults and $5.00 for children six through sixteen to

Be My Loveville Valentine

In 1989 Eva C. Hall decided the postmark from her zip code, 20656, should be red and have a cherubic arrow-shooter aiming toward a heart, particularly around the first half of February. It's understandable; 20656 is Loveville, named after Kingsley Love, the town's first postmaster. Hall has worked at the post office for thirty years, and she receives mail from around the world so special cards and letters will have a special stamp for Valentine's Day. About 30,000 pieces of mail will be handstamped at this post office, which normally sees about 400 pieces a day. Most come from visitors from nearby Washington, Virginia, Pennsylvania, and, of course, Maryland, but other letters have come from as far away as Japan. The post office is at 27780 Point Lookout Road, Loveville 20656. Call (301) 475–5243.

Buzzy's Country Store

As you head toward Point Lookout, at the very southern tip of St. Mary's, you're likely to find Ridgell's Country Store and its proprietor, Clarence "Buzzy" Ridgell. This is the place to find beer, souvenirs, pennants, bait, wine, and other "stuff." You'll also see, plastered, after a fashion, on the ceiling, his collection of more than 400 hats, from as far away as Australia and Russia. If you have a cap you want to donate, feel free to do so. You can find Buzzy at 12665 Point Lookout Road, Scotland 20687, (301) 872–5430.

tour on Saturday and Sunday. Call (301) 373–2280 or (800) 681–0850; or visit www.sotterley.com.

At the ***St. Clements Island Potomac River Museum*** you can discover the landing site of Maryland's first European settlers. Historic churches abound. St. Mary's City is actually a small town—just St. Mary's College, a post office, Trinity Episcopal Church, and Historic St. Mary's City, an outdoor living-history museum. Scant development and modernization has meant that St. Mary's is the only early permanent English settlement that has remained largely undisturbed; thus it is a favorite of archaeologists, who have uncovered millions of artifacts in a relatively short time.

You can see the replica of the square-rigged **Maryland Dove,** one of the two ships that brought the first settlers and supplies from England; the reconstructed State House of 1676; the Godiah Spray Tobacco Plantation; archaeological excavations; the Margaret Brent Memorial Garden; Farthing's Ordinary (a seventeenth-century inn exhibit and modern restaurant); and a visitors center with an archaeology exhibit hall, guided walking tours, and museum gift shop. It's difficult to believe you're barely an hour from Washington, D.C. (well, depends on the traffic), while walking through this seventeenth-century capital. The 800 acres of unspoiled tidewater landscape whisper tranquillity.

The exhibits are open March 24 through the last weekend in November, Wednesday through Sunday 10:00 A.M. to 5:00 P.M. Call (301) 862–0960 or (800) SMC–1634, or log on to www.webgraphic. com/hsmc.

With more miles of shoreline than square miles of land and a college campus full of students, you know this has to be a good party town (the college shudders at that reputation). One can study only so long. St. Mary's College was formerly St. Mary's Female Seminary, and it is considered one of the best buys in education, with an excellent teacher-student ratio and a small enrollment of about 1,300 students. Of course, as a student or parent of a student, that is the reputation that should interest you.

The **Freedom of Conscience *Statue*** at the entrance to the college was erected by the counties of Maryland and symbolizes the religious freedom on which the state was founded. In 1649, at the request of town officials from St. Mary's City, a guarantee of freedom of conscience to all Christians (freedom of other religions came later) was enacted by the state legislature.

The Potomac and Patuxent Rivers, the creeks, the streams, and the Chesapeake Bay are ideal for biology and marine-science studies. But the bay also makes this area ideal for sailing, so it is frequently invaded by sailors seeking a home port.

Freedom of Conscience Statue

The annual Governor's Cup Regatta is considered one of the ten best sailing parties of the year by national sailors. The water is also perfect for those interested in sailboarding. With St. Mary's mild winters, students can enjoy boating about six months of the school year.

On the banks of the St. Mary's River is a 40-foot ***circle labyrinth,*** with a path that leads to the center, or rosette, and back out again. It's modeled after one on the floor of Chartres Cathedral in France. Labyrinths have been around for thousands of years, as seen in the Hopi medicine wheel. The labyrinth emphasizes tranquillity while you clear your mind and meditate. Unlike a maze, there's only one path and you can't get lost. Call (301) 863–8403 for more details. The labyrinth is on private property, next to the Historic St. Mary's City Visitor Center, 18751 Hogaboom Lane, St. Mary's City. Call (301) 862–0990.

All is not water, water, everywhere, in St. Mary's County; some of the area is devoted to produce farms. One of the major enticements of the county is the ***Charlotte Hall Farmers Market,*** with its Amish goods, produce, antiques, and curios. As with most farmer's markets, the earlier you arrive, the better the selection.

The market, open year-round on Wednesday and Saturday from 8:00 A.M. to 5:00 P.M., is on Route 5 in Charlotte Hall. Call (301) 884–3108.

The ***Captain Tyler passenger ferryboat*** runs between Point Lookout State Park and Smith Island, with the one-hundred-minute ride departing at 10:00 A.M. and returning at 4:00 P.M. It operates daily Memorial Day through Labor Day, other times on Saturday and Sunday, and can carry 150 passengers. The cost is $25 for adults and $10 for children; bicycles are permitted and are included in the fare. For more information call Tyler's Cruises, Rhodes Point 21858, (410) 425–2771, or visit www.smithislandcruises. com.

For a picturesque view, you'll want to stop at ***Point Lookout State Park*** at the confluence of the Potomac River and the Chesapeake Bay. The lighthouse here is unique and was the first permanent light built on the Potomac River. It's the only accessible lighthouse in its original location in southern Maryland. This is a great spot for picnicking, fishing, and enjoying the nearby campground (if you're really crazy about mosquitos). The six-acre park is open daily from

Trivia

The old sailor's rhyme was "Point Lookout, Point Lookin, Point no Point, Point Again." I've seen the first three on a map, but not the fourth. Perhaps it was just rhyme or had some deeper, older meaning I never learned.

sunrise to dusk. The park's phone number is (301) 872–5688; www.dnr. state.md.us.

Trivia

The Piney Point Lighthouse was known as the Lighthouse of Presidents because starting with James Madison, presidents and other notables spent their summers at Piney Point.

The ***Piney Point Lighthouse Museum*** is where you can see exhibits describing the construction and operation of the lighthouse (which was in use from 1836 through 1964) and the role of the United States Coast Guard. The lighthouse museum and gift shop are open daily from 1:00 to 6:00 P.M. Located on Lighthouse Road, Piney Point 20674; (301) 769–2222; www.somd.lib.md.ns/STMA/Government/Rec/ullos.htm.

The **Black Panther** is a U-1105 German submarine from the World War II era that featured a rubber coating that made it "invisible" to the detection devices of the day. The sub was captured at the end of the war, and after going over it with a fine-toothed comb, the United States Navy sank it off the coast of Piney Point. Now it's Maryland's first Historic Shipwreck Diving Preserve and a National Historic Landmark. For more information, call the St. Clement's Island Potomac River Museum at (301) 769–2222.

For additional tourism information write to St. Mary's County Division of Tourism, P.O. Box 653, Leonardtown 20650. Call (800) 327–9023.

PLACES TO EAT IN SOUTHERN MARYLAND

BENEDICT
Chappelear's,
7350 Benedict Place,
(301) 274–9828

Tony's Riverhouse,
7320 Benedict Avenue,
(301) 274–4440

BROOMES ISLAND
Stoney's Seafood House,
39393 Oyster House Road,
(410) 586–1888

CALIFORNIA
Aloha Restaurant,
Route 235,
23415 Three Notch Road,
(301) 862–4838

Lenny's,
22576 Macarthur Boulevard,
(301) 737–0777

CHESAPEAKE BEACH
Abner's Seaside Crab House,
3748 Harbor Road,
(410) 257–3689 or
(301) 855–6705

Chaney's on the Chesapeake,
8323 Bayside Road,
(301) 855–2323

Rod-N-Reel,
Route 261 and Mears Avenue,
(410) 257–2735 or
(301) 855–8351

Smokey Joe's,
Route 261 and Mears Avenue,
(410) 257–2427

Wesley Stinnett's,
8617 Bayside Road,
(410) 257–6100

CHARLOTTE HALL
Charlotte Hall House of Ribs,
Route 5,
(301) 884–6124

Hensen's Charcoal Steakhouse,
Route 5,
(301) 884–7549

Clements
Abell's,
23945 Colton's Point Road,
(301) 769–4010

Cobb Island
Captain John's Crab House,
16215 Cobb Island Road,
(301) 259–2315

Drayden
Still Anchors,
46555 Dennis Point Way,
(301) 994–2288

Hollywood
Clarke's Landing,
24580 Clarke's Landing Road,
(301) 373–8468

La Plata
Casey Jones Restaurant,
417 East Charles Street,
(301) 932–6226

Leonardtown
Cafe Des Artistes,
41655 Fenwick Street,
(301) 997–0500

Willow's Restaurant,
24509 Point Lookout Road,
(301) 475–6553

Lexington Park
Emily's Oriental Express,
432 Great Mills Road,
(301) 737–5232

Linda's Cafe,
21779 Tulagi Place #A,
(301) 862–3544

Peking Restaurant,
21775 Great Mills Road #900,
(301) 863–6190

Lusby
Vera's White Sands,
1200 White Sands Drive,
(410) 586–1182

Mechanicsville
Bert's 50s Diner,
28760 Three Notch Road,
(301) 884–3837

Cape St. Mary's Marina,
Route 472 Sandgates Road,
(301) 373–2001

Captain Leonard's,
Route 235 and Morganza Turner Road,
(301) 884–3701

Copsey's Seafood,
29876 Three Notch Road,
(301) 884–4235

Drift Inn,
41396 Riverview Drive Road,
(301) 884–3470

North Beach
Neptune's Seafood Pub,
8800 Chesapeake Avenue at First Street,
(410) 257–7899

Thursday's Bar and Grill,
Seventh Street and Bay Avenue,
(410) 286–8695

Piney Point
Oakwood Lodge,
17275 Lighthouse Road,
(301) 994–2377

Pope's Creek
Capt Billy's Crab House,
Pope's Creek Road,
(301) 932–4323

Robertson's Crab House,
Pope's Creek Road,
(301) 934–9236

Prince Frederick
Adams,
the Place For Ribs,
2200 Solomons Island Road North,
(410) 586–0001

Old Field Inn,
485 Main Street,
(410) 535–1054,
(301) 855–1054, or
(800) 698–1054

Stoney's Seafood House,
Fox Run Shopping Center,
(410) 535–1888

Ridge
Scheible's,
48342 Wynne Road,
(301) 872–5185

Spinnakers,
16244 Millers Wharf Road,
(301) 872–4340,
www.spinnakersrestaurant.com

St. George Island
Evans Seafood,
Route 249,
(301) 994–2299

St. Mary's City
Brome-Howard Inn,
18281 Rosecroft Road,
(301) 866–0656,
www.bromehowardinn.com

Solomons
Boomerangs Original Ribs,
13820 Solomons Island Road,
(410) 326–6050

Bowen's Inn,
14630 Solomons Island Road South,
(410) 326–9880

Captain's Table,
275 Lore Road,
(410) 326–2772

Catamarans Seafood and Steaks,
14470 Solomons Island Road South,
(410) 326–8399

C.D. Cafe,
14350 Solomons Island Road,
(410) 326–3877

DiGiovanni's Dock of the Bay,
14556 Solomons Island Road,
(410) 394–6400,
www.digiovannis restaurant.com

Dry Dock Restaurant,
251 C Street,
(410) 326–4817

Lighthouse Inn,
14640 Solomons Island Road South,
(410) 326–2444,
www.lighthouse-inn.com

Solomons Pier Restaurant & Lounge,
14575 Solomons Island Road South,
(410) 326–2424

Valley Lee
Cedar Cove Inn,
Route 249 Cedar Cove Marina,
(301) 994–1155 or
(800) 705–2628

Where to Stay in Southern Maryland

Bel Alton
Bel Alton Motel,
9295 Crain Highway,
(301) 934–9505

Broomes Island
Island Creek Bed and Breakfast,
9435 River View Road,
(410) 286–0950

Bryantown
Wiltshire Plains Bed and Breakfast,
4710 Bryantown Road,
(301) 638–7773 or
(800) 808–7773

California
Myrtle Point Bed and Breakfast,
24000 Patuxent Boulevard,
(301) 862–3090 or
(800) 249–3090

Chesapeake Beach
Tidewater Treasures Bed and Breakfast,
7315 Bayside Road,
(410) 257–0784

Dunkirk
Haven's Rest Bed and Breakfast,
1961 Haven Lane,
(301) 855–2232

Hughesville
Shady Oaks Bed and Breakfast,
7490 Serenity Drive,
(301) 932–8864 or
(800) 597–0924

Huntington
Back Woods Bed and Breakfast,
2135 Deer Run Court,
(410) 535–4627

Serenity Acres Bed and Breakfast,
4270 Hardesty Road,
(410) 535–3744,
www.bbonline.com/md/serenity

Indian Head
Indian Head Inn,
4640 Strauss Avenue,
(301) 743–5405

Mechanicsville
Wide Bay Cottage at Dameron,
997 Old Route 3,
(301) 884–3254

North Beach
Westlawn Inn Beach House Bed and Breakfast,
9200 Chesapeake Avenue,
(301) 855–2607,
www.westlawninn.com

Prince Frederick
Baycliff Bed and Breakfast,
168 Windcliff Road,
(410) 535–2278

Cliff House,
156 Windcliff Road,
(410) 535–4839,
www.bbonline.com/md/cliffhouse

Ridge
Bard's Field of Trinity Manor,
15671 Pratt Road,
(301) 872–5989,
www.erols.com/ajpratt

St. George's Island
Potomac View Farm,
15914 Camp Merryelande Road,
(301) 994–2311

St. Leonard
Jeff's Bed and Fix Your Own Breakfast,
6040 Bayview Road,
(410) 535–5308

St. Mary's City
Brome-Howard Inn,
18281 Rosecroft Road,
(301) 866–0656,
www.bromehowardinn.com

Scotland
St. Michael's Manor,
50200 St. Michael's Manor Way,
(301) 872–4025

Solomons
Adina's Guest House,
14236 Solomons Island Road,
(410) 326–4895

Back Creek Inn,
210 Alexander Street,
(410) 326–2022,
www.bbonline.com/md/back-creek

By-the-Bay Bed and Breakfast,
14374 Calvert Street,
(410) 326–3428,
www.chesapeake.net/~bythebay-bandb

Grey Fox Inn,
14560 Solomons Island Road South,
(410) 326–6826

Locust Inn Rooms,
14478 Solomons Island Road South,
(410) 326–9817

Solomons Victorian Inn,
125 Charles Street,
(410) 326–4811,
www.chesapeake.net/solomons/victorianinn

Solomons Holiday Inn Select,
155 Holiday Drive,
(800) 356–2009 or
(410) 326–6311,
www.ameritel.net/hisolomons

Webster House Bed and Breakfast,
14364 Sedwick Avenue,
(410) 326–0454,
www.solomons-island.com/webster

Tall Timbers
Potomac View Farm Bed and Breakfast,
44477 Tall Timbers Road,
(301) 994–2311,
www.erols.com/campmd

Waldorf
Holiday Inn Waldorf Hotel,
1 St. Patrick's Drive,
(800) HOLIDAY or
(301) 645–8200

Other Attractions in Southern Maryland

Academy of Natural Sciences,
St. Leonard,
(410) 586–9700

African-American Heritage Museum,
La Plata,
(301) 843–0371

All Faith Episcopal Church,
Charlotte Hall,
(301) 884–3773

All Saints Episcopal Church,
Avenue,
(301) 769–4288

All Saints Episcopal Church,
Sunderland,
(410) 257–6306

American Chestnut Land Trust,
Prince Frederick,
(410) 586–1570,
www.anserc.org/aclt

American Indian Cultural Center,
Waldorf,
(301)372–1932

Calvert Cliffs Nuclear Power Plant,
Lusby,
(410) 495–4673,
www.calvertcliffs.com

Cecil's Old Mill,
Great Mills,
(301) 994–1510

Chesapeake Beach Railway Museum,
Chesapeake Beach,
(410) 257–3892

Chesapeake Beach Water Park,
Chesapeake Beach,
(410) 257–1404,
www.cal.md.us/cced/guide/waterpark.htm

Chesapeake Biological Lab Visitor Center, Solomons, (410) 326–7282

Christ Church, La Plata, (301) 932–1051

Christ Episcopal Church, Chaptico, (301) 884–3451

Christ Episcopal Church, Port Republic, (410) 586–0565

Dent Chapel, Charlotte Hall, (301) 884–8174, ext. 403

Emmanuel United Methodist Church, Huntingtown, (410) 535–3177

Friendship House, La Plata, (301) 934–2251 or (800) 933–9177

Greenwell State Park, Hollywood, (301) 872–5389, www.dnr.state.md.us

Joseph C. Lore & Sons Oyster House, Solomons, (410) 326–2042

Kings Landing Park, Huntingtown, (410) 535–2661

Middleham Episcopal Church, Lusby, (410) 326–4948, www.chesapeake.net/~stpete

(Dr. Samuel) Mudd Home Museum, Waldorf, (301) 934–8464, www.somd.lib.md.us/museums.mudd.htm

North End Gallery, Leonardtown, (301) 475–3130

Old Jail Museum, Leonardtown, (301) 475–2467

One-Room Schoolhouse, Port Republic, (410) 586–0482

Patuxent Naval Air Museum, Lexington Park, (301) 863–7418

Port Tobacco Courthouse and Museum, Port Tobacco, (301) 934–4313

Port Tobacco One-Room School, Port Tobacco, (301) 932–6064

St. Andrews Episcopal Church, California, (301) 862–2247, www.eaglenet.com/andrews

St. Clement's Island and Potomac River Museum, Coltons Point, (301) 769–2222 www.somd.lib.md.us/STMA/Goverment/Rec/potomoc.htm

St. Francis Xavier Church, Leonardtown, (301) 475–9885

St. George Episcopal Church, Valley Lee, (301) 994–0585

St. Ignatius Catholic Church, Chapel Point, (301) 934–8245

St. Ignatius Church, St. Inigoes, (301) 872–5590

St. Mary's County Historical Society, Leonardtown, (301) 475–2467, www.somd.lib.md.us/smchs

St. Mary's River State Park, Great Mills, (301) 872–5688

Smallwood's Retreat, Marbury, (301) 743–7613

Smallwood State Park, Marbury, (301) 743–7613 or (800) 784–5380, www.dnr.state.md.us

Thomas Stone National Historical Site, Port Tobacco, (301) 934–6027

Trinity Episcopal Church, St. Mary's City, (301) 862–4597

Calendar of Annual Events in Southern Maryland

January

Winterlights: A Celebration of Chesapeake Bay Lighthouse, *Solomons, (410) 326–2042, www.calvertmarinemuseum.com*

March

Maryland Days, *St Mary's City, (800) 762–1634 or (301) 862–0990*

April

Bay County Boat Show, *Hollywood, (301) 373–5468*

Celtic Festival and Highland Gathering, *St. Leonard, (410) 257–9003, www.cssm.org*

Earth Day Family Open House, *St. Leonard, (410) 586–9700*

Gardenfest, *Solomons, (410) 544–4526*

John Wilkes Booth Escape Route Tour, *Clinton, (301) 868–1121, www.surratt.org*

Maryland Archaeology Month, *statewide, (410) 514–7661*

Right of Way Hike, *Chesapeake Beach, (410) 257–3892 or (301) 855–6472*

Solomons Spring Launch, *Solomons, (410) 326–2525, www.sba.solomons.md.us*

Sunrise Service, *Point Lookout State Park, (301) 872–5688*

World Carnival, *St. Mary's College, (301) 862–0203*

May

African-American Family Community Day, *St. Leonard, (410) 586–8501*

Antique Vehicle Run, *Chesapeake Beach, (410) 257–3892 or (301) 855–6472*

International Museum Day, *Solomons, (410) 326–2042*

Kids' Fishing Derby, *Smallwood State Park, (301) 888–1410*

Lighthouse Days, *Piney Point, (301) 769–2222*

Memorial Day Celebration, *La Plata, (301) 934–8421*

Memorial Day Outside Antique Sale, *Huntingtown, (410) 257–1677*

Patuxent Family Discovery Day, *Solomons, (410) 326–2042*

Quilt and Needlework Show, *Hollywood, (301) 373–2280 or (800) 681–0850, www.sotterleycom*

Southern Maryland Annual Spring Festival, *Leonardtown, (301) 994–0525*

Spring Festival, *Cedarville State Forest, (301) 888–1410 or (800) 784–5380*

Spring Games, *Waldorf, (301) 934–0137*

Strawberry Festival, *St. Leonard, (410) 586–1716*

Welcome Summertime Memorial Day Weekend, *Chesapeake Beach, (410) 257–2735*

June

Blue and Gray Days, *Point Lookout State Park, (301) 872–5688*

Cobb Island Day, *Cobb Island, (301) 259–2078 or (301) 259–2955*

Children's Day on the Farm, *St. Leonard, (410) 586–8501, www.jefpat.org*

Confederate POW Commemoration, *Point Lookout State Park, (757) 427–5065*

County Heritage Festival, *Leonardtown, (301) 884–3024*

Midsummer Village Faire, *St. Mary's, (800) 762–1634 or (301) 862–0990*

North Beach House and Garden Tour, *North Beach, (410) 257–6127*

St. Mary's County Crab Festival, *Leonardtown, (301) 475–8403*

Calendar of Annual Events in Southern Maryland (Cont'd)

July

Family Day on the Bay, *Chesapeake Beach, (301) 855–8351 or (410) 257–2735*

Fourth of July Celebration, *Indian Head, (301) 753–6633, www.somd.lib.md.us/indianhead*

St. Clement's Island Museum Anniversary Week, *Colton's Point, (301) 769–2222*

Sharkfest, *Solomons, (410) 326–2042*

Solomons July Fourth Celebration, *Solomons, (410) 326–2549, www.sba.solomons.md.us*

Tidewater Archaeology Dig, *St. Mary's City, (800) 762–1634 or (301) 862–0990*

August

Bayfest, *North Beach, (301) 855–6681 or (410) 257–9618*

Cradle of Invasion, *Solomons, (410) 326–2042*

Jousting Tournament, *Port Republic, (410) 535–1710*

St. Mary's College Governor's Cup, *St. Mary's City, (301) 862–0280, www.smcm.edu*

St. Mary's County Fair, *Leonardtown, (301) 475–8434*

September

Artsfest, *Solomons, (410) 326–4640*

Battle of St. Leonard, *St. Leonard, (410) 586–8501*

Calvert County Fair, *Barstow, (410) 535–0026*

Charles County Fair, *La Plata, (301) 932–1234*

Jazz Down by the Riverside, *St. Leonard, (301) 855–9394, www.jefpat.org*

Labor Day Weekend, *Chesapeake Beach, (410) 257–2735, (301) 855–8351, or (877) RODNREEL, www.rodnreelinc.com*

Lackey Athletic Boosters Association, *Indian Head, (301) 753–6720*

Solomons Island Biathlon, *Solomons, (410) 326–7214, clb.umces.edu*

War of 1812 Re-enactment, *St. Leonard, (410) 586–8500, www.jefpat.org*

Waterside Concert, *Solomons, (410) 326–2042, www.calvertmarinemuseum.com*

October

Blessing of the Fleet, *Colton's Point, (301) 769–2222*

Charles County Wine Festival, *La Plata, (301) 645–0558 or (800) 766–3386*

Grand Militia Muster, *St. Mary's City, (800) 762–1634 or (301) 862–0990*

Haunts of Smallwood, *Marbury, (301) 888–1410 or (800) 784–5380*

Patuxent River Appreciation Days Festival, *Solomons, (410) 326–2042, www.calvertmarinemuseum.com*

Point Lookout Ghost Walk, *Point Lookout State Park, (301) 872–5688, www.dnr.state.md.us*

Southern Maryland Farm Life Festival, *Charlotte Hall, (301) 863–2905*

St. Mary's County Oyster Festival, *Leonardtown, (301) 863–5015*

Woodland Indian Culture Days, *St. Mary's City, (301) 862–0990 or (800) 762–1634*

November

Eastern States Archaeological Federation, *Solomons, (410) 514–7661, www.qua50.com*

Festival of Trees, *Waldorf, (301) 934–1268 or (301) 609–TREE*

Calendar of Annual Events in Southern Maryland (Cont'd)

Lighthouse Open House, *Point Lookout State Park, (301) 872–5688*

Road Rally, *North Beach, (301) 855–6681 or (410) 257–9618*

Veteran's Day Parade, *Leonardtown, (301) 475–9791*

December

A Plantation Christmas, *Hollywood, (301) 373–2280 or (800) 681–0850, www.sotterley.com*

Colonial Christmas at Smallwood, *Marbury, (301) 888–1410 or (800) 784–5380, www.dnr.state.md.us*

Garden in Lights, *Solomons, (410) 326–4640*

Madrigals and Carols, *St. Mary's City, (301) 862–0990 or (800) 762–1634*

Solomons Christmas Walk and Boat Parade, *Solomons, (410) 326–2549*

Eastern Shore

Welcome to the Eastern Shore, the southern part of the ***Delmarva Peninsula*** (*DEL*aware, *MAR*yland, and *V*irgini*A*). This is where you see as well as hear about those unfamiliar boats, the skipjack, the bugeye, and the bungy. You will also see "June bugs," the thousands of kids who invade the ocean beaches and boardwalks every summer to work at jobs and on tanning.

Explore and enjoy the dissimilarities you will find within a few short miles. Stop by a library to see a mural painted by an artist who became so popular that the library could not afford another mural like it. Find budding artists at the Dorchester Arts Center. Search for bald eagles and great blue herons, mingle with area residents at the general store, and see centuries-old homes that have not needed restoration because they have been so well maintained over the years. Ride the ferryboats, eat at some of the best seafood restaurants in the country, examine the fine local examples of duck-decoy carving, and take a peek at some of the prettiest passenger boats and ferryboats being built these days.

Take time to locate the Mason-Dixon line; it surprises most people that the line not only separates Pennsylvania and Maryland, but it also delineates the Delaware–Maryland border. Last but not least, get some sand between your toes and contemplate the treasures of America in Miniature. On the eastern side of the Chesapeake Bay lies the Eastern Shore, a very distinct and separate entity from the "western shore." People here are dedicated to the ways of the watermen and to the riches the land can bring, although farming here means just about anything that grows (except tobacco).

At the eastern end of the William Preston Lane Jr. Memorial Bridge—the Chesapeake Bay Bridge—is Kent Island, where the first European settlement in Maryland was founded in 1631. When the settlers came, they found the Nanticoke and Choptank tribes, which are now immortalized by Indian lore exhibits and two rivers named after the tribes.

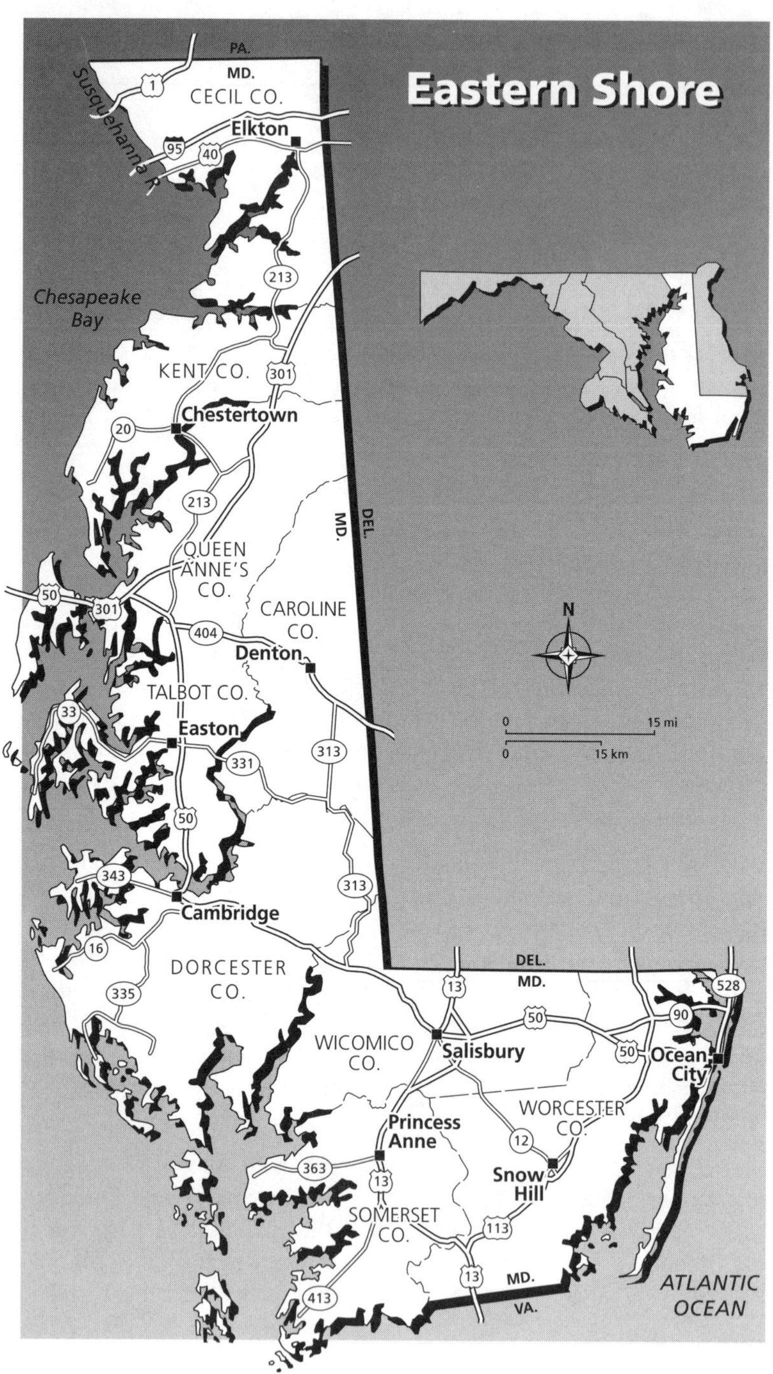
Eastern Shore
PA.
MD.
CECIL CO.
Susquehanna R.
Elkton
Chesapeake Bay
KENT CO.
Chestertown
QUEEN ANNE'S CO.
CAROLINE CO.
Denton
TALBOT CO.
Easton
Cambridge
DORCESTER CO.
WICOMICO CO.
Salisbury
Princess Anne
SOMERSET CO.
WORCESTER CO.
Snow Hill
Ocean City
DEL.
MD.
VA.
ATLANTIC OCEAN
N
0
15 mi
15 km
1
95
40
213
301
20
50
404
33
331
313
343
16
335
13
528
90
12
363
113
413

History surrounds the bay's little towns and 500 sheltered harbors. The bay is home to boatbuilders, sailors, fishermen (10,000 fishermen earn their livelihood from the bay), and sportsmen. The waterways are often as secluded as in the days when pirates and buccaneers hid in the bays and inlets. Some say there may still be buried treasure stashed in the sand dunes. At other times the waterways can compete with traffic-bound interstate freeways for congestion.

Judy's Favorite Attractions on the Eastern Shore

Blackwater National Wildlife Refuge

Eastern Shore Early Americana Museum

Plumpton Park Zoo

Ward Museum of Wildfowl Art

Wye Oak State Park

Hunters flock here every fall, for this is a major stop for migrating birds on the Atlantic flyway. To conserve and protect those birds that are not so abundant, nearly $2 million has been raised for conservation projects along the flyway.

On the flat-as-a-pancake terrain are farmlands, stately manors, and, once again, small towns. It seems that most of Maryland is filled with small towns. And, fortunately, the towns of the Eastern Shore are always sponsoring festivals celebrating the richness of the land or the sea.

My Eastern Shore excursion starts at the top of the bay and works its way down and to the east, over to the Atlantic Ocean.

Cecil County

Starting at the top of the state, at the head of the Chesapeake Bay, we begin at Cecil County.

Fair Hill Nature and Environmental Center is a facility located in the northern half of the 5,600-acre Fair Hill Natural Resources Management Area in northeastern Cecil County. One of the state's remaining covered bridges is at Fair Hill, which was a 7,000-acre estate owned by William DuPont Jr. The entire Maryland portion was purchased by the state as a Natural Resource Area. In the northern reaches of the property, near the Pennsylvania border, is the 1850s covered bridge. The headquarters building was formerly used by William DuPont Jr. as his hunting lodge and is next to the covered bridge over Big Elk Creek. There are two Mason-Dixon line markers on the property.

Trivia

Located in the northeastern corner of Maryland, midway between Baltimore and Philadelphia, Cecil County is the only Maryland county that is considered part of the Wilmington, Delaware, New Jersey, and Maryland primary metropolitan statistical area.

This is an outdoor education school with programs designed to encourage awareness, understanding, and appreciation of the natural world, our natural resources, and the impact of people on the environment. The indoor and outdoor classrooms are open Monday through Friday and on occasional weekends and evenings for members of the Fair Hill Environmental Foundation Inc. (a private, nonprofit support group) and for groups by reservation.

Program subjects might include bird identification, wildflowers, marsh studies, landscaping, animal designs for survival, aquatic studies, basic entomology, clean water watch, ecology, forestry, and soil studies.

The Fair Hill Nature and Environmental Center is at 375 Fair Hill Drive, Elkton 21921, and is open from 8:30 A.M. to 4:30 P.M. Monday through Friday. Call (410) 398–1246 for additional information.

Across Route 273 is the ***steeplechase track at Fair Hill***, an exact replica of Aintree, where England's Grand National is held. Since it opened in 1933 there have been a number of steeplechase races annually, and the May event is the only steeplechase in the United States that permits

A Beloved Place

Fair Hill Nature and Environmental Center will look familiar to those of you who saw the Oprah Winfrey film Beloved, *for about half of the movie was shot on the property. According to Carol Cebula, Fair Hill office administrator, the house was built from scratch and was "aged" for the movie. Only those rooms used in the movie were actually decorated; the rest were left bare. The back of the house was constructed of plywood so the cameras could have access for filming.*

The movie's other buildings, particularly the log structures, were imported from North Carolina, where they had been dismantled and shipped to Maryland to be reassembled. The farm animals were brought in and the garden was planted.

A barn, smokehouse, outhouse, corn crib, carriage shed, and other farm structures were built, two wells were drilled, telephone cables were installed, the heating and air conditioning were upgraded, roadways were laid, and a new Chevy Tahoe was given to the center. In all, Fair Hill received about $1 million in cash and donated items.

All of this for about two weeks' worth of shooting! Ed Walls, the former Fair Hill manager, was in the movie as a ticket taker in the carnival scene and was the only staff member who had a part in the movie.

If you hurry, you can see the temporary buildings—they'll probably be demolished some time in 2001. Drive to the butterfly field off Bluestone Road.

pari-mutuel wagering. Fair Hill is also the home of the National Steeplechase and Hunt Association, which moved from Belmont, New York, in June 1989.

The ***Mitchell House*** is a two-and-a-half-story stone dwelling believed to have been built in 1764 (based on a fireback date), although it has had considerable alterations since then. The house has been a Revolutionary War hospital (run by its owner, Dr. Abraham Mitchell) for Continental soldiers, a hotel, a post office, and a store.

Anthony Graziano purchased the building from the state of Maryland in 1978 when it was in dilapidated condition, and he has proudly restored it. Now the house is the ***Fair Hill Inn,*** a fine restaurant that features an Italian continental menu but specializes in Maryland seafood. Just perusing the menu, which includes Veal Imperial (a Fair Hill delight), pasta marinara (scallops, shrimp, clams, and mussels served over pasta), and seafood Beatrice (lobster tail, scallops, shrimp, and crabmeat cooked with brandy, flamed with Pernod, for two), is enough to encourage *buon appetito.*

The Fair Hill Inn is open for lunch Tuesday through Friday from 11:30 A.M. to 2:30 P.M., for dinner Tuesday through Sunday from 4:30 to 9:00 P.M., and for Sunday brunch from 11:30 A.M. to 2:30 P.M. Reservations are advised; call (410) 398–4187. The inn is located at the junction of Routes 273 and 213, Fair Hill 21921.

South of Fair Hill is Elkton, and if you have seen such movies as *The Manchurian Candidate, Guys and Dolls, The Philadelphia Story, Pillow Talk,* and *Solid Gold Cadillac,* then you have heard people talking about eloping to Elkton or going to "that town in Maryland" to get married. Until the late thirties the town of Elkton was known as the Marriage Capital of the World. Some 10,000 people a year were wed here, and one assumes most of them were eloping. They came to Elkton because it was the first county seat south of New York that did not require a waiting period or blood test before the ceremony was performed.

Only one wedding chapel remains, the ***Little Wedding Chapel.*** This is where Babe Ruth and Joan Fontaine were married (no, not to each other), among dozens of notables, and this is where nearly 1,000 couples are still married each year. Stop by to talk with Barbara Foster and hear some of her many stories, witness a wedding or two, or plan for your own nuptials to be held here.

The Little Wedding Chapel is located at 142 East Main Street, Elkton 21921. The phone number is (410) 398–3640.

Detouring a little before heading down the Eastern Shore, for we are on a romantic subject, we can visit the other covered bridge (or "kissing" bridge) in Cecil. ***Gilpin's Falls covered bridge*** has a 119-foot span and a 13½-foot roadway, and it is adjacent to Route 272 over Northeast Creek, ½ mile north of Bayview. Reportedly, the bridge's arches were made from single timbers, which were curved to shape by balancing them on stumps and pulling their ends down. The bridge was constructed in the 1850s, abandoned in the 1930s, and left to disintegrate until 1959, when it was restored. Traffic along Route 272 bypasses the bridge, which is within a few yards of the roadway.

Gilpin's Falls covered bridge is on Route 272, 5 miles north of the town of North East, or 2 miles north of I–95. (410) 996–6292.

Now, head west just a little more to visit the ***Day Basket Factory.*** Established in 1876 in the town of North East, the factory still makes oak splint baskets the old-fashioned way. Shortly after the Civil War, Edward and Samuel Day came to North East from Massachusetts to make their baskets because the wood was plentiful, the transportation was good, and the demand for their wares, particularly from cotton pickers, was great. Business boomed, and during World War I the factory had thirty-five people on its payroll turning out 2,000 baskets a week. There are now four or five basket makers there who produce old-time baskets, from lunch and market styles to fruit and bread baskets. Antiques are tucked into nooks surrounding the baskets.

Depending on the wood supply, hobbyists will be pleased to know they have pliable number 1 oak strips, hand-split in any dimension, for chair seats or baskets or whatever you need. You can watch the

Water Power

The Susquehanna River separates the western border of Cecil County from the eastern border of Harford County. At one time there were two covered bridges crossing the Susquehanna River, but the last one was flooded with the construction of the **Conowingo Hydroelectric Plant.** *Built in 1928, Conowingo is one of the largest hydroelectric plants in the northeast, if not in the country, and the biggest fish lift in the United States. The enormous dam forms a freshwater lake 14 miles long, impounding some 105 billion gallons of water. It is a noted freshwater fishing spot. There's a public swimming pool, open from Memorial Day through Labor Day. The plant is located on U.S. Route 1 in Conowingo. Call (410) 457–5011.*

process (you must be at least eighteen) Monday through Friday from 8:30 A.M. to 4:00 P.M. The shop is open from 10:00 A.M. to 6:00 P.M. Monday through Saturday in the summer and until 5:00 P.M. in the winter, but there are no workers in the factory on Saturday. Please call ahead (410–287–6100) to let them know if you want a tour. The factory is located at the corner of Irishtown Road and Mauldin Avenue, North East 21901.

Trivia

The Principio Iron Furnace on the shore of the Susquehanna River in Perryville was an important Cecil County ironwork site from 1725 until 1925. The Maryland Commission for Celebration 2000 gave $15,000 toward this site so the property can be protected and future development can be determined.

Plumpton Park Zoo, the second largest zoo in Maryland, is a rural zoological garden that features plants as well as exotic and native animals, including emus, wallabies, llamas, bison, Persian sheep, Chinese deer, miniature donkeys, pygmy goats, wild turkeys, and Australian black swans in a country setting.

Eighteenth-century buildings and ruins are on the grounds, including the 1734 mill that houses the gift shop. The zoo has an adopt-an-animal program, with prices ranging from $25 for an Amazon parrot or Australian black swan to $250 for a giraffe or a Siberian tiger, with options in between.

Plumpton Park Zoo is open daily from 10:00 A.M. to 4:00 P.M. March 1 through September 30, and from 10:00 A.M. to 4:00 P.M. Wednesday through Sunday the rest of the year. It's closed on Thanksgiving and Christmas. Admission is $6.50 for adults, $5.50 for seniors sixty and over, and $3.25 for children two through twelve. Group tours are available by reservation. Contact the zoo at 1416 Telegraph Road (Route 273), Rising Sun 21911, or call (410) 658–6850.

Heading farther south is Chesapeake City, where you'll come across the ***Chesapeake and Delaware Canal.*** On October 17, 1829, it made water transportation in the northern part of the bay even more important. At that time the canal had four locks, but the Corps of Army Engineers lowered the canal to sea level in 1927.

Receiving considerably less publicity than the C&O Canal, the 13-mile C&D Canal cuts off some 350 miles of water navigation for ships going between Philadelphia and Baltimore, and the 22,000 vessels that use it annually make it one of the busiest waterways in the world.

The C&O Canal Museum in Chesapeake City, located next to the canal, reviews its history. The museum is open Monday through Saturday from 8:00 A.M. to 4:15 P.M. and Sunday from 10:00 A.M. to 6:00 P.M. It is closed on Sunday from Thanksgiving through Easter. Call (410) 885–5622 for more information.

South Chesapeake City is on the National Register of Historic Places, with picturesque Victorian architecture, antiques, waterfront restaurants, art galleries, and inns.

I find the other, or north, side of the canal equally interesting—at least the views are. During the ride or walk across the bridge, 135 feet in the air, you can see the canal's course for miles. From the north side you can see the pilots on their pilot boats going to and from the ships navigating the canal. Stop by the Pilot House for information and a schedule on ships coming through.

For additional information write to Tourism Coordinator, Cecil County Chamber of Commerce, 1 Seahawk Drive, Suite 114, North East 21901, or call (800) CECIL–95 or (410) 966–6290.

Kent County

Kent County has the largest proportion of farmland to total acreage of the Upper Eastern Shore counties, yet it is bordered on the north by the Sassafras River, on the south by the Chester River, and on the west by the Chesapeake Bay, so you can understand its multiple focal points. There might be an Old-Fashioned Fourth festival in Rock Hall, an Eastern Shore fish fry, and a Kent County Watermen's Association workboat race and docking course competition, all on the same summer weekend. After the harvest, it is time for snow goose and deer hunting. For those who prefer architectural history to land and water sports, Chestertown, the county seat of the smallest county in the state, is said to be the tenth favorite historic place in America because of the large number of restored eighteenth-century homes.

When driving through Kent County, it is wonderful to take time to see local sights such as the picturesque view of waterfront homes at Chestertown; the Eastern Neck National Wildlife Refuge; the Geddes-Piper House, a Philadelphia-style town house; the Kitty Knight House; the 3,000-acre wildlife research and demonstration area known as Chesapeake Farms (formerly Remington Farms); the Rock Hall Museum; and Washington College, the tenth oldest college in this country, which George Washington helped found.

On the second and fourth Saturdays of the month, ***Harry Rudnick and***

Sons auctions antiques, furniture, glass, china, Oriental rugs, and almost everything else anyone wants to sell. Frank Rudnick, the son of the late Harry Rudnick, says, "We have dealers, local people, and antique-shop owners, and they come from Pennsylvania, Maryland, Delaware, Virginia, D.C.—all over."

The auction starts at 9:00 A.M. and continues to about 4:00 or 4:30 P.M. "We sell about eight hundred, nine hundred, a thousand items a day," says Rudnick. Whenever there is a sale, the lunchroom is open for breakfast and lunch and the menu changes every week. "Some days," adds Rudnick, "the women prepare spaghetti, fried chicken, or turkey, and there's hamburgers, hot dogs, and homemade soup."

Harry Rudnick and Sons is on Main Street, P.O. Box 190, Galena 21635. Call (410) 648–5601.

At the ***Kent Museum*** are indoor and outdoor exhibits of farm machinery from the last two centuries. The county gave a group of local farmers one hundred acres, twenty-five acres of which they ran on a volunteer basis to help defray the museum's operating costs. It was started about two dozen years ago, and people from the area and as far away as Pennsylvania have donated equipment to it. Two early farm tractors mark the entrance, so you can't miss it.

Inside and outside the 40-by-150-foot building are exhibits on equipment used in planting and harvesting corn, wheat, soy, and other grains. You will see threshers, tools from preindustrial days, and modern-day combines and reapers. Other exhibits explain the work done by hand planters, automated corn planters, and tractors (the earliest tractor on display is a 1947 model).

On the first Saturday in August is a threshing dinner. Of course, if you just happen by at other times of the year when workers are planting or otherwise tending to the fields, you can watch them at work then, too.

No admission is charged, but contributions are accepted. Kent Museum is open 10:00 A.M. to 4:00 P.M. the first and third Saturday of the month April through September, and it is located on Route 448 at Turner's Creek Public Landing, near Kennedyville. Call John Clendaniel at (410) 778–3257 or Mrs. William Payne at (410) 348–5721 for additional information.

Bicycle tours are popular in Kent County, and the tourism office has prepared a booklet, *The Kent County Bicycle Tour,* for your information. Included are nine routes developed by the Baltimore Bicycling Club that range from 11 to 81 miles in length.

Routes include the 11-mile Pomona Warm-Up, which follows winding country roads, along the Chester River, and the 81-mile Pump House Primer through northern Kent County and Cecil County. In addition to tourism information, specific directions, maps, and a listing of restaurants, hotels, motels, campgrounds, and bed-and-breakfast establishments are available from the Kent County Tourism Office.

If you'd like to see a full-size replica of a 1767 schooner, then head to the ***Schooner Sultana Project*** where children and adults receive a hands-on education about the history and natural environment of the Chesapeake Bay and its watershed. The schooner is under construction at the Sultana Shipyard in Chestertown. For more information contact the Chester River Craft and Art Inc., P.O. Box 524, Chestertown 21620; (410) 778–5954, www.schoonersultana.com. Internships have been available, and completion and launching are scheduled for the summer of 2001.

As you travel through Rock Hall, in southwestern Kent County, you may notice ***Tallulah's on Main,*** a gallery/gift shop and a five-suite hotel, and wonder about the name. According to Jim Messersmith, owner of Tallulah's, the famed movie star Tallulah Bankhead used to shop at this location when it was a general store; she bought her meats and gourmet items next door when it was Myer's meat market. Many of the locals still remember her frequent visits, and her grandnieces visit the gift shop and gallery. Jim says they liked the name, but "most of all felt that she needed to be honored still as a great actress and woman of our time." The folks at Tallulah's have several books about her life and wonderful stories. Tallulah's also rents a house on the beach with a beautiful due-west sunset view all year long. It's located at 5750 Main Street, Rock Hall 21661; (410) 639–2596; www.rockhallmd.com.

For additional county information write to Kent County Tourism Office, 400 High Street, Chestertown 21620, call (410) 778–0416 or visit www.kentcounty.com.

Queen Anne's County

The ***Old Wye Grist Mill*** is the oldest business in Queen Anne's County, in operation since 1664, 1671, or 1680, depending on whose reports you read. At least three mills have been located in this area for more than 300 years, giving the town of Wye Mills its name. Among its historic claims is the fact that ground cornmeal from this mill was purchased by Robert Morris, financier of the American Revolution, to be used as provisions for George Washington's army at Valley Forge in 1778.

Preservation Maryland, an organization to preserve the state's history and culture, has had the pleasure of working on this mill, which is particularly fascinating because as new equipment was developed, the old equipment was not hauled away or discarded. Therefore, there is a continuum of equipment to show the progress of milling over the years. The organization has completed work on the hydraulics and done most of the interior restoration and soon will transfer ownership to the Friends of Wye Mill. During your visit you can try your skill at Maryland's preindustrial crafts, such as weaving, broom making, and hand milling. Also, depending on the season, you can buy cornmeal and a variety of flours—buckwheat, whole wheat, and sometimes rye.

The Wye Mill is open weekends, 10:00 A.M. to 4:00 P.M., and Monday through Friday from 10:00 A.M. to 1:00 P.M. April through November, and by appointment at other times. There is no admission charge, but they do ask for a donation. The mill is on Route 50, south of Route 662. The mailing address is P.O. Box 277, Wye Mills 21679, or you can contact the mill at (410) 827–6909 or 685–2886.

Queen Anne's is known for its sprawling countryside and 900 farms, terrific access to the bay and bay tributaries, and the genteel lifestyle it promotes. Kent Narrows, formerly known for its horrendous weekend beach traffic jams, has become a minor destination of its own, with plenty of historic sites, fine boating, golf, and dining.

The meeting place of the Eastern Shore since 1955, however, has been ***Holly's Restaurant,*** noted for having the best milk shakes in the state. The tables are wooden and devoid of such frills as tablecloths, and the waitresses are friendly. You will find Holly's off Route 50 at 108 Jackson Creek Road, Grasonville 21638. Call (410) 827–8711.

Birdlife photographers and observers will enjoy the Wildfowl Trust of North America's ***Horsehead Wetland Center*** and the adjacent captive wildfowl collection in Grasonville. Surrounded by more than 500 acres of natural beauty, the center has a fascinating and colorful flock of wildfowl, including ducks, geese, and swans, and nearby are deer, red foxes, river otters, and bald eagles living in the brackish marsh, pine forest, shrub habitat, meadow, and shallow water impoundment. Special screening allows you to quietly enter blinds so you can observe wildlife without disturbing it. Nature trails, wetland boardwalks, the observation towers, and viewing blinds offer a variety of ways to see the wildlife and a panoramic view of Chesapeake Bay.

The Wildfowl Trust of North America, founded in 1979, is responsible for the center, and you can be sure of programs, guided walks, workshops, a

Trivia

St. Michaels was named after the Episcopal parish established in 1677, named for St. Michael the archangel.

wetland festival, and lectures promoting stewardship of our dwindling wetland resources. A gift shop and a shaded picnic area are also on-site.

Horsehead Wetland Center is ½ mile from Route 18, off Perry Corner Road. Admission is $5.00 for adults, $4.00 for seniors age fifty-five or older, and $3.00 for children age eighteen and younger. Dogs are not permitted. The center is open 9:00 A.M. to 5:00 P.M. daily. It is closed Independence Day, Thanksgiving, Christmas, and New Year's Day. For more information write to the Executive Director, The Wildfowl Trust of North America, 600 Discovery Lane, P.O. Box 519, Grasonville 21638, or call (410) 827–6694 or (800) CANVASBACK.

For more tourism information write to Queen Anne's County Department of Business and Tourism, 425 Piney Narrows Road, Suite 3, Chester 21619. Call (410) 604–2100 or (888) 400–RSVP, e-mail tourism@gac.org, or log on to www.gac.org.

Talbot County

Tourists coming through this area—about 100,000 each year going to St. Michaels—stop to see the Chesapeake Bay Maritime Museum, the Customs House, St. Michaels Square Museum, the Robert Morris Inn, and Tilghman Island (with a meal at Harrison's Chesapeake House). The Chesapeake Bay Maritime Museum receives by far the most tourists, and well it should.

The Town that Fooled the British

St. Michaels is known as the "Town that Fooled the British," and although the tale may be apocryphal, it has been around for so long that people will swear on their mothers' graves that it's true. So you will hear that during the War of 1812 this town "was an important shipbuilding center of privateers, blockade runners and naval barges. This activity caused an attempt by the British naval forces to destroy the shipyards and the boats under construction. On the morning of August 10, 1813, a number of British barges manned by marines shelled the town and attacked a fort on the harbor side. Residents, forewarned, had hoisted lanterns to the masts of ships and in the tops of the trees causing the cannons to overshoot the town. This first 'blackout' was effective and only one house was struck. It is known as the 'Cannonball House.' St. Michaels is now known as 'The Town that Fooled the British.'"

But there are two small, privately owned museums that may also be worth your time. Millie Curtis's ***Museum of Costume*** in St. Michaels contains some unique displays. On exhibit are gowns worn by former presidents' wives, pantaloons worn by Mrs. Abraham Lincoln, and a vest worn by Clark Gable in *Gone With the Wind.*

Rooms are filled with ornate nineteenth- and early twentieth-century gowns. Curtis has been accumulating her collection since 1940, and has been known to greet guests wearing one of her costumes. Also of interest is the setting, representing life as it was for the wealthy and the not-so-wealthy. Ms. Curtis herself is a wealth of information and a fascinating conversationalist, so you might want to plan a little extra time to enjoy your trip to the past.

The white frame house was erected by shipbuilder and sea captain Lewis Tarr in 1843. It is restored, so you can see the original pine floors, the board-and-batten doors, and other aspects of the architecture.

The Museum of Costume is open weekends 11:00 A.M. to 4:00 P.M., April through November. The suggested donation is $2.00. Children under ten are admitted free. The address is 400 St. Mary's Square, St. Michaels 21663. Call (410) 745–5154.

The St. Mary's Square Museum exhibits items of significance to the local history and culture, not just of St. Michaels, but of the land between Tilghman and Royal Oak, called the Bay 100—that portion of land that could be defended by one hundred armed men. Two buildings, originally part of a steam and gristmill, are used for this museum, one of them dating from 1820 and one from 1860. The latter is referred to as the "Teetotum" building because it is shaped like a child's four-sided top of that name. In the 1820 building are artifacts from 1800 to 1850, in the kitchen area are items from 1850 to 1900, and in the Teetotum room are articles from colonial days to about 1950.

This museum was opened in 1964 by a group of local citizens, and although it sits on the original St. Mary's Square and is on city property, the museum is entirely self-supported. A group of twenty board members runs the operation.

The museum is open May through October on Saturday, Sunday, and holidays from 10:00 A.M. to 4:00 P.M. and by appointment. There is no admission charge, but donations are accepted. For additional information call (410) 745–9561.

Laura Ashley fans rejoice. As you may recall, Sir Bernard Ashley (who with his late wife, Laura, founded the clothing and furnishings empire) had added more rooms to his ***Inn at Perry Cabin*** in St. Michaels, all decorated in Laura Ashley prints. When Orient-Express Hotels bought the twenty-five-acre waterfront property in January 2000, there was some concern that they would change the decor. Fear not. According to general manager Stephen Creese, he has been busy updating draperies and upholstery, and tending to all those other details of maintaining a property of this quality, and it's all in Laura Ashley designs. Master chef Mark Salter remains, creating magical cuisine for your dining pleasure. So you still have a choice of forty-one individually and sumptuously decorated rooms and suites that include many Laura Ashley design touches. There's also an indoor pool and exercise room. The food is superb, the wine cellar extraordinary, and the setting as picture-perfect for a wedding as anyone could wish. Bring your boat and dock at the inn's slips, pick up one of the inn's bicycles to explore the countryside (nice and flat, and very pastoral), or just come to relax.

This is hospitality in a fine tradition. Inn at Perry Cabin is at 308 Watkins Lane, St. Michaels 21663. The phone number is (410) 745–5178 or (800) 722–2947.

If hot (and I don't mean weather) tempts your taste buds, then a stop in St. Michaels isn't complete until you've visited ***Flamingo Flats.*** Their motto is: "Where taste is paramount and life's too short to eat boring food." Opened in 1988, Flamingo Flats has hot sauce and salsa specialties; cigars; a tasting bar with more than 2,000 salsas, hot sauces, marinades, and barbecue sauces; more than 500 mustards; more than 75 jars with olives as a base; and hundreds of cookbooks, gifts, and jewelry items.

Among the sauces you'll find are Chile Today Hot Tamale, Gator Hammock Gator Sauce, Jump Up and Kiss Me, Lottie's Bajan Cajan, Matouk's Hot Calypso, Ring of Fire, and Rothschild's Fiery Raspberry Salsa. If you have an asbestos tongue, step up to the tasting bar and go to town. The shop specialty is its own Cannonball sauce. Cannonball is a combination of carrots, onions, lime juice, tomato, vinegar, and habanero peppers. It's a sauce more for tasting than for destroying your intestinal lining.

Flamingo Flats is located at 100 South Talbot Street, St. Michaels 21663. Call (410) 745–2053 or (800) HOT–8841.

Bed-and-breakfast establishments seem to belong in large Victorian homes, and the ***John S. McDaniel House Bed and Breakfast,*** owned and operated by Dawn Rehbein, fits that description to a T. Built about 1890, the house has a high octagonal tower (a great sitting room), a hip roof with dormers, and a porch that runs across the front and part of the south side of the house. Each of the eight guest rooms is spacious and bright and equipped with air-conditioning and a ceiling fan. Fortunately, the house is located within walking distance of historic Easton.

The John S. McDaniel House Bed and Breakfast is located at 14 North Aurora Street, Easton 21601. Call (410) 822–3704 or (800) 787–4667 for information and reservations.

Another wonderful lodging place in Easton is the ***Tidewater Inn and Conference Center.*** The Tidewater looks ages old and is filled with eighteenth-century furnishings, but it actually was built in 1949 and enlarged in 1953. And although the property is relatively new, you wouldn't be blamed if you felt the company of past cotillions, proms, and weddings. It's a question of whether the service, the restaurant, or the ambience wins the contest for "best" feature of this hotel. The service has been impeccable every time I've stopped by. The menu changes with the seasons, and the kitchen staff will work to prepare what you want the way you want it.

A grand time to be here is during duck season, when hunters stay, enjoy a 4:30 A.M. hunt breakfast on a chilly autumn morning, then leave before dawn to sit out in the blinds and await their prey. The hotel will arrange guide services and kennel the dogs.

Another marvelous feature of the Tidewater is its convenience to shopping, the restored 1921 Avalon Theater, and the Academy Art Museum. All in all, the Tidewater Inn is a superb place to stay as a base for your Eastern Shore sightseeing. It's located at 101 East Dover Street, Easton 21601; call (410) 822–1300 or (800) 237–8775. The inn's Web site is www. tidewaterinn.com.

One of the ten remaining ferries in service in Maryland is the ***Oxford-Belleview Ferry,*** which crosses Tred Avon River and connects Oxford to Bellevue. It has been operating since 1683 and is said to be the oldest "free-running" (not cable-connected), privately owned ferry in the country. It operates March 1 through mid-December. Generally, the ferry schedule starts at 7:00 A.M. on weekday mornings and 9:00 A.M. on weekends and runs until sunset, except during June, July, and August, when it runs until 9:00 P.M.

It costs $5.00 for car and driver one-way and $8.00 round-trip, plus 50 cents per passenger each way. Bicycles are $2.00 one-way, $3.00 round-trip, and foot passengers are $1.00 each. Motorcycles are $3.00. This is a particularly photogenic ferry crossing at sunset, when the boats are all at their Oxford harbor moorings with their masts standing out against the skyline. To reach the Tred Avon Ferry from Easton, take Route 33 and Route 333; from Bellevue take Route 33 and Route 329 to Royal Oak and follow the signs. Call (410) 745–9023 for more information.

Next to the Oxford landing is the ***Customs House,*** a replica of the original built in pre–Revolutionary War days when Oxford was an official port of entry. It's open from 3:00 to 5:00 P.M. Friday through Sunday, April through October. (410) 226–5760.

Almost as good as a platter of crabs are the biscuits from ***Orrell House and Bakery***. Hundreds of dozens of these heavy biscuits, which started as a source of pin money for Mrs. Orrell about fifty years ago, go out to local stores and shops around the country. The recipe, which combines flour, water, salt, lard, sugar, and baking powder, originated in southern Maryland and the Eastern Shore during plantation days. It produces a biscuit that is soft and doughy on the inside and hard on the outside. There are some who say these biscuits are not any good until they feel like hockey pucks, and many swear by them as teething biscuits.

Believe me, just because they feel hard does not mean they have gone stale. A special pick is used to prick the tops of the biscuits (in an O and cross design) so they will not blister and burn.

The bakery is open on Wednesday from 7:00 A.M. to 2:00 P.M., Thursday

Wye Is This Oak So Famous?

You have heard that big oaks come from little acorns, and, of course, the converse is true—little acorns come from big oaks. The Maryland Forest, Park and Wildlife Service gathers the acorns, plants them, and lets them grow for a couple of years until they are established seedlings. You can purchase a Wye Oak seedling from the state for about $6.00 (plus tax if you live in Maryland). They are shipped in March in time for spring planting. They cannot be shipped to Arizona, California, Florida, Louisiana, or Oregon due to quarantine restrictions. These are the cutest little trees, no bigger in diameter than your little finger, but they produce mature-size leaves, about six or seven of them the first year. They do not grow as rapidly as, say, a maple tree, but they are of substantial size within a decade. And, who knows, 400 years from now there may be a champion tree in your yard. To order Wye Oak seedlings, write to the Nursery Manager, Buckingham Forest Tree Nursery, Harmans 21077. You must give a full street address; a post office box number is inadequate for delivery.

from 2:00 to 11:00 P.M., and Friday from 7:00 A.M. to noon. The address is Orrell House and Bakery, P.O. Box 7, Wye Mills 21679. Turn right at the stoplight at Chesapeake College and drive to the famous Wye Oak Tree. Orrell House is between the oak and Wye parish. Call (410) 822–2065.

Wye Oak State Park is considered a "big little" place: The park's total size is only twenty-nine acres, but it contains the 450-year-old Maryland state tree, the Wye Oak. This tree measures a huge 37 feet in circumference and is considered to be the largest and finest of its species in the United States. The state bought the tree and one acre around it in 1939—the first time any state ever purchased one tree just to preserve it. Over time, more land was added to make this a state park. It was the first state park to be fully accessible to the handicapped, perhaps because it's so small that accessibility was easy to create. Wye Oak State Park on Route 662. Call (410) 634–2810, or visit www.dnr.state.md.us.

For more tourism information write to Talbot County Office of Tourism, Easton Airport, U.S. Route 60, Easton 21601, or call (410) 770–8000.

Caroline County

Caroline County is the only Eastern Shore county not directly on the ocean or the bay, but there are calm waters, such as the Choptank and Tuckahoe Rivers and Marshyhope Creek, state parks for canoeing and fishing, and an active crabbing and fishing industry. The prime interest here is agrarian, and the crops are bountiful. Corn, soybeans,

The Green Garden County

According to George Sands of the Caroline County Library: "On March 24, 1981, the County Commissioners of Caroline County adopted a resolution establishing an official motto for 'Caroline the Green Garden County of Maryland.' This was carried out in conjunction with the library publication of an Agricultural Directory. The research showed that at the time Caroline County was first in Maryland in production of vegetables for markets and processing. It is among the top 3 percent in the U.S. in acreage of garden vegetables and at or near the top in Maryland and the nation in a number of related vegetable production areas. The term was coined by Bud Hutton."

cucumbers, tomatoes, peas, beans, sweet corn, cantaloupes, peaches, and melons fill the fields and make a stop at a local produce stand an essential part of anyone's visit.

Across from the Caroline County Courthouse in Denton is the ***Museum of Rural Life***. Even county residents realize that the farming folk who have populated Caroline for the past three centuries may as well have been "consigned to a black hole of obscurity." The county has produced no national leaders, scientists, engineers, patriots, or even notorious rogues. Tombstones are the only proof that people have indeed lived here throughout the history of the United States.

Now, thanks to J. O. K. Walsh, the Denton Jaycees, the County Historical Society, and countless others, a determined effort has produced this museum, a tribute to those anonymous farming families who created Caroline County history.

The museum combines one of the original dwellings on Court House Square with new construction. There's a reception area, a gallery for rotating exhibits, and an audiovisual room. The museum explores the various aspects and changes in rural life since European settlers arrived here in the 1600s. Hundreds of artifacts, documents, and photographs have been collected. You may even uncover some of the history behind the fireworks-induced conflagration of July 4, 1865.

If for some reason you can't find the answer to your Caroline County history question here, talk with Walsh. He's known as the person who "knows more about Caroline history than anyone." The museum is at 16 North Second Street, Denton 21629. Call (410) 479–2055.

The historical marker next to the ***Choptank Electric Cooperative*** on Routes 404 and 328, just west of Denton, marks the modest but historic ***Neck Meeting House.*** Built in 1802 by members of the Society of Friends, the meetinghouse is believed to be the oldest house of worship in Caroline County. Most of the funds raised for the aluminum marker came from the recycling of aluminum cans by local residents.

The Choptank Electric Cooperative is refurbishing the small building, and if you would like to look inside, stop by the cooperative for the key.

The ***Slo Horse Inn*** is located in a quiet country setting on a twelve-acre horse farm between Ridgely and Denton. Owner Cat (Catherine) Sebasco says it was a horse farm featuring some of the slowest Thoroughbred racehorses ever born. "They were not known for winning," says Cat.

So she and husband Jesse kicked the horses out to pasture and converted

Maryland's Snail-Order Company

On the Eastern Shore of Maryland, where there probably are more chickens than people, Ed Chupek raises gourmet escargots (Helix aspersa). Chupek lives on an eighty-acre farm with his wife, two sons, a steer, and hundreds of snails. He's the only escargot "farmer" licensed by the Department of Agriculture in Maryland. In fact, he's the only domestic provider of escargots south of the Mason-Dixon line.

Although his company, U.S. Snails, is relatively young, he already has such clients as the Inn at Little Washington in Washington, Virginia; Inn at Perry Cabin in St. Michael's, Maryland; the Willard Room in Washington, D.C.; Harry Browne's in Annapolis; Fisherman's Inn, Kent Island, Maryland; and Bis, Bistro Lepic, and the Park Hyatt, all in Washington, D.C. The list continues, but I'm sure you have the idea. U.S. Snails will sell to consumers as well as commercial establishments.

His snails are fed "only the finest grains and vegetables and are purged with basil for several days before processing." When an order arrives, the snails are blanched in lemon water for three minutes, then packaged and shipped. These fresh, tiny escargots are much more tender than any canned or frozen snails on the market.

To order his snails, call Ed Chupek at (410) 673–2349.

the stable into four bedrooms, each with private bath, TV, coffeepot, and refrigerator. You can choose king, queen, double, or twin-bedded accommodations, or combine two rooms for a family or two couples. "It's very casual out here," she says. In fact, when Cat moved to Caroline from Washington, D.C., she felt like she was trying to "tap dance to a waltz." Now she has acclimated to the different pace and loves it.

Take Holly Road off Route 404 and continue for exactly 1⁹⁄₁₀ miles; look for a large white farmhouse, with a post-and-rail fence, on the right. Call (410) 634–2128.

Ashly Acres produced the first miniature horses to participate in an inaugural parade—former president Bush's. This nine-acre farm is owned by Robin Stallings, Karen Kilheffer, and Ashly Wayne Asbury, who breed, raise, and show quality registered miniature horses.

A miniature horse is a true horse, not a pony or a dwarf, and is very gentle. According to Ashly Acres, the ancestor of the modern miniature horse was bred for the royal courts of Europe during the seventeenth century. The horses were often passed from one sovereign to another as diplomatic tokens of goodwill. When the power and wealth of the royalty began to decline, a few horses found their way into the traveling circuses

Trivia

George Martinak deeded land to the state in 1961 for preservation as a recreational facility and a natural area for the enjoyment of all. It was named Martinak State Park after him.

of Europe. Some were used as pit ponies in the coal mines. The selective breeding process was interrupted, and the breed almost became extinct.

The American miniature horse is a scaled-down model of a full-size horse and can measure no more than 34 inches at the withers. Foals usually weigh between eighteen and twenty-five pounds and stand between 16 and 22 inches at birth. They come in all colors, and although they can be ridden by very small children, they usually are used in harness where they can easily pull a full-size adult. They function best as lovable exotic pets.

In the early 1900s a Virginian named Normal Fields imported some miniature horses with a shipment of pit ponies. He was so taken with them that he started a breeding program that continued for thirty-five years. Another Virginian, Smith McCoy, started with ten or twelve horses under 32 inches and built one of the largest miniature horse herds in the United States.

Trivia

There are more than 240,000 acres of public land in the Maryland State Forests and Parks system, meaning there is a state forest or park within forty-five minutes of nearly every Marylander.

The address for Ashly Acres is R.D. 1, Box 207CC, Denton 21629. Tours for twenty-five people or more are available by appointment; call (410) 479–1159 to ask if you can join one.

In June 1984, in the quiet hours of an early Sunday night, a thirty-five-ton limb from Maryland's state tree crashed to the ground. Being practical, the state decided that some of the limb should be made into souvenirs, such as gavels; but 70,000 pounds of tree would make a lot of gavels. The Maryland Forest, Park and Wildlife Service sent a two-ton chunk of wood to sculptor Steven Weitzman to create the ***Wye Oak Sculpture***.

He carved the wood into a monument in his shop at Seneca Creek State Park in Gaithersburg. On April 3, 1985, his sculpture of two children leaning over a shovel in the act of planting a tree was moved to its permanent home at ***Martinak State Park,*** 2 miles east of Denton. The children, carved larger than life-size, are standing beneath a white oak tree in this 10-foot-tall statue that measures about 4½ feet from front to back.

Trivia

The Adkins Arboretum at Tuckahoe State Park, west of Denton, was conceived and funded by the late Leon Andrus of Cheston-on-Wye. He suggested that it be named in honor of the Adkins family, who has produced civic leaders for generations.

Wye Oak Sculpture

Martinak is bordered by the Choptank River and Watts Creek, and you can drop a line for bass, perch, sunfish, and catfish (a Maryland Chesapeake Bay Sportfishing License is required), camp in one of the sixty-three campsites for tent or trailer camping April through October, stay in a year-round cabin, launch your boat, rent a boat, go hiking, picnic, enjoy a ball game, or recreate on the playground. You'll also be able to see the reconstructed hull of a wrecked bungy, a type of boat used on the bay in the early nineteenth century.

The park is open from sunrise to sunset daily, except Christmas week. Martinak State Park is on Deep Shore Road, off Route 404, Denton 21629. Call (410) 479–1619 or (888) 432–2267; www.dnr.state.md.us.

Seven miles west of Denton, off Route 404, is ***Tuckahoe State Park.*** Tuckahoe Creek meanders through this park, and a sixty-acre lake offers fishing and boating opportunities on twenty acres of open water. There are thirty-five campsites and four sites for youth groups. A central bathhouse with showers and toilet facilities is available. The Adkins Arboretum encompasses 500 acres of parkland and nearly 3 miles of walkways through the trees and shrubs. Canoes are available for rental from May to October. There are also other recreational options, including archery, hiking, a playground, a ball field, an equestrian center, hiking trails, a pet loop, and picnicking. Tuckahoe State Park is located in Queen Anne. Call (410) 820–1668 or (888) 432–2267; www.dnr.state.md.us.

For additional tourism information write to Caroline County Economic Development Commission, P.O. Box 207, Denton 21629, or call (410) 479–2230.

Dorchester County

When you cross the Choptank River bridge, you'll see something that looks like a large sailing yacht. It's the Visitors Center at ***Sailwinds Park,*** and the mistake is understandable because the center lies amid a spectacular 110-foot fiberglass sail. Here you will find visitor information on the Eastern Shore region, indoor and outdoor interpretive exhibits, a children's playground, a beach, and a boardwalk that links to the Choptank Fishing Pier. Such diverse events as the Seafood Festival, a Native American powwow, the Choptank River Beer and Wine Festival, the Harriet Tubman Festival, and more are held here. Sailwinds Park is at 200 Byrn Street, Cambridge 21613. Phone (410) 228–SAIL.

Because Dorchester County is blessed with fairly flat terrain and lots of water, the county has created two brochures of interest to boaters and bikers. *Water Trails* lists canoe and kayak launches, boat ramps, and facilities. *Cycling Trails* shows the well-paved, lightly traveled, and scenic accesses to the county. The most often used routes are highlighted, and alternate roads are shown to shorten or lengthen your ride. Either brochure can be obtained by calling (800) 552–TOUR or (410) 228–1000.

Years before I thought about writing this book, I stopped at the ***Dorchester County Public Library*** and admired a wonderful mural of Eastern Shore scenes being painted by Chesapeake Bay artist John Moll. That creation has stayed in my mental and metal filing drawers all these years.

Moll's lithographs are known for their faithful characterizations of the skipjacks and bay lighthouses he loved. His Christmas cards with Oxford and Annapolis scenes or Baycraft portraits are still popular, and John Moll oils hang in the permanent collection of the Eastern Academy of Arts, in the visitor center at Sailwinds Park, and in the historic Robert Morris Inn in Oxford. This gives you an idea how popular the artist is whose work is on the Dorchester County Public Library walls. The address of the library is 303 Gay Street, Cambridge 21613. Phone (410) 228–7331.

The ***Dorchester Arts Center*** was founded in 1970 and has between 400 and 500 members (mostly from the Cambridge area) including potters, photographers, quilters, stained-glass artists, and basket makers. In addition to regular classes in these and other crafts, the center has two galleries where local work is exhibited and sold. Each month a new exhibit opens with a reception. During the year, the center sponsors a variety of music, dance, and educational programs, a number of which are free to the public.

Each September the sidewalks along historic, brick High Street, with its beautiful period homes, are festooned with the best work of 125 or more of Dorchester County artists.

The center, located at 120 High Street, Cambridge 21613, is open Monday through Friday from 10:00 A.M. to 2:00 P.M. and Saturday from 11:00 A.M. to 3:00 P.M. Call (410) 228–7782 for more information.

Interesting tours are conducted through the ***Brooks Barrel Company,*** one of the last remaining slack cooperages now operating in America, and the only one in Maryland. Paul Brooks founded the company in 1950, making "hand-crafted wooden barrel product . . . Nature's Way" with equipment dating from the turn of the twentieth century. These planters, kegs, and barrels are made of natural yellow pine from Delmarva. Planning to grow strawberries next year? Try one of the 12-inch by 18-inch strawberry kegs with holes.

After touring the plant you'll realize what's involved every time you look at a candy barrel, view the miniseries made from Alex Haley's book *Queen,* or watch Robert Redford's movie *A River Runs Through It.*

Tours (which can be very noisy) are available Tuesday through Thursday for $3.50. Brooks Barrel Company Inc. is at 5228 Bucktown Road, Cambridge 21613-1056. Call (410) 228–0790 or (800) 398–BROOKS.

Another place of interest is the ***Harriet Tubman birthplace.*** Tubman has been called the "Moses of her People" because of her work in the Underground Railroad that helped free more than 300 slaves. A slave herself, Tubman ran away only to return to Delmarva nineteen times to free others. During the Civil War she served in the Union army as a nurse, scout, and spy. A marker denotes the Harriet Tubman birthplace on Green Briar Road in Bucktown. Call (410) 288–0401.

For more information about Harriet Tubman and the Underground Railroad, stop by the ***Underground Railroad: Harriet Tubman Museum.*** A grant of $25,000 from the Maryland Commission for Celebration 2000 will allow archaeologists to "locate structures, graves, and artifacts associated with Tubman's life and better protect and interpret this nationally significant site." There's a gift shop with items from such countries as Kenya and Nigeria, Native American goods, and local products.

There is no admission fee, and the museum, located at 424 Race Street, Bucktown 21613, is open Monday and Saturday from 10:00 A.M. to 2:00 P.M. and Tuesday through Friday from 9:00 A.M. to 5:00 P.M. (410) 228–0401.

Annie Oakley Lived Here

As you're driving through the area, you might stop by 28 Bellevue Avenue on Hambrooks Bay in Cambridge. For about five years, beginning in 1912, this was the home of Wild West sharpshooter Annie Oakley. It was designed and built by Oakley and her husband, Frank Butler, when they retired to Cambridge. The bungalow was typical of the period, except for a few features characteristic of the Butlers' unique lifestyle. You can drive by and see the second floor balcony from which Oakley could shoot ducks on the Bay.

It makes one wonder, why here? According to Thomas A. Flowers, the Old Honker, in his book Shore Folklore: Growing Up with Ghosts, 'n Legends, 'n Tales, 'n Home Remedies, *Oakley and Butler moved here because in her travels all over the world, she "had never seen a more beautiful spot than Hambrooks Bay." Butler was known to fish for perch in the bay, and Oakley's black-and-white bird dog Dave was known to stand so stock still that Oakley could shoot an apple off his head.*

South of Cambridge is the ***Blackwater National Wildlife Refuge,*** a marvelous sanctuary of more than 22,000 acres. The refuge boasts the largest nesting population of bald eagles in the East, north of Florida. There is a $3.00 charge per car and a $1.00 charge per person on foot or bicycle unless you have a Golden Age, Golden Eagle, Golden Access, or Blackwater National Wildlife Refuge Pass, or a current Federal Duck Stamp. There is no admission fee to visit the welcome center. Besides the bald eagle and the great blue heron, you will see black ducks, the endangered Delmarva fox squirrel, and countless other animals and birds. Do stop by in November and December when the Canada geese fly overhead. Bring your insect repellent in July and August.

Take Route 16 west to Route 335 in Church Creek and turn left onto Key Wallace Drive. Follow the signs to the refuge, located at 2145 Key Wallace Drive, Cambridge 21613. The refuge is open daily, Labor Day through Memorial Day, from dawn to dusk. Call (410) 228–2677 for additional information.

The food is good where the locals gather, and one of these gathering places is on Taylor's Island at ***Taylor's Island General Store,*** just across Slaughter Creek Bridge, southwest of Cambridge. The best sandwiches and soups in the area are served here, and you will not go wrong with Erlyne Twining's crab soup, oyster chowder, chili, or lima bean soup; meat-based soups sell for $2.00 and nonmeat soups sell for $1.50. The crab cakes contain a quarter pound of crab meat each and go for $3.00. Quite a bargain.

A Bridge Too Far?

South of Taylor's Island you run into some barrier islands that achieved infamy beyond their size in the summer of 1980. Seems it was decided that a new bridge should be built over Narrows Ferry between Middle Hooper Island and Lower Hooper Island. No problem with that; the old one was a forty-year-old, one-lane, rickety, planked-pine swing bridge. But by the time planners and builders and others were involved, this concrete-and-steel span arching 27 feet above the narrow channel ended up costing more than $3 million, up from an estimate of $500,000.

Thomas A. Flowers, a county commissioner who relates in his book Shore Folklore: Growing Up with Ghosts, 'n Legends, 'n Tales, 'n Home Remedies *that his four-sentence dedication before about twenty people was picked up by Walter Cronkite, the* Los Angeles Times, People *magazine, and other noted publications. Among those commenting on this structure was Robert "Bob" C. Reid, one of my first editors, who at the time of the dedication was the Annapolis Bureau Chief of the* Frederick Post. *One of the finest writers I've ever met or read, Reid's article started, "Suddenly, there it is, rising from the swampland. It's a magnificent monument to nothing. It's like finding the Taj Mahal popping up over the next sand dune on the Sahara Desert, or the 'Love Boat' cruising down a trout stream in the mountains of West Virginia."*

And now for a few of Flowers's words of invocation. "Father, today we are gathered here to dedicate a bridge that is a monument to man's stupidity, a monument to man's waste, a monument to governmental interference and inefficiency, for there is no need for such an elaborate structure as this is and which is so out-of-keeping in the peaceful and lovely environment of South Dorchester."

Flowers is now president of the Dorchester County Commissioners. He is still busy dedicating bridges, attending other notable events, and speaking his mind.

Erlyne, her husband, Perry, and their son Terry also sell ice, beer, soda, gas, and groceries and have an interesting display of "old-time stuff" from former general stores.

You will find signs that spell it Taylors Island—usually state signs—and people who spell it Taylor's—usually the locals, because they say the land originally was called Taylor's Folly after the Mr. Taylor who bought the land. I side with the locals on this one. Taylor's Island General Store is on Route 16, Taylor's Island 21669; (410) 397–3733.

And, as long as you're on Taylor's Island, stop by the museum, located in a 1916 school, showing local and regional antiques and memorabilia. There's no admission fee, but you have to call for an appointment. (410) 397–3338, (410) 397–3262, or (800) 522–TOUR.

Trivia

James B. Richardson, a master shipwright known along the waterways as "Mr. Jim," built the 1971 reproduction of the Spocott Windmill, likening it to the wooden boats he has built and repaired. The mill has canvas sails with a wingspan of 52 feet. The wide sails turn a wooden shaft and a series of wooden gears that turn the upper millstone, grinding the grain against the bottom millstone. These post windmills appeared in England at the end of the twelfth century, and it's estimated that there were about eighteen post windmills in the county.

Six miles west of Cambridge on Route 343 is ***Spocott Windmill,*** the only existing post windmill in the state for grinding grain. There used to be eighteen of these windmills, each resting on a single pole at the base, throughout Dorchester. When you stop by you can also see a tenant farmhouse (circa 1775), a one-room Victorian-era schoolhouse (1870), and a country store museum. The windmill was reconstructed in 1971, based on a windmill built here about 1850 by John H. L. Radcliffe, which was destroyed in the blizzard of 1888. You're invited to tour the windmill, climb its steep steps, and dowdle around for as long as you like. Corn is ground on special occasions. Check with the Spocott Windmill Foundation about special events, such as Spocott Windmill Day. The Spocott Windmill is at Route 343, Cambridge 21613. (410) 228–7090.

East New Market, originally Crossroads, could easily be called Churchtown or Churchville, for at each of the four entrances to the town stands a church. On Route 16 South, it is Trinity United Methodist; Route 16 North, St. Stephen's Episcopal; Route 14 West, First Baptist; and Route 14 East, Salem German Evangelical and Reformed Church. These churches reflect the diverse denominations represented in this area.

Indians dwelled here; the first European mention of the region was in a grant to Henry Sewell dated 1659 in London, England. The first white settler is believed to have been a Quaker, John Edmondson, who came from Virginia in the 1660s to seek religious freedom. Edmondson was followed by the O'Sullivane family, and this historic district contains almost all of their early residences.

In addition to the churches, the town is known for its historical architecture, and the entire town is designated a historic district. Colonial homes are the core of the town's architecture, but among the almost seventy-five buildings are a number from the eighteenth, nineteenth, and twentieth centuries. Many of the brick walks laid in 1884 still exist.

The East New Market Heritage Foundation sponsors an annual Candlelight Tour in late December. Call (410) 228–1000 for details.

For additional tourism information write to Dorchester County Tourism, 2 Rose Hill Place, Cambridge 21613, call (410) 228–1000 or (800) 522–TOUR, or visit www.tourdorchester.org.

Wicomico County

For a long time Salisbury was known as the last great gasp going east (or the first coming west) on the way to the beach at Ocean City. Now it's a community in its own right with a world-renowned museum, a zoo that doesn't overwhelm you with its size, and some interesting shopping. You could spend your vacation here and avoid the hot, sweaty, shoulder-to-shoulder, sand- and sunblock-covered visitors catching the rays on the shore.

For an impressive look into the peninsula's past, stop by the ***Edward H. Nabb Research Center for Delmarva History and Culture,*** where you can find some of the nation's oldest artifacts. Genealogists from around the world visit this center at Salisbury State University.

The center, at 1101 Camden Avenue, Salisbury State University, Salisbury 21804, is named for Cambridge attorney Edward H. Nabb, whose forebear came to the Eastern Shore in the early eighteenth century as an indentured servant. In endowing the center with a $500,000 challenge grant Nabb said, "Let's face it. This [the Chesapeake Bay region] is where the United States began. There should really be a center somewhere here as a repository for that information."

Because many settlers came up the Chesapeake before moving elsewhere, the Eastern Shore is an important national genealogical source for family history. They even have some records the Salt Lake City–based Church of Jesus Christ of Latter-day Saints genealogical resource center doesn't have. The Nabb Center has copies of the oldest continuous sets of courthouse records in the continental United States, dating from 1632.

Trivia

Edward H. Nabb, an octogenarian, has a pilot's license and is the only person on Earth to receive all three of the world's top power-boating awards: induction into the Power Boat Racing Hall of Fame and American Power Boat Association Honor Squadron; and the Medal of Honor of the Union of International Motor Boating. He was one of the last people to "read" for the bar in Maryland, attending some classes, but never officially enrolling toward a law degree. For more than forty years he has been a member of Maryland's oldest law firm, Harrington, Harrington and Nabb.

Recognizing the center's potential, the late Wilcomb Washburn, head of the American Studies Program at the Smithsonian Institution, donated his personal library of more than 10,000 volumes before his death, and the Donner Foundation of New York has established a $75,000 Washburn memorial at the center.

The center, at 1101 Camden Avenue, Salisbury State University, Salisbury 21804, is open Monday from 9:30 A.M. to 9:00 P.M., Tuesday through Friday from 9:30 A.M. to 4:30 P.M., and by appointment. It may be closed during school breaks, so for more information call (410) 543–6312.

The ***Country House*** in Salisbury is the largest country store in the East and delights all the senses with sounds of soothing music, the smell of potpourri and candles, and the feel of quality merchandise. You'll discover every colonial home furnishing you could wish to find as well as beautiful decorative accessories and old-time candy. Looking for that perfect something for your kitchen, bedroom, or bathroom? It should be here. You can select from an array of curtains, lighting fixtures, pottery, collectibles, furniture, shelving, rugs, baskets, and dried flowers. There are also some Victorian-style items, and the Christmas section is open year-round.

Owners Mike and Norma Delano handpick every item in the store, and they love to stop and talk with their customers. The shop is open Monday through Saturday 10:00 A.M. to 5:30 P.M.; on Friday night it's open until 8:00 P.M. From Thanksgiving to Christmas the store stays open until 8:00 P.M. Monday through Friday. You'll find the Country House at 805 East Main Street, Salisbury 21804. Call (410) 749–1959 or log on to www. thecountryhouse.com.

Salisbury Pewter, formed in 1980, is a company of dedicated workers who believe that although modern technology can be helpful, the most important part of their business is to maintain the heritage of their craft. Many of their methods have been handed down for centuries, and each piece of pewter they create is meticulously handcrafted and contains no lead. They offer a customizing service, and there is one wall with letters of appreciation from elected high officials for a series of pewter pieces created for an appreciation award. On weekdays you can see the crafters working pewter from raw product to a finished piece of art.

The shop is open Monday through Friday from 9:00 A.M. to 5:30 P.M., Saturday from 10:00 A.M. to 5:00 P.M. Call the store for Sunday hours. Salisbury Pewter is on Highway 13 North, Salisbury. The mailing address is P.O. Box 2475, Salisbury 21801; call (410) 546–1188 or (800) 824–4700 (out of state).

If you hate a zoo that rambles forever and ever and tries to be encyclopedic in its collection, you'll love the smallness and intimacy of ***Salisbury Zoo and Park***. Founded by the city to advance animal conservation and environmental awareness, the zoo has about 400 mammals, birds, and reptiles native to the Americas, with exhibits of spectacled bears, monkeys, jaguars, bison, bald eagles, and a wonderful waterfowl collection.

The snug twelve-acre facility embraces a branch of the Wicomico River and has plenty of shade trees, exotic plants, and wildlife, making for a cool, peaceful setting for family outings. No gift or food concessions are in the zoo, but there are plenty nearby, and picnic tables and toilet facilities are inside the park.

Located at 750 South Park Drive, Salisbury 21804, admission and parking are free. Pets are not permitted. The zoo is open daily from Memorial Day to Labor Day from 8:30 A.M. to 7:30 P.M. and until 4:30 P.M. the rest of the year. It is closed on Thanksgiving and Christmas. Group guided tours are available by appointment; call (410) 546–3440 or visit www.salisburyzoo.org.

Of major note is the ***Ward Museum of Wildfowl Art,*** which houses what is perhaps the largest collection of decorative bird carvings in the world, including many antique decoys. The museum is named for internationally renowned waterfowl carvers and painters Lem and Steve Ward of Crisfield, Maryland. During their lifetimes they produced more than 25,000 decoys and decorative birds, which the men called "counterfeits." Their workshop has been re-created, and on display are more than one hundred fine examples of their old classic hunting decoys as well as their decoratives. Lem did most of the painting, while Steve did most of the carving. Steve died in 1976, and Lem died in 1984 at the age of eighty-eight.

The museum has changing exhibits featuring oils of wild animals or the art of the Northwest Indians. You can experience the story of this Native American art form, decoy carving, from its beginning to the present. And if you don't want to venture into the wetlands yourself with the bugs and the mud, in the museum you can experience the sights and sounds of the wetland habitat of native American wildfowl. Even the setting is close to spectacular. The waterfront setting overlooks a bird sanctuary where ducks, geese, herons, ospreys, and songbirds flock, as though to perform for you. An on-site gift shop has a wide selection of wildfowl-related items.

Located at 909 South Shumaker Drive, Salisbury 21804, the museum is open Monday through Saturday from 10:00 A.M. to 5:00 P.M. and Sunday from noon to 5:00 P.M. Guided group tours are available. Admission is

If It Looks Like a Duck . . .

The Ward Foundation was established to save the art form of decoy carving, which has grown from the carving of working decoys designed to catch birds to the decorative carving of collector's items. The foundation's annual summer seminars at 909 South Shumaker Drive, Salisbury 21804, offer hands-on instruction by some of the most talented artists and teachers in the field, such as Ernie Muehlmatt, Pat Godin, Bill Koelpin, Bob Guge, Larry Bath, and Jim Sprankle. Intensive weeklong sessions cover such topics as anatomy and research, shaping, texturing, burning, priming and painting, and various brush techniques. Room and board are provided on campus. For information about the seminars, contact the Ward Foundation at (410) 742–4988.

$7.00 for adults, $5.00 for seniors age sixty and older, $3.00 for college students, and $3.50 for children age five through eighteen. It's still a great value at any price. Preschoolers are free. For more information contact the Ward Foundation at (410) 742–4988 or www.ward museum.org.

If you have ever heard the railroad expression about "highballing it down the road" and wondered what it meant, take a visit to Delmar to see the ***High Ball.*** (Delmar lies in both Delaware and Maryland; State Street straddles the border. There was a time when the two halves—two mayors, two town councils, two school systems—fought over municipal functions, but things have been patched up for some time.)

Along the tracks near State Street you will see a large white ball, which was raised on high to signify that the line was clear, giving rise to the term "highballing." A small museum is housed in the caboose next to the tracks, and it is open by appointment. Call George Truitt at (302) 846–2654.

Driving along the flat stretch of Route 54 west of Delmar near Mardela Springs, you will parallel the southern end of the north-south section of the ***Mason-Dixon line***. One could even say this is the cornerstone of the Mason-Dixon line. A double crownstone was installed in 1768 by Charles Mason and Jeremiah Dixon to settle the boundary disputes between the Penn and Calvert families, whose coats of arms it bears. There is a small parking lot and a brick and wrought-iron pavilion protecting the stones.

Called the Middle Point monument because it marks the middle of the

Delmarva Peninsula, the crownstone also is a triangulation point of the National Geodetic Survey. The stone was broken off at ground level by vandals in 1983, and another stone originally set by colonial surveyors in 1760 was defaced by removal of the Calvert coat of arms. The Maryland Department of Natural Resources and Delaware's State Boundary Commission jointly replaced the monument on October 24, 1985.

Skipjacks can be seen in the watermen's villages of Deal Island, Chance, and Wenona. Over Labor Day weekend this last fleet of working sailboats races in the Tangier Sound off Deal Island in the annual Skipjack Races.

Two ferryboats continue service in this part of Maryland, survivors of the many that once linked water-isolated communities on the Wicomico River, between Wicomico and Somerset Counties. Both are small, both are free, and both operate all year, weather conditions and tides permitting.

The ***Upper Ferry*** crosses between Allen and Route 349 in Salisbury and takes about three minutes. It is an outboard motor-propelled cable ferryboat with no name. A ferry has been running here since at least 1897; the current one has a capacity of two cars plus six passengers,

Skipjack

with a maximum vehicle size of five tons gross weight. Bicycles are permitted.

The Upper Ferry runs Monday through Friday March through September from 7:00 A.M. to 6:00 P.M. and the rest of the year from 7:00 A.M. to 5:30 P.M. Monday through Friday and 7:00 A.M. to 1:00 P.M. on Saturday. Call (410) 334–2798.

The ***Whitehaven–Mt. Vernon Cable Ferry***, called the Whitehaven Ferry, is 6 miles downriver from the Upper Ferry and connects Whitehaven to Widgeon; it has been operating since 1690. The modern ferryboat, the *Som-Wico,* takes about five minutes for a crossing and can hold three cars plus ten passengers. Bikes are permitted.

Whitehaven is the oldest incorporated town on the river and once was a vital deepwater port and shipbuilding area. Both ferries are run by the Wicomico County Road Department. Call (410) 548–4872 for more information.

Contact Lewis R. Carman, Tourism Director, at the Convention and Visitor Bureau, P.O. Box 2333, Salisbury 21802-2333, for more details on tourism, or call (410) 548–4914 or (800) 332–8687.

Worcester County

The town of Berlin in Worcester (pronounced like "rooster") County has no connection to the city in Germany; instead, it is a corruption of Burley Inn, the name of the site on which it was constructed. A guided map for a ***Berlin walking tour*** includes a town park and monument dedicated to Comm. Stephen Decatur, a native of Berlin. The oldest homes were built during the Federal period, later homes adopted the Victorian style, and twentieth-century homes are typified by the "bungalow." The walking tour brochure can be picked up at local Berlin businesses.

A typical Federal-style post-and-beam house is the ***Taylor House Museum***. It was built about 1825 and now is used as the town museum. The gable-front house features a Palladian window with Victorian glass, restored wood graining, and a magnificent front doorway with butterfly medallions, sunbursts, and fluted, engaged columns. The house was supposed to be destroyed and replaced by a new post office and parking lot, but it was saved in 1981 by the Berlin Heritage Foundation. With $100,000 in private donations from the community, the house was restored from its dilapidated condition.

Although Robert J. Henry, who was instrumental in bringing the railroad to Berlin, lived in the house, the most famous occupant was Calvin B. Taylor, the founder of the Calvin B. Taylor Banking Company, which is still in existence. Much of the house and appointments are original to the times that various occupants lived in the house, including C. B. Taylor's bank desk, with its hidden doors on the side and front.

The Taylor House is at 208 North Main Street, Berlin 21811, at the intersection with Baker Street, across from the Stevenson Methodist Church. The house is open Monday, Wednesday, Friday, and Saturday, mid-May through the end of October, from 1:00 to 4:00 P.M. and for such special events as concerts. Call (410) 641–1019. There is no admission charge, but a $2.00 donation is suggested.

In the middle of the historic district is the ***Atlantic Hotel,*** a faithfully restored 1895 Victorian hostelry that was rescued from the depths of distress to become this showpiece, which was named to the National Register of Historic Places in 1980. Each of the sixteen guest rooms (each with private bath) is beautifully furnished with antiques and is unique in its decor. Rich green and burgundy, delicate rose and aqua, deep mahogany tones, tassels, braid, lace, and crochet help transport you to a gentler time and quieter pace.

A parlor—for reading, letter writing, or conversation—is on the second floor. As a concession to our lives, new owner Gary Webosha had a television set placed in every room. Continental breakfast provided.

The Atlantic Hotel and all of Berlin will look familiar to you if you saw

Atlantic Hotel

the Richard Gere and Julia Roberts movie *Runaway Bride.* The town was called Hale in the movie and all the shops were renamed; only the Atlantic kept its own identity. The Atlantic Hotel Inn and Restaurant is located at 2 North Main Street, Berlin 21811. Call (410) 641–3589 or (800) 814–7672 for information or reservations.

Seven miles east of Berlin is ***Assateague Island National Seashore*** and the Assateague State Park, reached by Route 611. Nearly two million people visit this seashore annually. A two-room visitors center is open for interpretive classes and exhibits, which include a small "touch tank" of marine life. During a visit here you can take a guided walk; view a demonstration on how to catch blue crabs, clams, and ribbed mussels (mighty tasty steamed or sautéed in butter); or join a naturalist at the Old Ferry Landing to explore the 3⁄4-mile width of Assateague Island. You will travel by foot and bike or car from the salt marsh to the pounding surf, discovering relationships between the various barrier island life zones.

The famed ***Chincoteague ponies*** can be seen on Assateague, for two herds of the wild ponies make their home here. The herds are separated by a fence at the Maryland–Virginia state line. Managed by the National Park Service on the Maryland side, horses are often seen around roads and campgrounds. The horses sold at auction every July are on the Virginia side. No road connects the two states within the park. Supposedly, the horses are descended from domesticated stock that grazed on the island as early as the seventeenth century; Eastern Shore planters put them here to avoid mainland taxes and fencing requirements. Smaller than horses, these shaggy, sturdy ponies are well adapted to their harsh seashore environment. Marsh and dune grasses supply the bulk of their food, and they obtain water from freshwater impoundments or natural ponds.

Although they appear tame, they are unpredictable and can inflict serious wounds by kicking and biting. The Park Service strongly recommends that you do not pet or feed the ponies.

While at the park, you may see great blue herons, snowy egrets, dunlins, American widgeons, black-crowned night herons, peregrine falcons, and numerous other birds on the Maryland side, but they are more easily seen on the Virginia side.

Legend has it that Edward Teach (Blackbeard the Pirate) kept one of his fourteen wives, a base of operations, and buried treasure on Assateague.

The Assateague Island National Seashore visitor center is open daily from 9:00 A.M. to 5:00 P.M.; 7206 National Seashore Lane, Berlin 21811.

Call (410) 641–1441 or (800) 365–2267 or log on to www.nps.gov/asis. The Assateague State Park, 7307 Stephen Decatur Highway, Berlin 21811, can be reached at (410) 641–2120 or (888) 432–2267; www.dnr.state.md.us.

The ***Viewtrail 100*** signs you will see on secondary state and county roads mark a scenic bicycle trail, which is maintained by the Worcester County Extension Service. You can join the trail in Berlin as it sweeps down to Pocomoke City, past the access to Furnace Town, Nassawango Creek Cypress Swamp, Milburn Landing on the north bank of the Pocomoke River, Mt. Zion One-Room School Museum, and many other interesting attractions.

The ***Pocomoke River*** is the northernmost swamp river on the East Coast, and along its banks are cypress trees that were used to make our country's first ships. Here you can view eagles, egrets, hawks, and vultures, as well. For more Maryland bike trail information, call (800) 252–8776.

The ***Beach to Bay Indian Trail*** is a self-guided driving trail that goes from Crisfield on the Chesapeake Bay in Somerset County up to Princess Anne, Pocomoke City, Snow Hill, Berlin, and Ocean City. It was opened in 1988 and is jointly sponsored by Somerset and Worcester Tourism, Ocean City, the State of Maryland, and the departments of Transportation, Natural Resources, and Housing and Community Development.

A carved-wood relief sculpture in polychrome, called **The Power of Communication**, hangs over the postmaster's door in the Pocomoke City Post Office. Perna Krick of Baltimore executed the commission in 1940. The figure of a Native American with an airplane reflects the history of the area, from early tradition to the development of communication, from primitive methods to present-day service.

Ms. Krick was born in Ohio in 1909 and attended the Dayton Art Institute. She studied under J. Maxwell Miller at the Rinehard School of Sculpture in Baltimore, receiving two European traveling scholarships. By the time she received this commission from the Federal Works Agency, her work had been exhibited at the Baltimore Art Museum, the Pennsylvania Academy of Fine Arts, and the Architectural League in New York.

Ocean City is a family-oriented town on the ocean. It lies 7 miles east of Berlin. Thousands of college kids ("June bugs") come here every summer to work and vacation. There is plenty to do, from kite flying (probably my favorite activity), to boating, fishing, golfing, and checking to make sure the draft beer is kept at the right temperature. As with any resort, there are dozens (if not hundreds) of restaurants, eateries, bars, and food stands along the 3-mile boardwalk, and you have to try some of the famous saltwater taffy and Thrasher's french fries with vinegar. Rather than trying to drive through traffic, which can be terrible in the summer, try the bus. As they say in Ocean City "Avoid the fuss, take the bus." Ride all day for only $1.00. Call (410) 723–1606 for the schedule.

One of the traditional sights around Ocean City is the airplanes flying advertising banners about 200 feet above sea level. Robert Bunting of Berlin bought a small crop duster in 1982 and started airplane advertising by flying up and down the beach with banner messages. The business is so popular that a half dozen banner-bearing, single-engine aircraft are used for this kind of advertising. Each banner must have forty or fewer letters. Some carry marriage proposals; others tell you about the newest restaurant in town.

If you would like to have one carry your message for the world to see while the plane flies "low and slow," it will cost between $50 and $160 per banner. If you go watch the ground crew rig the planes, you will see them set the banner between two upright poles that are 6 feet apart. (It is said that if the ground crew is feeling prankish, they will close the poles only 2 feet apart.) Then the plane flies about 85 miles per hour to pick up the banner. Usually the pilot makes it on the first trip, but it has taken as many as six tries to hook a banner. You are looking at some first-class flying.

Between Memorial Day and Labor Day, each pilot logs about 500 hours, flying from 10:00 A.M. to 4:00 P.M., seven days a week, and together the pilots can fly as many as 110 banners in one day, although the average is about forty-five to fifty.

The Ocean City restaurant that has to be a first on anyone's list is ***Phillips Crab House.*** Eating at this restaurant, which was started by Shirley and Brice Phillips from Hooper's Island on Chesapeake Bay, has been a ritual in Ocean City since 1956. The two of them have become such an institution and such an integral part of their community that they were honored in 1989 by the Ocean City Good Will Ambassadors Grand Ball and again in 2000 by the Maryland Tourism Council during National Tourism Week, as the most prominent tourism industry family.

Phillips has branched out with several locations, among them in Baltimore's Harborplace, Washington, D.C., and Norfolk. But the Ocean City location is the one to visit. It was a shingle-covered shack in the boonies when it opened. Now it is in the middle of everything that is happening and can seat 1,400 diners at one time. Despite its size, you will have to arrive early or plan to wait a while, because there is always a line for dinner. This is where you come to eat crabs, piled in mounds on broad sheets of paper that cover tables that once held sewing machines.

If steamed crabs, spiced shrimp, and crab cakes don't appeal to you, there is always fried chicken or Virginia baked ham served with corn on the cob, watermelon, and cole slaw. A children's menu is also available.

Phillips Crab House is at Twenty-first Street and Philadelphia Avenue, Ocean City 21842. For information call (410) 289–6821.

Those of you who served aboard the ***USS* 324**, a World War II submarine that was built in 1944 and saw battle in the Java and South China Seas, will find her serving a new function as a reef in the Atlantic Ocean about 15 miles off Ocean City. The *Blenny* was scuttled in 1989 also about 15 miles offshore. It acts as a base for algae and soft coral growth, which will attract small fish and then larger fish, fishermen, and divers.

Ocean City is not just for summer fun. It is a year-round community that sponsors a great number of activities during the winter season, including workshops, entertainment, an annual Christmas parade, a traditional lighting and trimming of a 30-foot tree on the beach, and the placement of holiday decorations throughout the town. Call (800) 62–OCEAN for details about this and numerous other events.

One of the unfortunate duties of Ocean City is lifesaving, for some people will do stupid things, and some people will be the victims of circumstances even without being stupid. The ***Ocean City Life-Saving Station Museum,*** located on the south end of the boardwalk, shows some early lifesaving equipment and sands from around the world, shipwreck artifacts, antique bathing suits, models of old Ocean City hotels and businesses, photos of famous storms, and tales (not tails) of mermaids.

It's open all year, with hours of 11:00 A.M. to 10:00 P.M. daily during the summer. Admission is $2.00. Call (410) 289–4991 for off-season hours and information, or log on to www.beachinet/~ocmuseum.

A brochure about Christmas in Ocean City (as well as in Berlin, Snow Hill, and Pocomoke) is available from the Ocean City Public Relations Office, P.O. Box 158, Ocean City 21842. You can call the office at (410) 289–2800.

For additional information on Worcester County, contact the Maryland Lower Shore Tourist Information Center, U.S. Route 13 North, 144 Ocean

Highway, Pocomoke City 21851 (410–957–2484), or Worcester County Tourism, P.O. Box 208, Snow Hill 21863 (800–852–0335 or log on to www.skipjack.net/le_shore.visitworcester).

Somerset County

Every endeavor from the sublime to the ridiculous is represented at two Somerset County museums, and both museums are well documented in most state tourism brochures. These two museums may contain items about the same time, place, and people, but they sure do come out different.

Depending on your available time (you'd need at least two weeks to see and learn about the thousands of items in this collection), you will want to stop by the ***Eastern Shore Early Americana Museum*** at Route 667 and Old Westover Road, in Hudsons Corner. Pack rats and Americana lovers have Lawrence W. Burgess to thank for being a certifiable scavenger. This museum, housed in a converted poultry house, is a monument to the art of accumulation. It contains a little bit of everything, from political buttons to oyster-tonging forks. The museum is open 1:00 to 4:00 P.M. daily April 1 through October 31, and is located at 30195 Rehoboth Road, Marion Station 21838; (410) 623–8324.

On the other hand, there is the ***Crisfield Historical Museum*** in Crisfield, with its exhibits pertaining to the late Maryland governor J. Millard Tawes, the history and development of the Crisfield seafood industry, local art and folklore, and the anthropological history of the area.

The Crisfield Museum, 3 Ninth Street, Crisfield 21817, is open daily during the summer from 9:00 A.M. to 6:00 P.M. and during the winter Monday through Saturday from 9:00 A.M. to 4:30 P.M. Call (410) 968–2501 for more information.

With a little time, you also might want to stop by the ***Teackle Mansion*** on Sunday afternoon. This is a very elaborate example of the Federal style of architecture in 1802 and then in 1818 and 1819, erected by Littleton Dennis Teackle (1777–1848), an influential man of the early 1800s. Teackle and his wife Elizabeth Upshur Teackle (1783–1835), moved to this area from Accomack County in Virginia, shortly after they were married in 1800. Teackle was a merchant, statesman, and entrepreneur, owning agriculture and timber lands, and trading with merchants in England and the Caribbean. He established the Bank of Somerset in 1813 and served for many years in the Maryland House of Delegates.

The mansion was sold and eventually became apartments, until Maude Jeffries and her sister Catherine Ricketts founded Olde Princess Anne Days Inc. The funds this organization raised bought and restored the mansion. An infusion of $25,000 from the Maryland Commission for Celebration 2000 will support an archaeological survey of the property that will map and retrieve sensitive archaeological resources.

Located at 11736 Mansion Street, Princess Anne 21853, the mansion is open on Wednesday, Saturday, and Sunday from 1:00 to 3:00 P.M. May through November, and by appointment. Call (410) 651–2238 or (800) 621–9189 for information.

The Teackle Mansion is also the home of the Somerset County Historical Society (410–651–2238) from April to November.

You also might want to try some seafood, for Crisfield is the self-proclaimed "Seafood Capital of the World," or take a ferry out to Smith Island. For both of these pleasures, you could not come to a more perfect place. As you drive down to the end of Main Street to watch the boating activity, stop for a meal at the ***Original Captain's Galley Restaurant.*** The owners are not immodest when they claim that this is the "home of the world's best crab cake." The crabs are caught and picked fresh daily from the Chesapeake waters, and then the meat is lightly seasoned with herbs and spices. For a real treat, try the 100 percent backfin crabmeat, fried or broiled.

Owner Jim Dodson's soft-shell crab sandwich is no slouch either, and on cold days there is nothing better than one of the apple dumplings to warm up the insides. The local artwork is also a special treat. As you dine on delectable seafood, you can watch the watermen of the Chesapeake bring in the bounty of its waters.

The Original Captain's Galley is at the end of Main Street, well within sight of the pavilion at the end of the city wharf. Located at 1021 West Main Street, Crisfield 21817, it overlooks beautiful Tangier Sound. Call (410) 968–3313 for information or reservations.

Two of Maryland's ten ferries—the Whitehaven and Upper Ferries—operate between Somerset and Wicomico Counties. Check the Wicomico County section for additional details.

For additional tourism information write to Somerset County Tourism, P.O. Box 243, Princess Anne 21853. Call (410) 651–2968 or (800) 521–9189 (nationwide).

PLACES TO EAT ON THE EASTERN SHORE

BERLIN
Atlantic Hotel Inn and Restaurant,
2 North Main Street,
(410) 641–3589

CAMBRIDGE
Port Side Seafood Company,
201 Trenton Street,
(410) 228–9007

CHESTERTOWN
Blue Heron Cafe,
236 Cannon Street,
(410) 778–0188

CRISFIELD
The Original Captain's Galley,
Main Street,
(410) 968–3313

ELKTON
Fair Hill Inn,
Routes 273 and 213,
(410) 398–4187

EASTON
Tidewater Inn,
101 East Dover Street,
(410) 822–1300 or
(800) 237–8775

GRASONVILLE
Holly's,
108 Jackson Creek Road,
(410) 827–8711

Fisherman's Village,
3116 Main Street,
(410) 827–8807

Harris' Crab House,
433 Kent Narrows Way North,
(410) 827–9500

OCEAN CITY
Captain's Galley II,
12817 Harbor Road,
(410) 213–2525

Captain's Table,
1500 Baltimore Avenue,
(410) 289–7191

Christopher's Tutti Gusti,
3322 Coastal Highway,
(410) 289–3318

Crab Alley,
9703 Golf Course Road,
(410) 213–7800

Duffy's Love Shack,
102 Worcester Street,
(410) 289–1400

Dumser's Dairyland,
Ocean City Boardwalk,
(410) 289–0934

Embers,
24th and Coastal Highway,
(410) 289–3322

Fager's Island,
59th Street, In-the-Bay,
(410) 524–5500

Galaxy Bar & Grille,
6601 Coastal Highway,
(410) 723–6762

Harrison's Harbor Watch,
Boardwalk South,
(410) 289–5121

Hobbit,
81st & Bay,
(410) 524–8100

Mo's Seafood Factory,
82nd Street on the Bay,
(410) 723–2500

Paul Revere's Smorgasbord,
Second Street and Boardwalk,
(410) 524–1776

Phillips Crab House,
2004 21st Street,
(410) 289–6821

Phillips By the Sea Restaurant,
Oceanfront at 13th Street,
(410) 289–9121 or
(800) 492–5834

Phillips Seafood House,
141st Street and Coastal Highway,
(410) 250–1200 or
(800) 799–2722

Seacrets,
49th and the Bay,
(410) 524–4900

Shenanigan's Irish Pub and Seafood House,
Boardwalk and Fourth Street,
(410) 289–7181

Wharf Restaurant and Lounge,
12801 Coastal Highway,
(410) 250–1001

OXFORD
Le Zinc,
101 Mill Street,
(410) 226–5776

Pier Street Restaurant,
West Pier Street,
(410) 226–5171

Robert Morris Inn,
North Morris Street,
(410) 226–5111

Schooner's Landing,
Tilghman Street,
(410) 226–0160

Rock Hall
America's Cup Cafe,
5745 Main Street,
(410) 639–7361

Old Oars Inn,
5731 Main Street,
(410) 639–2541

P.E. Pruitt's,
20899 Bayside Avenue,
(410) 639–7454

Waterman's Crab House,
21055 Sharp Street Pier,
(410) 639–2261

St. Michaels
208 Talbot Street,
208 Talbot Street,
(410) 745–3838

Bistro St. Michaels,
403 South Talbot Street,
(410) 745–9111

Inn at Perry Cabin,
308 Watkins Lane,
(410) 745–5178

Justine's Ice Cream Parlour,
101 South Talbot Street,
(410) 745–5416

Poppi's,
207 North Talbot Street,
(410) 745–3158

Stevensville
Hemingway's Restaurant,
(Exit 37S) off Route 50,
357 Pier 1,
(410) 643–CRAB

Kentmorr Restaurant and Crab House,
910 Kentmorr Road,
(410) 643–2263

Taylor's Island
Taylor's Island General Store,
Route 16,
(410) 397–3733

Tilghman Island
Harrison's Chesapeake House,
Chesapeake House Drive,
(410) 886–2121

Tilghman Island Inn,
21384 Coopertown Road,
(410) 886–2141 or
(800) 866–2141

Places to Stay on the Eastern Shore

Berlin
Atlantic Hotel Inn and Restaurant,
2 North Main Street,
(410) 641–3589,
www.atlantichotel.com

Holland House Bed and Breakfast,
5 Bay Street,
(410) 641–1956

Merry Sherwood Plantation,
8909 Worcester Highway,
(410) 641–2112 or
(800) 660–0358,
www.merrysherwood.com

Betterton
Lantern Inn Bed and Breakfast,
115 Ericsson Avenue,
(410) 348–5809 or
(800) 499–7265,
www.bbonline.com/md/lanterninn

Bishopville
Grove Market,
12402 St. Martin's Neck Road,
(410) 352–5055

Cambridge
Anchorage Bed and Breakfast,
5667 Augustine Herman Highway,
(410) 275–1972

Cambridge House Bed and Breakfast,
112 High Street,
(410) 221–7700,
www.cambridgehousebandb.com

Cambridge Inn,
2831 Ocean Gateway,
(410) 221–0800

Commodores Cottage Bed and Breakfast,
215 Glenburn Avenue,
(410) 228–6938 or
(800) 228–6938

Glasgow on the Choptank,
1500 Hambrooks Boulevard,
(410) 288–0575 or
(800) 373–7890

Lodgecliffe on the Choptank,
103 Choptank Terrace,
(410) 228–1760

Relax Inn,
2917 Ocean Gateway,
(410) 228–4444 or
(888) 735–2980

CENTREVILLE
Rose Tree Bed and Breakfast,
116 South Commerce Street,
(410) 768–3991

CHESAPEAKE CITY
Blue Max Inn,
300 South Bohemia Avenue,
(410) 885–2781,
www.bluemaxinn.com

Chesapeake City Bed and Breakfast,
208 Bank Street,
(410) 885–2200

Inn at the Canal,
104 Bohemia Avenue,
(410) 885–5995,
www.chesapeakecity.com/inn@thecanal/inn.html

Ship Watch Inn,
401 First Street,
(410) 885–5300,
www.chesapeakecity.com

CHESTER
Chesapeake Bay Waterfront Bed and Breakfast,
101 Swan Cove Lane,
(410) 757–0248

CHESTERTOWN
April Inn,
407 Campus Avenue,
(410) 778–5540,
www.EasternShore.com

Brampton Inn,
25227 Chestertown Road,
(410) 778–1860,
www.bramptoninn.com

Claddaugh Farm Bed and Breakfast,
160 Claddaugh Lane,
(410) 778–4894,
www.chestertown.com

Foxley Manor,
609 Washington Avenue,
(410) 778–3200,
www.chestertown.com

Great Oak Lodge and Restaurant,
22170 Great Oak Landing Road,
(410) 778–2100,
www.chestertown.com

Great Oak Manor,
10568 Cliff Road,
(410) 778–5943 or
(800) 504–3098,
www.greatoak.com

Hill's Inn Bed and Breakfast,
114 Washington Avenue,
(410) 778–1926,
www.chestertown.com

Inn at Mitchell House,
8796 Maryland Parkway,
(410) 778–6500,
www.chestertown.com/mitchell

Laurentum Inn Bed and Breakfast,
954 High Street,
(410) 778–3236 or
(800) 742–3236,
www.chestertown.com

Parker House,
108 Spring Avenue,
(410) 778–9041,
www.chestertown.com/parker

Pratt-Perry House,
224 Washington Avenue,
(410) 778–2734 or
(800) 720–8788,
www.chestertown.com

River Inn at Rolph's Wharf,
1008 Rolph's Wharf Road,
(410) 778–6347 or
(800) 894–6347,
www.chestertown.com

White Swan Tavern,
231 High Street,
(410) 778–2300,
www.chestertown.com/whiteswan

Widow's Walk Inn Bed and Breakfast,
402 High Street,
(410) 778–6455 or
(888) 778–6455,
www.chestertown.com

CHURCH CREEK
Loblolly Landings and Lodge,
2142 Liners Road,
(410) 397–3033 or
(800) 862–7452

CRISFIELD
Bea's Bed and Breakfast,
10 South Somerset Avenue,
(410) 968–0423,
www.beasbandb.com

Cole House Bed and Breakfast,
Route 209,
(410) 928–5514

Leonora's Crisfield Inn,
209 West Main Street,
(410) 968–2181

Washington Tull House,
3296 Sackertown Road,
(410) 968–1891

DENTON
White Pillars Inn,
206 South Fifth Street,
(410) 479–3292

EASTON
Ashby "1663" Bed and Breakfast,
27448 Goldsborough Neck Road,
(410) 822–4235 or
(800) 458–3622,
www.ashby1663.com

Bishop's House Bed and Breakfast,
214 Goldsborough Street,
(410) 820–7290 or
(800) 223–7290,
www.traveldata.com/inns/data/bishop.html

Chaffinch House Bed and Breakfast,
132 South Harrison Street,
(410) 822–5074 or
(800) 861–5074,
www.echo-sol.com/chaffinch

Double Mills Guest House,
26877 Double Mills Road,
(410) 349–2267

McDaniel House Bed and Breakfast,
14 North Aurora Street,
(410) 822–3704 or
(800) 787–INNS

Tidewater Inn and Conference Center,
101 East Dover Street,
(410) 822–1300,
www.tidewaterinn.com

ELKTON
Garden Cottage at Sinking Springs Farm,
843 Elk Forest Road,
(410) 398–5566

GALENA
Carrousel Horse,
145 Main Street,
(410) 648–5476,
www.chestertown.com/carhorse/carrousel.html

Rose Hill Farm Bed and Breakfast,
13842 Gregg Neck Road,
(410) 648–5334,
www.easternshorelodging.com

GRASONVILLE
Lands End Manor on the Bay,
232 Prospect Bay Drive,
(410) 827–6284

HENDERSON
Chesapeake Inn Bed and Breakfast,
16090 Oakland Road,
(410) 758–1824 or
(800) 778–INNS

HURLOCK
North Fork Bed and Breakfast,
6505 Palmers Mill Road,
(410) 943–4706 or
(800) N–FORK–BB

NORTH EAST
North Bay Bed and Breakfast,
9 Sunset Drive,
(410) 287–5948,
www.northbayinc.com

OCEAN CITY
There are dozens, if not hundreds, of hotels, motels, boardinghouses, apartments, bed-and-breakfasts, and condo units for rent in Ocean City. They are bayside or oceanside, seasonal and year-round. They are available on a weekly basis (Saturday to Saturday, Sunday to Sunday), a full weekend only, or by the night. For your first visit, you might want to contact the Chamber of Commerce (410–213–0552) or one of about a dozen vacation rental establishments and ask for information about this resort area.

Ambassador Inn,
North Fifth and Philadelphia Avenue,
(410) 289–6100

Atlantic House Bed and Breakfast,
501 North Baltimore Avenue,
(410) 289–2333,
www.atlantichouse.com

Coconut Malorie Resort,
200 59th Street,
(800) 767–6060,
www.coconutmalorie.com

Commander Hotel,
1401 Baltimore Avenue,
(410) 289–6166 or
(888) 289–6166,
www.commanderhotel.com

Fenwick Inn,
13801 Coastal Highway,
(410) 250–1100 or
(800) 492–1873,
www.fenwickinn.com

Harrison Hall Hotel,
15th Street,
Boardwalk,
(410) 289–6222 or
(800) 638–2106

Inn on the Ocean,
1001 Atlantic Avenue,
(410) 289–8894 or
(888) 226–6223,
www.bbonline.com/md/ontheocean

Lighthouse Club Hotel,
201 60th Street,
(410) 524–5400 or
(888) 371–5400,
www.fagers.com

Princess Bayside Beach Hotel,
4801 Coastal Highway,
(410) 723–2900 or
(800) 854–9785,
www.princessbayside.com

Talbot Inn,
311 Talbot Street,
(410) 289–9125 or
(800) 659–7703

Wellington Hotel,
900 Baltimore Avenue,
(410) 289–9189,
www.ocean-city.com/wellington.html

OXFORD

1876 House Bed and Breakfast,
110 North Morris Street,
(410) 226–5496,
www.bbhost.com1876house

Combsberry 1730,
4837 Evergreen Road,
(410) 226–5353,
www.combsberry.com

Nichols House,
217 South Morris Street,
(410) 226–5799,
www.oxfordmd.com/nicholshouse

Oxford Inn,
504 South Morris Street,
(410) 226–5220,
www.oxfordmd.com/oxfordinn

Robert Morris Inn,
314 North Morris Street,
(410) 226–5111,
www.robertmorrisinn.com

POCOMOKE CITY

Littleton's Bed and Breakfast,
407 Second Street,
(410) 957–1645,
www.bnbinns.com/littletons.inn

PRINCESS ANNE

Hayman House Bed and Breakfast,
30491 Prince William Street,
(410) 651–2753,
www.virtualcities.com

Hyland House,
27070 Annie Hyland Road,
(410) 651–1056

Washington Hotel Inn,
11784 Somerset Avenue,
(410) 651–2525

Waterloo Country Inn,
28822 Mount Vernon Road,
(410) 651–0883,
www.waterloocountryinn.com

QUEENSTOWN

Irishtown Bed and Breakfast,
511 Pintail Point Farm Lane,
(410) 827–7029

Queenstown Inn Bed and Breakfast,
7109 Main Street,
(410) 827–3396 or
(800) 720–8788

Stillwater Inn Bed and Breakfast,
7109 Second Avenue,
(410) 827–9362,
www.bbonline.com/md/stillwater

RIDGELY

Dunning Studio Bed and Breakfast,
24451 Burnt Mill Road,
(410) 634–2491

Slo Horse Inn,
11649 Holly Road,
(410) 634–2128,
www.oldbayrealty.com/slohorse.html

ROCK HALL

Bay Breeze Inn,
5758 Main Street,
(410) 639–2061,
www.rockhallmd.com

Black Duck Inn,
21906 Chesapeake Avenue,
(410) 639–2478,
www.rockhallmd.com

Carriage House,
5877 Coleman Road,
(410) 639–2855

Huntingfield Manor,
4928 Eastern Neck Road,
(410) 639–7779 or
(800) 720–8788,
www.huntingfield.com

Inn at Osprey Point,
20786 Rock Hall Avenue,
(410) 639–2194

Mariner's Motel,
5681 Hawthorne Avenue,
(410) 639–2291,
www.rockhallmd.com

Moonlight Bay Inn,
6002 Lawton Avenue,
(410) 639–2660,
www.kentcounty.com

North Point Marina Hotel,
5639 Walnut Street,
(410) 639–2907,
www.rockhallmd.com

Swan Haven Bed and Breakfast,
20950 Rock Hall Avenue,
(410) 639–2527,
www.rockhallmd.com/swanhaven

Swan Point Inn Bed and Breakfast,
Route 20 and Coleman Road,
(410) 639–2500,
www.rockhallmd.com

Tallulah's,
5750 Main Street,
(410) 639–2596,
www.rockhallmd.com

SALISBURY

Landon Cottage,
21902 Sherwood Landing Road,
(410) 886–2551

Lowes Wharf Marina Inn,
21651 Lowes Wharf Road,
(410) 745–6684 or
(888) 484–9267,
www.loweswharf.com

Moorings Bed and Breakfast,
7857 Tilghman Island Road,
(410) 745–6396 or
(800) 316–6396,
www.morringsbb.com

SMITH ISLAND

Ewell Tide Inn,
4063 Tyler Road,
(410) 425–2141,
www.smithisland.net

Inn of Silent Music,
2955 Tylerton Road,
(410) 425–3541,
www.bbonline.com

Janice Marshall's Overnight Lodging,
3008 Union Church Road,
(410) 425–3701

Smith Island Motel,
4018 Smith Island Road,
(410) 968–1933

Tourist Home,
2 Tyler Road,
(410) 968–2990

ST. MICHAELS

Barrett's Bed and Breakfast Inn,
204 North Talbot Street,
(410) 745–3322,
www.barrettbb.com

Brick House,
202 North Talbot Street,
(410) 745–2799 or
(877) 466–0100

Captain's Quarters,
115 East Chew Avenue,
(410) 745–9152

Chew Inn Bed and Bath,
114 East Chew Avenue,
(410) 745–3243,
www.members.home.net/wilsonlsu

Cygnet House,
201 Carpenter Street,
(410) 745–2929

Dr. Dodson House Bed and Breakfast,
200 Cherry Street,
(410) 745–3691,
www.drdodsonhouse.com

Escape Hatch,
700 South Talbot Street,
(410) 745–6360

Fleet's Inn,
200 East Chew Road,
(410) 745–9678

Getaway Bed and Breakfast,
Waterfront Estate,
(410) 756–2094

Hambleton Inn,
202 Cherry Street,
(410) 745–3350,
www.hambletoninn.com

Harris Cove Cottages Bed & Boat,
8080 Bozman–Neavitt Road,
(410) 745–9701,
www.bednboat.com

Inn at Perry Cabin,
308 Watkins Lane,
(410) 745–2200 or
(800) 722–2949,
www.perrycabin.com

Kemp House Inn,
412 South Talbot Street,
(410) 745–2243

Old Brick Inn,
401 South Talbot Street,
(410) 745–3323,
www.oldbrickinn.com

Parsonage Inn,
210 North Talbot Street,
(410) 745–5519 or
(800) 394–5519,
www.parsonage-inn.com

Rigby Valliant House Bed and Breakfast,
123 West Chestnut Street,
(410) 745–3977,
www.stmichaelsmd.org/members/rigby/rigby.html

St. Michaels Harbour Inn,
101 North Harbor Road,
(410) 745–5102 or
(800) 955–9001,
www.harbourinn.com

Tarr House Bed and Breakfast,
109 Green Street,
(410) 745–2175

Thomas Harrison House on the Harbor,
201 Green Street,
(703) 387–3008

Two Swan Inn,
208 Carpenter Street,
(410) 745–2929

Victoriana Inn,
205 Cherry Street,
(410) 745–3368,
www.virtualcities.com/ons/md/2/mdz9601.htm

Wades Point Inn on the Bay,
Wades Point Road,
(410) 745–2500 or
(888) 923–3466,
www.wadespoint.com

Snow Hill

Chanceford Hall,
209 Federal Hill,
(410) 632–2900,
www.chancefordhall.com

River House Inn,
201 East Market Street,
(410) 632–2722,
www.riverhouseinn.com

Stevensville

Kent Manor Inn,
500 Kent Manor Drive,
(410) 643–5757 or
(800) 820–4511

Taylor's Island

Becky Phipp's Inn,
Taylor's Island Road,
(410) 221–2911

Tilghman Island

Black Walnut Point Inn,
Black Walnut Road,
(410) 886–2452,
www.tilghmanisland.com/blackwalnut

Chesapeake Wood Duck Inn,
Gibsontown Road,
(410) 886–2070 or
(800) 956–2070,
www.woodduckinn.com

Lazyjack Inn,
5907 Tilghman Island Road,
(410) 886–2215 or
(800) 690–5080,
www.lazyjackinn.com

Norma's Guest House,
2146 Dogwood Harbor,
(410) 886–2395

Sinclair House Bed and Breakfast,
5718 Black Walnut Point Road,
(410) 886–2147 or
(888) 859–2147,
www.tilghmanisland.com/sinclair

Trappe

Country Bed and Breakfast,
5991 Ocean Gateway,
(410) 822–0587

Vienna

Nanticoke Manor,
Church Street at Water Street,
(410) 376–3432

Tavern House,
111 Water Street,
(410) 376–3347

Whitehaven

Whitehaven Bed and Breakfast,
23844-48 River Street,
(410) 873–3294 or
(888) 205–5921,
www.whitehaven.com

Wingate

Wingate Manor Bed and Breakfast,
2335 Wingate-Bishops Head Road,
(410) 397–8717 or
(888) 397–8717,
www.triple1.com/usa/mdwingate.htm

Winntman Island

Watermark Bed and Breakfast,
8956 Tilghman Island Road,
(410) 745–2892 or
(800) 987–8436,
www.watermarkinn.com

WITTMAN
Inn at Christmas Farm,
8873 Tilghman Island Road,
(410) 745–5312 or
(800) 987–8436

OTHER ATTRACTIONS WORTH SEEING ON THE EASTERN SHORE

107 Tory House,
Charlestown,
(410) 287–8262

Annie Taylor House Museum of Rural Life,
Denton,
(410) 822–7039

Art Institute and Gallery,
Salisbury,
(410) 546–4748

Avalon Theatre,
Easton,
(410) 822–0345,
www.avalontheatre.com

Betterton Beach,
Betterton,
(410) 778–1948

Brannock Maritime Museum,
Cambridge,
(410) 228–6938 or
(800) 228–6938

C&O Canal Museum,
Chesapeake City,
(410) 885–5621

Chesapeake City Historic District,
Chesapeake City,
(410) 885–2415

Chesapeake Farms,
Chestertown,
(410) 604–2100

Chesapeake Bay Maritime Museum,
St. Michaels,
(410) 745–2916,
www.cbmm.org

Chesapeake Farms,
Chestertown,
(410) 778–1565

Chesapeake Railroad,
Greensboro,
(410) 482–2330

Chipman Cultural Center,
Salisbury,
(410) 742–0100

Christ Church,
Easton,
(410) 822–2677

Christ Episcopal Church,
Cambridge,
(410) 228–3161

Church Hill Theatre,
Church Hill,
(410) 758–1331

Cost House & Hall Memorial Garden,
Pocomoke City,
(410) 957–3110

Cray House,
Stevensville,
(410) 653–3261

Customs House,
Oxford,
(410) 226–5760

Cypress Park Nature and Exercise Trail,
Pocomoke City,
(410) 957–1919 or
(410) 957–1333

Delmarva Shorebirds,
Salisbury,
(410) 219–3112 or
(888) BIRDS–96,
www.theshorebirds.com

Dorchester Heritage Museum,
Cambridge,
(410) 228–1899 or
(800) 522–TOUR

Dudley's Chapel,
Sudlersville,
(410) 604–2100

Durding's Store,
Rock Hall,
(410) 778–7957

Eastern Neck Wildlife Refuge,
Rock Hall,
(410) 639–7056

Elk Neck State Park,
North East,
(410) 287–5333,
www.dnr.state.md.us

Emmanual Episcopal Church,
Chestertown,
(410) 778–3477

Fairmount Academy,
Upper Fairmount,
(410) 651–0351 or
(800) 521–9189,
www.skipjack.net/le_shore/visitsomerset

Frontier Town Cowboy Golf/Waterpark,
Ocean City,
(410) 289–7877,
www.frontiertown.com

Frederick Douglass Marker,
Easton,
(410) 822–4606,
www.talbotchamber.org

Furnace Town Historic Site, Snow Hill, (410) 632–2032, www.dol.net/~ebola.ftown.htm

Geddes-Piper House, Chestertown, (410) 778–3499

H.M. Krentz Skipjack Charter, Tilghman, (410) 745–6080

Historical Society of Cecil County, Elkton, (410) 398–1790, www.cchistory.org

Historical Society Museum, Easton, (410) 822–0773, www.hstc.org

Historic Holly Tree, Perryville, (410) 658–3000

Janes Island State Park, Crisfield, (410) 968–1565 or (888) 432–CAMP, www.dnr.state.md.us

Julia A. Purnell Museum, Snow Hill, (410) 632–0515

Kent Farm Museum, Hurlock, (410) 348–5239

Kent Island Federation of Art, Stevensville, (410) 643–7424

Kitty Knight House, Georgetown, (410) 648–5777

Little Red School House, Easton, (410) 822–4606 or (888) BAY–STAY, www.talbotchamber.org

Marion Station Railroad Museum, Mardela Springs, (410) 623–2420 or (888) 838–7638

Martin's National Wildlife Refuge, Smith Island, (410) 425–4971

Mason-Dixon 1768 Survey Markers, Mardela Springs, (410) 548–4914

Meredith House and Nield Museum, Cambridge, (410) 228–7953

Mount Harmon Plantation, Earleville, (410) 276–8819

Mount Zion One-Room School Museum, Snow Hill, (410) 632–1265

Museum of Eastern Shore Life, Centreville, (410) 822–6109

Nathan of Dorchester, Cambridge, (410) 228–7141, www.skipjack_nathan.org

National Railroad Historical Society Museum, Perryville, (410) 642–6066

No Corner for the Devil, Easton, (410) 822–4606 or (888) BAY–STAY, www.talbotchamber.org

Nutters Museum, Fruitland, (410) 546–0314

Old Stevensville Post Office, Stevensville, (410) 604–2100

Old Trinity Church, Church Creek, (410) 228–3583

Oxford House, Oxford, (410) 226–0191

Patty Cannon House, Reliance, (800) 522–TOUR

Pemberton Hall and Park, Salisbury, (410) 749–0124

Pickering Creek Environmental Center, Easton, (410) 822–4903, www.pickeringcreek.org

Pocomoke Cypress Swamps, Snow Hill, (410) 632–2566

Pocomoke River State Park, Snow Hill, (410) 632–2566, www.dnr.state.md.us

Pocomoke State Forest, Snow Hill, (410) 632–2566, www.dnr.state.md.us

Poplar Hill Mansion,
Salisbury,
(410) 749–1776

Port Deposit Historic District,
Port Deposit,
(410) 378–2121

Queen Anne's County Arts Council,
Centreville,
(410) 758–2520,
www.intercom.net/npo/qacas

Queen Anne's Courthouse at Queenstown,
Queenstown,
(410) 827–7646 or
(800) 987–7591,
www.courts.state.md.us

Queenstown Colonial Courthouse,
Queenstown,
(410) 827–7646

(James B.) Richardson Maritime Museum,
Cambridge,
(410) 221–1871 or
(800) 522–TOUR

Rock Hall Museum,
Rock Hall,
(410) 778–1399

Rockawalkin School,
Salisbury,
(410) 742–8805

Rodgers Tavern,
Perryville,
(410) 642–6066

St. Francis Xavier Shrine,
Warwick,
(410) 275–2866

St. Luke's Episcopal Church,
Chestertown,
(410) 556–6644

St. Mary's Museum,
St. Michaels,
(410) 745–9561

St. Paul's Episcopal Church,
Rock Hall,
(410) 778–1540,
www.kentcounty.com

Sheriff John F. Dewitt Museum,
Elkton,
(410) 398–1790

Sinking Springs Herb Farm,
Elkton,
(410) 398–5566

Smith Island Center,
Ewell,
(410) 425–3351

Smith Island Crabmeat Co-op Inc.,
Smith Island,
(410) 425–2035

Smith Island Cruises,
Crisfield,
(410) 425–2771

Stanley Institute,
Cambridge,
(410) 228–0401

Stevensville Train Station,
Stevensville,
(410) 643–3261

Sudlersville Train Station Museum,
Sudlersville,
(410) 438–3501

Sultana Shipyard,
Chestertown,
(410) 778–6461,
www.chesterriver.com/sultana

Tangier Island Cruises,
Crisfield,
(410) 968–2338 or
(800) 863–2338,
www.dmv.com/tangiercruises

Taylor Island Museum,
Taylor's Island,
(800) 522–TOUR

Tench Tilghman Monument,
Oxford,
(410) 822–4606 or
(888) BAY–STAY,
www.talbotchamber.org

Third Haven Friends Meeting House,
Easton,
(410) 822–0293

Trimper's Rides Amusements,
Ocean City,
(410) 289–8617

Tucker House,
Centreville,
(410) 758–1623

Upper Bay Museum,
North East,
(410) 287–2675

Washington College,
Chestertown,
(410) 778–2800

Waterman's Museum,
Rock Hall,
(410) 778–6697 or
(800) 506–6697,
www.havenharbour.com/hhwarmus.html

Wicomico Heritage Center,
Salisbury,
(410) 860–0447,
www.skipjack.net/le_shore.whs

William B. Mullins Education Center, Smith Island, (410) 968–1902

Wright's Chance, Centreville, (410) 643–8908

Wye Island National Resources Management Area, Queenstown, (410) 827–7577, www.dnr.state.md.us

Calendar of Annual Events on the Eastern Shore

February

National Outdoor Show, *Golden Hill, (410) 228–5413*

March

Artists of the Chesapeake, *Centreville, (410) 758–2520*

Elkton Salutes St. Patrick, *Elkton, (410) 398–1528*

St. Patrick's Day Parade and Festival, *Ocean City, (410) 289–6156*

April

Delmarva Birding Weekend, *throughout Eastern Shore, (800) 852–0335*

Main Street Stroll, *Elkton, (410) 398–1528*

Martinak Spring Fest, *Denton, (410) 820–1668*

Maryland Archaeology Month, *statewide, (410) 514–7661*

MD International Kite Festival, *Ocean City, (410) 289–7855*

Nanticoke River Shad Festival, *Vienna, (410) 873–2102*

Oxford Day, *Oxford, (410) 226–5730*

Salisbury Dogwood Festival, *Salisbury, (410) 749–0144*

Spocott Windmill Day, *Lloyds, (410) 228–7090*

Spring Festival, *Centreville, (410) 758–9933 or (410) 482–7579*

War World Championship Wildfowl Carving, *Ocean City, (410) 742–4988, ext. 106*

May

Antique Aircraft Fly–in, *Cambridge, (410) 228–5530*

Bridge Walk Rendezvous, *Stevensville, (410) 643–8530*

Chestertown Tea Party Festival, *Chestertown, (410) 778–0416*

Colonial Highland Gathering and Scottish Games, *Elkton, (302) 453–8998*

Kent Island Days, *Stevensville, (410) 643–5969*

May Fair, *Wye Mills, (410) 827–8484*

Memorial Day Weekend, *Berlin, (410) 641–4775*

Memorial Day Street Fest, *Elkton, (410) 398–4999*

Mid-Atlantic Maritime Festival, *Talbot, (410) 745–2916*

Native American Heritage and Pow Wow, *Marion, (410) 623–8329*

Springfest, *Ocean City, (410) 250–0125*

White Marlin Boardwalk Parade and Craft Festival, *Ocean City, (410) 289–1413*

June

Bay Country Music Festival, *Centreville, (410) 604–2100*

Berlin Village Fair, *Berlin, (410) 641–4775*

Crumpton Garden Tour and Auction, *Crumpton, (410) 928–3860*

Calendar of Annual Events on the Eastern Shore (Cont'd)

Cypress Festival, *Pocomoke, (410) 957–1919*

Elkton: Marriage Capital of the World, *Elkton, (410) 398–7007*

Galena Art Festival, *Galena, (410) 648–6959*

Lawn Fete, *Centreville, (410) 758–0143*

North East Flag Day Ceremony, *North East, (410) 287–5801*

Queen Anne's County Waterman's Festival, *Grasonville, (410) 827–8861 or (410) 827–0691*

Rock Hall Annual Rockfish Tournament, *Rock Hall, (410) 639–2662*

Tilghman Island Seafood Festival, *Tilghman, (410) 886–2677*

Tuckahoe Triathlon, *Tuckahoe State Park, (410) 820–1668*

July

Annual July Fourth Extravaganza and Fireworks, *Elkton, (410) 398–4999*

Bay Country Festival, *Cambridge, (410) 228–7762*

Caroline County Fair, *Denton, (410) 479–4030*

Chestertown Fireworks, *Chestertown, (410) 778–0500*

Fourth of July Fireworks Jubilee, *Ocean City, (410) 250–0125 or (800) OC–OCEAN, www.ocean-city.com*

Greek Festival, *Ocean City, (410) 524–0990 or (800) OC–OCEAN, www.ocean-city.com*

Independence Day Celebration, *Queenstown, (410) 604–2100*

J. Millard Tawes Crab and Clam Bake, *Crisfield, (410) 968–2500 or (800) 782–3913, www.skipjack.net/le_shore/visitsomerset*

Kent County Fair, *Chestertown, (410) 778–0767, www.kentcounty.com*

North East Water Festival, *North East, (410) 392–0155*

Ocean City Tuna Tournament, *Ocean City, (410) 213–1121*

Ocean Waiter/Waitress Charity Cup Race, *Ocean City, (410) 250–5512*

Rock Hall Fireworks and Fourth of July Celebration, *Rock Hall, (410) 778–0146, www.kentcounty.com*

Rock Hall Log Canoe Regatta, *Rock Hall, (410) 810–0707 or (800) 380–8614*

Sassafras Boat Parade, *Galena, (410) 648–5510*

Talbot County Fair, *Easton, (410) 822–1244*

August

Beach Polka Party, *Ocean City, (410) 524–6440*

Betterton Day Parade, *Betterton, (410) 788–0416*

Caroline Summerfest, *Denton, (410) 479–3721*

Celebrate Taneytown Festival, *Taneytown, (410) 751–1100, www.ci.taneytown.md.us*

Crab Feast and Seafood Festival Parade, *Port Deposit, (410) 378–5786*

Crab Days, *St. Michaels, (410) 745–2916*

Dorchester Chamber Seafood Feast-i-val, *Cambridge, (410) 228–3575*

Great Pocomoke Fair, *Pocomoke City, (410) 957–1919, www.pocomoke.com*

National Hard Crab Derby and Fair, *Crisfield, (410) 968–2500 or (800) 782–3913, www.skipjack.net/le_shore/visitsomerset*

Calendar of Annual Events on the Eastern Shore (Cont'd)

Peach Festival, *Stevensville, (410) 643–1650*

Rock Hall's Party on the Bay, *Rock Hall, (410) 778–5327, www.rockhallme.com*

Queen Anne's County Fair, *Centreville, (410) 758–0267*

Wesley Chapel Annual Fish Fry, *Rock Hall, (410) 778–6046*

Wheat Threshing, Steam and Gas Engine Show, *Federalsburg, (410) 754–8422*

White Marlin Open, *Ocean City, (410) 289–9229 or (800) OC–OCEAN, www.whitemarlinopen.com*

Worcester County Fair, *Snow Hill, (410) 632–1972*

Wye Field Day, *Queenstown, (410) 827–8056*

September

African-American Heritage Festival, *Berlin, (410) 641–3255*

Annual Benefit Boat Auction, *St. Michaels, (410) 745–2916*

Autumn in Delmar Country Craft Fair, *Delmar, (410) 228–6645 or (800) 239–6645*

Beachcomber Fun Run, *Ocean City, (410) 289–6834*

Berlin Fiddlers' Convention, *Berlin, (410) 641–4775*

Candlelight Walking Tour of Chestertown, *Chestertown, (410) 778–3499*

Chestertown Jazz Festival, *Chestertown, (410) 348–5528*

Delmarva Birding Weekend, *throughout Eastern Shore, (800) 852–0335*

Eastern Shore Fall Festival Championship Jousting Tournament, *Ridgely (410) 482–2176*

Fall Festival, *Elkton, (410) 392–2743*

Johnny Appleseed Festival, *Elkton, (410) 398–1349*

Kent Island Cup/Maryland Outrigger Challenge, *Chester, (410) 643–1306 or (410) 544–3804*

Labor Day Concert, *Ocean City, (800) OC–OCEAN, www.ocean-city.com*

Maryland State Surfing Championships, *Ocean City, (410) 213–0515*

Maryland Coast Day, *Berlin, (410) 629–1538 or (410) 213–BAYS*

Maryland State Surfing Championships, *Ocean City, (410) 213–0515*

Nause Waiwash Annual Native American Festival, *Cambridge, (410) 376–3889*

Old Queen Anne Days, *Centreville, (410) 758–1419 or (410) 758–0979*

Pemberton Colonial Fair, *Salisbury, (410) 548–4900*

Polkamotion-By-The-Ocean, *Ocean City, (410) 787–8675*

Port Deposit Heritage Day, *Port Deposit, (410) 378–2121*

Rock Hall Fallfest, *Rock Hall, (410) 778–0416 www.kentcounty.com*

Scorchy Tawes Pro-Am Fishing Tournament, *Crisfield, (410) 968–2500 or (800) 782–3913, www.skipjack.net/le_shore/visitsomerset*

Sunfest Kite Festival, *Ocean City, (410) 289–7855*

Sunfest, *Ocean City, (410) 250–0125*

Traditional Boat Festival, *St. Michaels, (410) 745–2916*

Tuckahoe Outlaw Days, *Denton, (410) 479–1183*

Calendar of Annual Events on the Eastern Shore (Cont'd)

Wetlands Fest, *Grasonville, (410) 827–6694*

Yesterdays, *North East, (410) 287–2658*

October

Autumn Walk at Leaf Thyme, *Elkton, (410) 398–5566*

Berlin Fall Festival, *Berlin, (410) 641–1064*

Chesapeake Celtic Festival, *Snow Hill, (410) 632–2032, www.furnacetown.cib.net*

Chestertown Wildlife Show, *Chestertown, (410) 778–0416*

Eastern Shore Seafood Fun Fest, *Wye Mills, (410) 643–8530, www.qacchamber.com*

Elkton Halloween Parade and Pumpkin Carving Contest, *Elkton, (410) 398–0550*

Fall Fest, *Denton, (410) 820–1668*

Ghost Walk, *Chesapeake City, (410) 885–2025*

Harvest Festival, *North East, (410) 287–2658*

Halloween Haunted Hayride, *Ridgely, (410) 634–2847, www.bluecrab.org/adkins*

Haunted House, *North East, (410) 287–5333*

J. Millard Tawes Oyster and Bull Road, *Crisfield, (410) 968–2501*

Martinak Fall Fest, *Denton, (410) 820–1668*

Mid-Atlantic Small Craft Festival, *St. Michaels, (410) 745–2916*

Mule Show, *Powellville, (410) 352–5779*

Ocean City Oktoberfest, *Ocean City, (410) 524–6440*

Olde Princess Anne Days, *Princess Anne, (410) 543–2100 or (800) 521–9189*

Queen Anne's County Seafood Funfest, *Stevensville, (410) 643–8530*

Rock Hall Fallfest, *Rock Hall, (410) 639–7943*

Seaside 10/5K Run, *Ocean City, (410) 250–0125 or (800) OC–OCEAN, www.ocean-city.com*

Tilghman Island Day, *Tilghman, (410) 886–2677*

Upper Shore Decoy Show, *North East, (410) 287–2675*

U.S. Offshore Powerboat Race, *Ocean City, (410) 289–2800 or (800) OC–OCEAN*

Wye Grist Mill Day, *Wye Mills, (410) 822–1910*

November

Christmas in Delmar Country Craft Faire, *Delmar, (410) 228–6645 or (800) 239–6645*

Day Basket Factory Open House, *North East, (410) 287–6100 or (800) 382–3105*

Festival of Trees, *Easton, (410) 819–FEST*

Festival of Trees, *Chestertown, (410) 778–0845*

Festival of Trees, *Salisbury, (410) 546–2241 or (800) 734–0300*

OysterFest, *St. Michaels, (410) 745–2916, www.cbmm.org*

Pocomoke City Parade, *Pocomoke City, (410) 957–1919*

Waterfowl Festival, *Easton, (410) 822–4567, www.waterfowlfest.org*

Winterfest of Light, *Ocean City, (410) 250–0125, www.ocean-city.com*

December

Candlelight Tour of Historic Homes and Churches, *Quantico, (410) 548–1930 or (410) 546–1557*

Calendar of Annual Events on the Eastern Shore (Cont'd)

Centreville Christmas Parade, *Centreville, (410) 758–1180*

Crumpton Candlelight House Tour, *Crumpton, (410) 928–5514*

Nineteenth Century Candlelight House and Walking Tour, *Chesapeake City, (410) 885–5377*

Ocean City Parade, *Ocean City, (410) 524–9000*

Delaware

The ***Delmarva Peninsula*** has always been DelMarVa to me, for DELaware, MARyland and VirginiA. It would never have occurred to me to question whether it should have or at some other time might have been VaMarDel or MarVa-Del or some other variation of the three states. Wade B. Fleetwood, who wrote a column about the people and places of the Eastern Shore, did question it, and now so have I. We have drawn no conclusion. It could be from north to south, or alphabetical, or political. I don't know. The only positive thing my research has given me is that it was referred to as that as early as 1870 when the fourteen counties of the Eastern Shore (three in Delaware, nine in Maryland, and two in Virginia) were discussing separate statehood. Why fight tradition?

Trivia

British captain Samuel Argall landed in a sheltered bay off the Atlantic Ocean during a ferocious storm in 1610. He named the bay De La Warr, after Thomas West, the third Baron of De La Warr and the governor of Virginia, a man who never had and never would step foot in the state. The name was shortened to Delaware and applied to the river that feeds the bay, and to the Native Americans who lived there.

So, if the Delaware of Delmarva comes first, why does this book list Maryland first? Because. *Maryland: Off the Beaten Path* was here first, and it wasn't until the third edition that it expanded its scope.

Trivia

Delaware is the second smallest state in the nation (Rhode Island is the smallest). It is about half the size of Los Angeles (Calif.) County.

Poor Delaware is just too tiny to claim its own volume. I know, someone out there is bound to say, "Well, all of Delaware is off the beaten path," and to a great extent that is very deliciously true. Nancy Sawin, a famed Delaware illustrator, has caught the state and the peninsula in many of her books. Her books can be difficult to find, but they're a treasure of information about everything from outhouses to swamps to lighthouses.

Despite Delaware's diminutive size, the Delaware Estuary is the major staging area for 80 percent of the snow geese in the Atlantic Flyway. Delaware also is known as the state without sales tax, and there are a

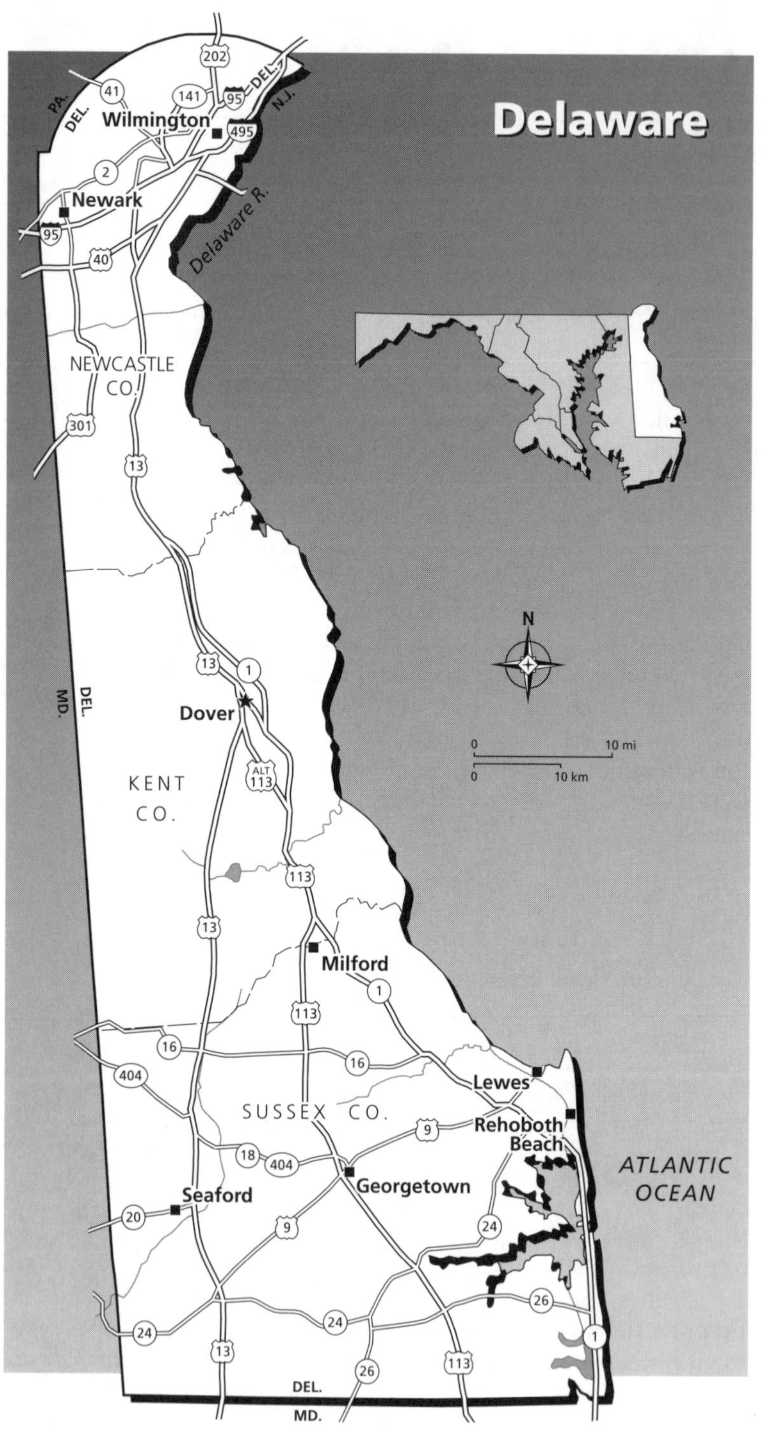

Delaware
PA.
DEL.
N.J.
DEL.
Wilmington
Newark
Delaware R.
NEWCASTLE CO.
MD.
DEL.
Dover
KENT CO.
Milford
Lewes
Rehoboth Beach
SUSSEX CO.
Georgetown
Seaford
ATLANTIC OCEAN
N
0
10 mi
0
10 km
DEL.
MD.

Judy's Favorite Attractions in Delaware

Delaware Agricultural Museum and Village

Dover Air Force Base

Trap Pond State Park

Zwaanendael Museum

number of outlet stores and malls, particularly at Rehoboth Beach (what else are you to do besides shop on a rainy day during your vacation?). For outlet information, call (888) SHOP–333 or visit www.shoprehoboth.com.

Everywhere you turn in Delaware there's a delightful treasure, whether it's watching children getting on a school bus, eyes and bodies filled with excitement and anticipation, or the changing song patterns of rain falling pitter patter on the car roof, interrupted by the overhanging trees dropping huge glops of water. The scenic ponds created to supply energy to the dozens of grist- and lumber mills are too perfect to be captured by mere artists or mere words. They have to be experienced firsthand. And the friendliness of everyone you meet is too precious to appreciate in one visit. You may have to move to Delaware and spend a lifetime in this Small Wonder and the First State (to ratify the Constitution).

New Castle County

Starting from the north of Delaware, we begin in Wilmington, the largest city in the state, and branch out and then south. Wilmington was laid out in 1731 by Quakers and was an important shipping center. Early in the 1800s, Eleuthère Irenée du Pont and his two sons moved into the area and, seeing the abundant waterpower potential, started their gunpowder business. Their influence on the development of the city and surrounding area can not be overstated. Eventually the du Ponts would be responsible for building public schools and creating some of the most incredible museums and museum settings.

Trivia

Delaware is also known as the Diamond State, because it was considered a "jewel" among states due to its strategic location.

Draped on either side of the Brandywine Creek that runs from the heart of Wilmington are Brandywine, Alapocas, and Rockford Parks. ***Brandywine Park*** was designed by Frederick Law Olmsted, creator of New York City's Central Park and the National Zoo in Washington, D.C. There's a playground here, a zoo, and the Josephine Garden, with its Japanese cherry trees. The park is open daily from dawn to dusk, with the zoo open from 10:00 A.M. to 4:00 P.M. There's no admission fee for the park, but between April and October the zoo is $3.00 for adults and $1.50 for those over sixty-one and between the ages of three and eleven.

Trivia

Downtown Wilmington, near the Amtrak station, is the site of a Wyland mural. Wyland was born in 1956 in Detroit, Michigan, and saw his first grey whales migrating off the California coast when he was fourteen. He started painting whales and dolphins when he was sixteen. By 1974 he had painted his first mural, an Alps mountain scene in Royal Oak, Michigan. The Wilmington painting, called Whaling Wall XLIV, Marine Mammals, *was done in 1993. It's located between Shipley and Market Streets on Martin Luther King Boulevard.*

It's free the rest of the year. The park is located at 1001 North Park Drive, Wilmington 19802. Call (302) 571–7747.

A little farther north is the ***Delaware Art Museum,*** with one of the country's most important assemblages of English pre-Raphaelite paintings in the Bancroft collection. American artists also are represented, and a hands-on section is great for children to learn about art.

Located at 2301 Kentmere Parkway, Wilmington 19806, the museum is open Tuesday through Saturday 9:00 A.M. to 4:00 P.M., until 9:00 P.M. on Wednesday, Sunday noon to 4:00 P.M. The museum is closed on New Year's Day, Thanksgiving, and Christmas. The admission for adults is $5.00; seniors over sixty, $3.00; and students with identification, $2.50. There's no admission fee after 4:00 P.M. on Wednesday or from 9:00 A.M. to noon on Saturday. Call (302) 571–9590 or visit www.delart.mus.de.us.

There are other special places to visit, and the ***Hagley Museum*** is one of them. Set on 240 landscaped acres at the original DuPont mills on Route 141 North, there are numerous exhibits showing the maturation of this country's economic growth.

When you consider how explosive gunpowder is, you can look at the architecture and design of the mills with great appreciation. The three side walls farthest from the water were made of heavy stone. The side wall along the creek was made of wood. When the inevitable explosion took place, it would blow out the less-sturdy wooden wall into the creek. This prevented the force of the explosion from blowing out walls that would have otherwise damaged nearby buildings.

The Hagley is open daily 9:30 A.M. to 4:30 P.M. from mid-March to December 30, and weekends 9:30 A.M. to 4:30 P.M. the rest of the year. The Hagley is closed Thanksgiving, Christmas, and New Year's Eve. Admission is $9.75 for adults,

Trivia

The Blue Hen chicken was adopted as Delaware's state bird on April 14, 1939, but its history as a symbol of the state dates from Revolutionary War days. The men of Capt. Jonathan Caldwell's company, recruited from Kent County, brought their fighting game chickens with them, and when the men weren't fighting the enemy they amused themselves with cock fights. The reputation for the tenacity of the cocks in their fights spread throughout the army, and the men of Delaware, equally tenacious, were compared to the fighting Blue Hens.

$7.50 for seniors and students, and $3.50 for children. A family rate is available at $26.50. Call (302) 658–2400 or log on to www.hagleylib.de.us.

Trivia

Wilmington was a major iron- and steel-working center where the entire suspended superstructure of the Brooklyn Bridge was manufactured.

Next to the Hagley is the ***Delaware Toy and Miniature Museum,*** with more than one hundred dollhouses and rooms, antiques, and newly crafted miniatures, which document European and American history from the eighteenth century forward. Within the collection are dolls, toys, trains, boats, and planes. Among the features are toys by Bliss, Hubley, Ives, A. C. Gilbert, Schoenhut, and McLoughlin. A permanent Victorian Christmas parlor is a particularly nostalgic scene, even if you never experienced one. There's no better way to connect the generations than by discussing the reminiscences of earlier times as prompted by the Nuremberg kitchens, the dollhouses, and period toys. If you like art in miniature, this is the place to visit.

A reference library and, of course, a museum sales shop are available for the incurable (myself included).

The Toy and Miniature Museum is located on Route 141. Admission is $5.00 for adults, $4.00 for those who are sixty-two and older, and $3.00 for those younger than thirteen. Reservations are required for a guided tour. The museum is open Tuesday through Saturday from 10:00 A.M. to 4:00 P.M. and Sunday from noon to 4:00 P.M. It is closed on Monday. (302) 427–TOYS (8697) or log on to www.thomes.net/toys.

Hockessin is a delightful little town just outside of Wilmington. As noted earlier, one of the pleasures of the Delmarva is the chance to pick up a Nancy Sawin book; she's done at least eleven, including *Delaware Sketchbook, Backroading Through Cecil* (MD) *County, Between the Bays* (Delaware and Chesapeake), and even one on outhouses entitled *Privy to the Council Seats of Yore,* with sketches of a variety of "necessary" buildings, from lean-tos and Alpine chalets to one that was fenced and shingled and one that had four columns on its porch.

Trivia

Locals who jog through Hockessin know there's an old gardener on Evanson Road who has nailed a basket to a tree on his property that is right next to the road. Every summer day there are fresh tomatoes, zucchini, chilis, and various other delights for any passersby to grab.

One of my great delights is driving through the state and trying to spot the objects Ms. Sawin has drawn. Sawin was born in Wilmington in 1917, and when she retired in 1974 from a life in education, she started writing and illustrating books on local history. Her home is adjacent to Sandford School, where she had been teacher, coach, and headmistress. She

Trivia

Old Swedes Church in Wilmington, built in 1698, is the oldest Protestant church still in use in the United States. The pipe organ was built by the Austin Company of Hartford, Connecticut, and has sixteen stops and sixteen ranks of pipe, for a total of 913 pipes.

refers to her home as a "semimuseum of early Americana," and some of the items therein are for sale.

Visitors are welcome, but please call first. Nancy C. Sawin, 147 Sawin Lane, Hockessin 19707; (302) 239–2416.

As you're driving around this area you may want to try the ***Back Burner*** restaurant. They have delicious seafood and meat entrees and friendly and attentive service. It's a small space, and people from Wilmington make a special drive "to the country" for the food. The Back Burner is at 425 Old Lancaster Pike, Hockessin 19707; (302) 239–2314.

A little north of Wilmington is the anomaly of modern government known as ***Arden***. It was one of three towns (along with Ardentown and Ardencroft, which would come later) created under the principles conceived by Philadelphia-born economist Henry George and his Theory of Single Tax. Born in 1839, George proposed that land only should be taxed, thereby creating the concept of the "single tax." Thus, in 1895 a group of single taxers from Philadelphia invaded Delaware with their political evangelism. Frank Stephens, a Philadelphia sculptor, with the help of architect Will Price and soap manufacturer Joseph Fels, acquired a Brandywine farm of 160 acres and started the village of Arden. It continues to this day as a single-tax entity.

Trivia

The only Revolutionary War battle fought in Delaware was the Battle of Cooch's Bridge (east of Newark), on September 3, 1777. It's said the new thirteen-star flag was first unfurled during this battle, a delaying action to slow the British advance toward Philadelphia. The area in which the Battle of Cooch's Bridge took place can be seen from a 90-foot observation tower in Iron Hill Park, west of SR 896 via Welsh Tract Road or Old Baltimore Pike in Newark.

Utopian in nature, the community also incorporated the artistic ideas of William Morris and the Arts and Crafts Movement, the Garden Cities planning ideas of Ebenezer Howard, and some social theories of Petr Alekseevich Kropotkin (1842–1921). Many of the homes are tiny, for they were summer places, but there definitely is a mix of new and old, fancy and ramshackle, set on lots of various sizes.

The three villages are surrounded by woodlands, including the Naaman's Creek natural area, designated as one of "Delaware's Outstanding Natural Areas." There are two things that drive the residents of Arden: the Arden Club and the Arden Community Recreation Association. Music, dance, theater, visual arts, and such crafts as pottery and ironwork are still highly valued in the three Ardens.

There is not much for the tourist to "see" in the way of historic buildings or museums, so you have to look at their activities calendar, scheduling your visit for the contra dancing/square dancing every month, the Arden Fair (the Saturday before Labor Day), the Shakespearean productions (*Merchant of Venice* and *Comedy of Errors* were presented recently) in the little (130-seat) outdoor theater on the Arden Green, and the Candlelight Music Dinner Theater in Ardentown that has shows throughout the year. Call (302) 475–2313 for information.

Trivia

Iron Hill, just south of Newark, is the home of one of the highest hills in the state (which isn't saying much). On a clear day, from the top of the Iron Hill Tower, you can see four states: New Jersey, Pennsylvania, Maryland, and, of course, Delaware.

Old New Castle, a section of New Castle, is filled with colonial-era homes and buildings that the Rockefeller Foundation initially wanted to restore as a living museum of colonial America. However, the locals raised such a fuss that the Rockefellers went to Williamsburg, Virginia, instead. Rather than reconstructing the history represented at Williamsburg, New Castle exudes the past from every brick and slather of mortar. It was here that William Penn set foot in North America for the first time. From those Quaker beginnings, the town became a trade center through shipping. A disastrous fire leveled the business area in 1824, but the town was restored when the railroad came through less than a decade later. The railroad was later rerouted into Wilmington, and the town has sat there ever since.

Among the houses that are open for your inspection and journey into the past are the Amstel House, the Dutch House, and the George Read II House and garden. You can also tour the restored Court House, or just spend a lazy afternoon on the green.

The ***Amstel House*** dates from the 1730s and was the home of colonial governor Nicholas Van Dyke. The furnishings show how life was during the colonial period, and includes a complete colonial kitchen. Yeah, we know George Washington was everywhere, and that includes attending a wedding here. Amstel House is at Fourth and Delaware Streets, New Castle 19720, and it's closed in January and February. (302) 322–2794.

In the ***Dutch House*** you are touring what is thought to be the oldest brick house in Delaware. Constructed in the late seventeenth century, it has been restored and contains wonderful decorative arts and historical items. It's located at 32 East Third Street, New Castle 19720; (302) 322–2794.

Trivia

New Castle was the original state capital of Delaware. In 1777 Dover was named the new capital. Delaware is one of four states in the country in which the initial letter of the capital is the same as the initial letter of the state. The others are Honolulu, Hawaii; Indianapolis, Indiana; and Oklahoma City, Oklahoma.

Both the Amstel and Dutch Houses are open March through December, Tuesday through Saturday 11:00 A.M. to 4:00 P.M. and Sunday 1:00 to 4:00 P.M. They're open on weekends the rest of the year but closed on holidays. Admission to each is $2.00 for adults and $1.00 for children under twelve, or you can get a combination ticket for $3.50 for adults and $1.50 for children.

George Read was one of the signers of the Declaration of Independence and the U.S. Constitution, and his son's home, called the ***George Read II House,*** was built over a seven-year period starting in 1797. It's a superb illustration of Federal-style architecture. Note the carved woodwork, fanlights, silver door hardware, and period furnishings as you tour through the twelve rooms (three of which are in the Colonial Revival style). A Philadelphia-style adaptation of a Victorian garden, designed in 1847, decorates the side and back yards. You have a choice of touring this home on your own or calling for an appointment for a guided tour. If you have the time, I recommend the latter.

March through December the George Read II House, at 42 The Strand, New Castle 19720, is open Tuesday through Saturday 10:00 A.M. to 4:00 P.M. and Sunday noon to 4:00 P.M. It's open on weekends in the winter but closed on holidays. The admission is $4.00 for adults, $3.50 for seniors and children thirteen to twenty-one, and $2.00 for children six to twelve. Call (302) 322–8411 or log on to www.hsd.org.

Surely you've noted that the top of the Delaware border, where it meets Pennsylvania, is the arc of a circle. The spire at the top of the ***New Castle Court House*** is the center point of the 12-mile radius that marks that arc. Although New Castle was the colonial capital of Delaware from 1732 to 1777, the courthouse is now restored to its 1804 appearance. Flags of the Netherlands, Sweden, Great Britain, and the United States represent the various governments that have had jurisdiction over New Castle.

Located at 211 Delaware Street, New Castle 19720, between Market and Third Streets, it's open Tuesday through Saturday 10:00 A.M. to 3:30 P.M. and Sunday 1:30 to 4:30 P.M.; closed on state holidays. There is no admission charge. Call (302) 323–4453 or (800) 441–8846.

If there's time, stop by the hexagon-shaped ***Old Library Museum*** (40 East Third Street, New Castle 19270; 302–322–2794), the Old Presbyterian Church, and the Original Ticket Office. Then reward yourself with a picnic stop at the green. Located on Delaware Street, between Third and Market Streets, it was laid out by Peter Stuyvesant in 1655.

For additional information write to the Wilmington Convention and Visitors Bureau, 1300 Market Street, Suite 504, Wilmington 19801, or call (302) 652–4088. You can also contact the New Castle Visitors Bureau, Box 465, New Castle 19720; (302) 322–8411 or (800) 748–1550.

On your way south on U.S. 1, you'll cross the Chesapeake and Delaware Canal at St. Georges on a bridge opened on December 23, 1995. Called the "relief route," the new U.S. 1 will extend from Tybouts Corner on the northern end to the Frederica/Felton area south of Dover. The bridge is a six-lane cable-stayed design. Lead engineer W. Denney Pate's previous cable-stayed bridges include the Sunshine Skyway in Tampa, Florida, Varina Enon bridge near Richmond, Virginia, Cochrane Bridge in Mobile, Alabama, and the Neches River bridge near Port Arthur, Texas.

Trivia

The Delaware State Seal was adopted on January 17, 1777, and contains the coat of arms. It also shows a farmer, corn, and a wheat sheaf (signifying the agricultural vitality of the state), a ship (symbolizing New Castle County's shipbuilding industry), a militiaman with his musket (honoring the role of the citizen-soldier in the maintenance of American liberties), an ox (representing animal husbandry), and water (for the Delaware River).

Kent County

Kent, the middle of the three Delaware counties, has Dover as its focus. This is the home of the Dover Air Force Base and some Amish families (with their attendant farmers markets and horse-drawn buggies); it is also the county seat. It's a hubbub of activity and constant change. Here you'll also find such unusually named places as Slaughter Beach, Seven Hickories, Dutch Neck Crossroads, and Little Heaven and an abundance of protected open spaces where you can explore what nature has left for you and the people of Delaware have kept protected for you.

Some of the information presented here is thumbnail in nature because it's easy to find your way around such places as Dover; other areas are a little more difficult to uncover and receive a bit more attention.

Trivia

"Woodburn," the official home of Delaware's governors, was built in 1790–1791 by Charles Hillyard and is considered one of the finest Middle Period Georgian homes in the state. Prior to being purchased by the state in 1965, the home was owned by an abolitionist, two U.S. Senators, three doctors, and a judge. It is located at 151 Kings Highway, Dover 19901; (302) 739–5656.

The town of ***Smyrna*** is pretty small, but it is growing. At the moment there's no department store, and a few other "big town" conveniences are missing. But the town's charm more than makes up for what it lacks. Actually, Smyrna is a historic town that straddles the two counties of New Castle and Kent. The line of demarcation is Duck Creek, located on the north side of the town.

On the south side of Smyrna, ***Lake Como*** (with a freshwater beach) is a beautiful, small lake surrounded by houses with well-manicured yards and the Delaware Home and Hospital. As one local said, "If I focus [into the past], I can see children playing with buckets and shovels in the sand, moms and dads and older kids in striped woolen swimwear walking on the beach, swimming in the cool waters, and diving off the end of the pier."

Trivia

Because of Delaware's liberal incorporation laws, more than half the country's Fortune 500 *companies have filed incorporation papers in the state.*

East of Smyrna, is an area that grew from the fur trapping and shipping trades of the early nineteenth century. You'll enjoy a visit here if you stop by the nearly 16,000-acre ***Bombay Hook National Wildlife Refuge,*** where you're sure to spot plenty of ducks, geese, and shorebirds during migrating season (more than one and a half million shorebirds traverse Delaware in the annual migration in late May and early June) and other wildlife year-round. More than 256 species of birds, 33 species of animals, and 37 species of reptiles and amphibians inhabit the refuge.

You can drive along the 12-mile loop or hike on the nature trails and climb the observation towers for a panoramic view. The refuge is open daily from dawn to dusk, and a visitors center is open daily during summer and on weekdays during winter. The admission to the refuge is $4.00 per private vehicle or $2.00 if you're on foot or coming in by bike. Those over age sixty-one and passengers with a Golden Age Passport or Duck Pass are free. The refuge is at 2591 Whitehall Neck Road, Smyrna 19977. (302) 653–6872.

The ***State House*** in Dover is the second oldest continuously used statehouse (the one in Annapolis, Maryland, is first). This restored 1792 structure has period furnishings and an exhibit of artifacts and historical items. Included in the tour is information about legislative and judicial activities, and how these actions affected the population, including slaves and free blacks. Guided thirty-minute tours upon demand are available between 10:00 A.M. and 4:30 P.M. Tuesday through Saturday and

1:30 to 4:30 P.M. on Sunday. The State House is located at South State Street, on the east side of the green. The entrance is at 406 Federal Street, Dover 19901. There is no admission charge. (302) 739–4266.

Free guided tours start from the Delaware Visitor Center and the private, nonprofit ***Sewell C. Biggs Museum of American Art,*** which is located behind the statehouse. Biggs, a native of Middletown, collected art from the eighteenth century to modern times and donated it to this museum, which is named in his honor. This building is made of brick and cast iron and was one of the first fireproof buildings in the state.

The Biggs Museum, 406 Federal Street, Dover 19903, is open Wednesday through Saturday from 10:00 A.M. to 4:00 P.M. and Sunday from 1:30 to 4:30 P.M. (302) 674–2111; www.biggsmuseum.org.

If you're at the State House, then you're in the ***Capital Green***, which was laid out in 1722. It is lined with historic buildings and is the very ground upon which the United States Constitution received its first signature in 1787. From here, Delaware's Continental Regiment mustered for the Revolutionary War, and from here they marched to join Washington's army. Political rallies still are held here, and in May there's Old Dover Days, with many private homes and buildings open to the public. If you're taking a guided tour, be sure to ask your leader about the woman who sent poisoned candy to her lover's family, resulting in the death of at least one person. This isn't a modern revenge happening; it took place in the 1890s.

At the ***Hall of Records,*** near Legislative Hall, is the public archives for the state. This is where you can find the original 1682 charter of King Charles II and William Penn's order for the platting of Dover.

The Hall of Records is at Legislative Avenue and Duke of York Street, Dover 19901; no charge. It's open Monday through Friday from 8:30 A.M. to 4:15 P.M. Closed on holidays. Call (302) 739–5314.

While in Dover, a must stop—if you're a fan of the TV show *Homicide* or other police-based shows, or your reading preferences tend toward procedurals—is the ***Delaware State Police Museum and Education Center.*** This state-of-the-art educational facility provides an opportunity to learn the history of the Delaware State Police law enforcement methods, a look at a 911 command and control console, and a display of uniforms and weapons. There are exhibits about substance abuse, highway safety efforts, and a variety of other important topics, with talks presented by specially trained troopers and volunteers. You can also catch a close-up view of patrol cars and motorcycles.

Trivia

The Lincoln Collection at the University of Delaware contains more than 2,000 items relating to the public and private life of Abraham Lincoln.

Located at the State Police Headquarters Complex, 1425 North DuPont Highway, Dover 19903, the museum is open Monday through Friday (except state holidays) from 11:00 A.M. to 3:00 P.M. and the third Saturday of each month. There is no admission charge. (302) 739–7700.

So, your life is filled with CDs—for music, for computer programs, and who knows what else? Your children have never even known an eight-track, much less heard of a Victrola. Now's the time to correct that. Stop by the ***Johnson Victrola Museum*** in Dover to see this tribute to Eldridge Reeves Johnson (a Delaware native who was an inventor, businessman, and philanthropist), the inventor and founder of the Victor Talking Machine Company (1901). Designed to look like a 1920s store, the museum has an extensive collection of phonographs, records, and memorabilia related to the company, including an original oil painting of Nipper, the dog who listened to "His Master's Voice."

The museum is open Tuesday through Saturday from 10:00 A.M. to 3:30 P.M. There's no admission charge (donations are accepted) to the museum, located at Bank Lane and New Street, Dover 19901. (302) 739–4266.

Go north of Dover about 2 miles and you'll see the ***Delaware Agricultural Museum and Village,*** covering 200 years of the agrarian heritage of Delaware, with dairy and poultry farming objects, horse-drawn equipment, and tractors from 1670 through the 1950s. There's a barbershop, farmhouse, general store, one-room schoolhouse, sawmill, train station, and blacksmith and wheelwright shops, all representing structures from the Civil War to the turn of the twentieth century.

Some of the programs that have been featured are "A More Abundant Life: Rural Delaware and Culture in New Deal Art," "The Ten Ton Tomato Club and Other Tales," and "Christmas on the Farm." Special events include "Fall Harvest Festival" and "A Farmer's Christmas."

The museum and village are located at 866 North DuPont Highway, Dover 19901. They're open Tuesday through Saturday 10:00 A.M. to 4:00 P.M. and Sunday 1:00 to 4:00 P.M. April through December. The rest of the year they're open Monday through Friday from 10:00 A.M. to 4:00 P.M. Closed on holidays. Admission fees are $3.00 for adults, $2.00 for seniors sixty and older and for children from six to seventeen. Call (302) 734–1618.

Head south of Dover about 4 miles if aviation is your passion. One of the more exciting places to visit is the ***Dover Air Force Base,*** particularly during the open house dates. That's when you'll see dozens of C5As or the C-5 Galaxy. Community Appreciation Days are held on the third Saturday of each month April through November, and some of the special exhibitions include a fire attack on an aircraft by the base fire department, an explosive ordnance robot demonstration, a security police K-9 demonstration, and a silent drill team (probably my favorite). The Aero club offers low-cost airplane rides.

Trivia

Each C5A or C-5 Galaxy, the largest cargo airplane in the world, at Dover Air Force Base is big enough to hold several football fields.

I know you've seen a lot of historic buildings around here, but this may be the first time you've seen a World War II hangar that's listed on the National Register of Historic Places. It was the site of the Army Air Force's rocket test center and is now the home of the ***Air Mobility Command Museum.***

Also on display at the museum is a collection of vintage planes from 1941, including a C-47 Gooney Bird and a B-17G. Other World War II artifacts also are on display.

The museum is open daily 9:00 A.M. to 4:00 P.M. and is closed on federal holidays. There is no admission charge. Best of all, photography is encouraged! Dover Air Force Base is on U.S. Route 113, and the museum is at 1301 Heritage Road, Dover 19902. Call (302) 677–5938 or visit www.amcmuseum.org.

South of the Air Force base is the ***John Dickinson Plantation,*** the boyhood home of John Dickinson, who in 1778 drafted the Articles of Confederation, for which he was known as the "Penman of the Revolution." His 1740s brick home and the reconstructed outbuildings are typical of eighteenth-century plantation architecture and lifestyle,

Horseshoe Crabs

The Delaware Bay area is home to the largest population of horseshoe crabs, which date from 250 million years ago. Actually related to scorpions, ticks, and land spiders, rather than crabs, they are not considered dangerous to humans. They grow when they molt (usually sixteen times until they become full-size adults), increasing in size by about one-fourth each time. During the high tides of the new and full moon, in the spring, thousands of horseshoe crabs descend on the Delaware Bay shoreline to spawn. Horseshoe crab eggs are important food for migratory shorebirds passing over the Delaware Bay during the spring mating season.

Trivia

Swedish immigrants built the first log cabins in America in Delaware, in 1638.

with the added benefit that the home is furnished with family pieces and period antiques.

March through December it is open Tuesday through Saturday 10:00 A.M. to 3:30 P.M. and Sunday 1:30 to 4:30 P.M.; free tours are available during those hours. It is closed on holidays. There is no admission charge. The John Dickinson Plantation is on Kitts Hammock Road, Dover 19901. Call (302) 739–3277.

Just southeast of Dover, in ***Magnolia,*** is the "town sign" that states: THIS IS MAGNOLIA, THE CENTER OF THE UNIVERSE, AROUND WHICH THE WORLD REVOLVES. Magnolia is noted as being one of those little peninsula towns that has not lost its personality in this modern age. The house you'll be looking at when you see this sign is the John B. Lindale House, a Victorian with really neat twin towers. It is a private residence, but you can still admire it.

A tribute to agriculture can be found in Harrington at the ***Messick Agricultural Museum,*** with its extensive display of farm implements of the early twentieth century. You'll see automobiles, a covered wagon, various engines, horse-drawn plows and vehicles, tools, tractors, and trucks. There's also an early-twentieth-century kitchen and smokehouse.

The museum, located at 317 Walt Messick Road, Harrington 19952, is open Monday through Friday from 7:30 A.M. to 5:00 P.M. and by appointment on weekends and holidays. There is no admission fee. (302) 398–3729.

There are a number of annual events in Harrington, including the Crab Feast in late August, Heritage Day in late September, and the Delaware State Fair in late July. This is a real old-fashioned state fair that still has strong agricultural roots and has not been "citified."

For additional information contact the Kent County Tourism Corporation, 9 East Lockerman Street, Box 576, Dover 19903, (302) 734–1736, or the Delaware Tourism Office, 99 Kings Highway, Box 1401, Dover 19903, (302) 734–1736.

Sussex County

Even if you've never heard of Sussex County, you've most likely heard of Rehoboth Beach and possibly even Bethany Beach, although both are billed as "quiet resorts." They are primarily residential and have been promoted as great family vacation and residential areas.

On the south side of the Fenwick Island Lighthouse is one of the original

Transpeninsular Line Markers, which was erected on April 26, 1751. This stone marked the east end of the 70-mile-long line that connected the Atlantic Ocean to the Chesapeake Bay, denoting what was then the southern border of Pennsylvania. Those three lower counties are now Delaware. A little more than a decade later, Mason and Dixon used the midpoint of the line when they surveyed the border between Pennsylvania and Maryland. The marker is 1 block south of Delaware Routes 1 and 54. Call the Bethany–Fenwick Island Chamber of Commerce, (302) 539–8129.

The 84-foot-tall white brick ***Fenwick Island Lighthouse,*** with a Third Order Fresnel lens projecting light 15 miles into the ocean, was commissioned on August 1, 1859, to protect ships from venturing onto the treacherous shoals extending 5 to 6 miles out from the Delaware coastline. It was automated in 1940, then decommissioned in 1978. A public outcry brought about the reinstallation of the original light, weighing about 1,500 pounds, and it has been in service since then. It's at the eastern terminus of the Mason-Dixon line at the Delaware–Maryland border. There's a cluster of buildings here, the lighthouse, two keepers' dwellings (now in private ownership), storage sheds, and the tower. The light is listed on the National Register of Historic Buildings. The Coast Guard deactivated it in 1978, but the Friends of the Fenwick Island Lighthouse has maintained it.

The lighthouse, between Delaware Route 521 and 146th Street, is open to the public on selected days and by appointment. There's no admission charge, but donations are accepted. For more information call the Bethany–Fenwick Island Chamber of Commerce, (302) 539–2100.

DiscoverSea is the place to visit to view hundreds of artifacts recovered from shipwrecks along the Delmarva coastline, dating from colonial days. Dedicated to preserving our maritime heritage, the museum opened in July 1995 after more than seventeen years of research and hard work. Stop by for a visit, a lecture, or a beach tour and travel to the past via this hands-on experience.

Open daily Memorial day through Labor Day from 9:00 A.M. to 9:00 P.M. and on weekends from 10:00 A.M. to 4:00 P.M. the rest of the year. There is no admission fee to DiscoverSea, which is located at 708

Trivia

The entrance to Bethany Beach, just south of the Delaware Seashore State Park, is marked by a 26-foot Native American totem pole. This greeting to Bethany Beach was sculpted by Dennis D. Beach and installed in the spring of 1994. It replaced a carving by Peter Toth, who donated his totem in 1976. Unfortunately, Toth's totem fell victim to termites and nasty storms. Chief Little Owl, *named for a chief of the Nanticoke tribe, represents an eagle protecting an Indian by clutching him to its breast.*

Trivia

When you catch sight of a T-shirt, sweatshirt, or cap with the legend "Slower Lower Delaware," you may have difficulty tracking down who first coined this phrase. But if you want it adorning a garment, a mug, license-plate frame, gourmet coffee, and more, get to Suzie's Tavern and Restaurant in Millsboro. Loyal customers started donning them here in 1991. Suzie's is on 226 Main Street; (302) 934–8188.

Ocean Highway, Fenwick Island 19944. Call (302) 539–9366 or (888) 743–5524 for additional information or log on to www.beach-net.com/discoversea.html.

If you'd like to try your hand at ***treasure hunting*** using a metal detector, the local beaches offer a potential bonanza, or at least a short entertainment. Your find may be change, jewelry, or an ancient relic, and you're particularly likely to find something after a crowded day on the beach or after a good Nor'easter. You can rent or buy a metal detector from Sea Shell City, with rentals going for about $20 for a half day and $35 for an entire day. When searching for treasure, remember, don't trespass, cover your holes, don't go across the sand dunes, don't litter, and stay out of legally protected historic or archaeological sites. If you're really considerate and others haven't been, you'll take whatever litter you may find and dispose of it. Sea Shell City is located at 708 Ocean Highway, Ocean View 19970. Call (302) 539–9366.

As one might expect, the town of Laurel (originally Laureltown) was so named because of the abundance of laurel bushes growing along Broad Creek. Settled in 1802, the town was the largest in Sussex County by 1859 and was once a thriving shipping center and port town. With more than 800 buildings on the National Register of Historic Places, it is the largest designated historic district in the state of Delaware. Many properties

A Cool Fund-raiser

In 1997 the Bethany-Fenwick Area Chamber of Commerce started a January 1 ***"Exercise Like the Eskimos"*** *to raise funds for scholarships for area high school seniors. By 1999 they were awarding $3,000, double what was given in the past. What's involved? It's running into the Atlantic Ocean (which is about forty degrees)! This polar bear stuff has always sounded to me like a cardiologist's heaven, but that's another story. Teams and individuals are invited to participate, with entry fees of $30 and $10 , respectively. Everyone registered gets a free hat. Hot chocolate and T-shirts are sold. Mangos' Oceanfront Restaurant serves a New Year's buffet, and part of that charge benefits the scholarship. If freezing your buns off sounds like a lot of fun, call the chamber of commerce at (302) 539–2100.*

were destroyed in the "Great Fire" of 1899, but others survived. Pick up a *Walking Tour of Historic Laurel* brochure from the historical society to see some of the fascinating moments from the past.

Trivia

The first beauty contest was held in Rehoboth Beach in 1880, and Miss United States was selected, with Thomas Edison as one of the judges.

As small as Bethel and the area around it are, there are enough people to see and talk to—and even things to do and learn—that you might find ways to spend an entire day there—even a lifetime. Start with the ***Laurel-Woodland Ferry,*** more commonly called the Woodland Ferry, that crosses the Nanticoke River just as boats have done since 1793. The cable-operated ferry is the last free river ferry in Delaware. The *Virginia C.*, apparently named for the wife of a former captain, is a 65-foot diesel-powered cable-guided ferry that can carry three or four cars on its six-minute ride across the river. Operated from sunup to sundown the ferry may make up to 300 trips on a busy day, saving its passengers a road trip of nearly 20 miles.

Signs on Route 78 in Laurel and Reliance, Route 490 south of Blades, and Route 80 at Seaford indicate if the ferry is running. Call the Seaford Chamber of Commerce at (302) 629–9690 for additional information.

On the western side of the Nanticoke is the town of ***Woodland,*** with a population of about one hundred people. As the Nanticoke is known for its shad and Woodland is known for its hospitality, you might want to schedule your visit for the annual spring shad supper held by the women of the Woodland Methodist Church.

While in Bethel you'll want to stop by ***Jeff Hastings' farm market*** to buy some fresh produce. He has been known to have some spectacular seedless watermelon. And just past his place is the ***Bethel Market*** on Main Street, which has soft ice cream that's pretty good, costs less than a dollar for a cone, and is made with real milk, not the skimpy, thin, fat-free stuff. You have to time your tastes to the days of the week. According to Mark Shaver (who has been connected with this family store for sixteen years), they used to have only vanilla. Then some customers started requesting chocolate, so he did that one day a week. Then they started clamoring for more. So now it's chocolate three days a week, on Monday, Wednesday, and Friday. The rest of the week it's vanilla. Shaver says they're too poor to afford two

Trivia

Emily P. Bissell (1861–1948) created the first Christmas seals when she drew pictures on stamps in 1907. She sold the stamps to raise funds to aid tubercular children. Emily lived in Delaware and was a cousin of a doctor at a tuberculosis sanitorium in Delaware along the Brandywine River.

Trivia

On the Saturday after Labor Day, Miltonians (residents of Milton) clean out garages, attics, and closets, and the **Town-Wide Yard Sale** *takes place.*

machines to make both every day. I would add that there isn't enough room in the store for two machines.

Across Main Street is the post office, where Bettie Stoakley has been postmaster since 1980, serving 120 families. Yes, it's an old house, and as you go in you'll notice the bottom tread and riser of some stairs that used to go up to a second floor. Stoakley says it's been that way since before she arrived.

In Laurel, Milton, Ridgeville, Milford, and other places, you'll see ***murals by Jack Lewis,*** a graduate of Rutgers with a master's degree in education. You'll find them on exterior walls, in banks, in the family court in Georgetown, and even in a prison. Lewis has been teaching art in the state for thirty years, and he participated in a Fulbright Scholarship exchange program. Lewis says, he's basically a watercolorist, and murals are not his chief interest. Fortunately, he has dabbled in the area of murals, for our enjoyment. Call (302) 337–8840 for more information.

Trivia

The town of Milton, settled in 1672 by English colonists, was known by several names over the years, until 1807 when the town was named after the English poet John Milton. With 198 of its homes on the National Register of Historic Places, it's said to have the finest concentration of nineteenth-century architecture in the country. Milton once had a thriving holly industry, providing holiday wreaths to much of the nation. The state tree is the American holly.

The Laurel area is noted for at least one other bit of historical trivia. On June 21, 1904, some signals were crossed and the schooner *Golden Gate,* traveling down the nearby Broad Creek, was struck by a mail train. Luckily the train engine automatically uncoupled, so the rest of the train didn't fall into the creek. This may be the only occurrence of a train and sailing ship colliding.

The ***Spring Garden Bed and Breakfast,*** with Gwen (or Gwenie) North as your hostess, is an excellent place to use as a base for your local explorations. Her half Victorian and half colonial home has been lovingly restored and is among the buildings on the National Register of Historic Places. North's family has been in this area since the seventeenth century, and Gwen has her finger on about as much history as you'll want. She was the first winner of the Governor's State Tourism Award. There are two bedrooms downstairs and four upstairs. The gardens are particularly inviting, and Gwen grows enough herbs to offer some to her guests so they'll remember her even when they return home.

Call Spring Garden, Delaware Avenue Extension, Laurel 19956, at (302) 875–7015 or (800) 797–4909. Talk to Gwen about the ***sweet potato houses,*** and if you're really interested, she'll tell you where to see some, or she'll call Kendall Jones for you, and he'll take you on a tour.

In a nutshell, or in a potato skin if you will, the life of a sweet potato is not easy. The seeds first must be started indoors in February. Then they must be transplanted to warm beds, then to the outdoors, and then harvested and dried. Sweet potatoes apparently are horrible if eaten when freshly harvested. They'll keep all winter if they're stored at a constant fifty-degree temperature. These buildings were constructed to hold the very productive sweet potato cash crop.

The buildings are usually two to three stories tall and are long and relatively narrow. The outer walls are made of three or more layers of wood siding. On the exterior is a horizontal layer, followed by a diagonal layer in the center, and a vertical layer on the inside. All this helped to insulate the building, and sometimes a form of tar paper or sawdust was used between the layers to further insulate it. Inside are a series of bins, about 3 feet by 9 feet, where the potatoes were stored. Sometimes access to the bins was from a central aisle, sometimes from a perimeter walkway. A stove at one end had to be tended morning and night once the first frost had set in. The second and third floors did not butt against the walls; this helped ventilation and ensured an even distribution of the heat to the upper and lower floors.

Sweet potato house

A blight hit the extremely labor-intensive crop in the 1940s and destroyed the industry. Now, some of the sweet potato or potato houses have been converted into office or living space. If you'd like to just drive by one, there's an excellent example across from the old Christ Church on Route 24, about a mile east of Route 13 just south of the intersection with Route 9. It's slightly different from most sweet potato houses because of the number of windows it has, but you'll get the idea.

Gwen's Spring Garden B&B is one of three (soon to be more) on a ***Bike and Bed program***. This four-day/three-night inn-to-inn bike touring experience averages 30 to 45 miles of back-roads pedaling. You'll go through small towns and past so many antiques stores that you wish you were in a car so you could cart home some of those treasures, or be glad you're on a bike and can't buy anything. You'll also go past a bison farm. The package includes three nights' accommodation, hotel tax, luggage transportation from inn to inn, three breakfasts and three dinners, snacks at each inn on arrival, detailed maps with points of interest, and secure bike storage. Call Ambassador Travel, Laurel 19956, at (302) 875–7015 or (800) 845–9939.

Eli's Country Inn near Greenwood also participates in the program. This is a painstakingly renovated farmhouse in the country, where you literally can hear the quiet.

Two rooms downstairs are accessible, and there is plenty of room on the porches and decks for sitting around in the afternoon if you don't want to go do something. With seventy-eight-plus acres planted with soybeans, fresh fruits, and vegetables, you can also do some gardening if you want. The organ is original, and the home has a vacuum cleaner motor powering it.

The Oklahoma Connection

When you try to trace Native American bloodlines from the original residents of Delaware, you have to go to Bartlesville, Oklahoma. Yes, that's where you'll locate the headquarters of the Delaware Indians. The Delaware or Lenni Lenape were a friendly tribe who gradually gave up their lands to the new settlers. They moved westward into Pennsylvania, then Ohio, then Indiana. Some even went to Canada (still occupying two small reserves in Ontario province). By 1820 they had crossed the Mississippi River into Missouri, then Kansas, and finally moved into Indian Territory in 1866. An 1867 agreement with the Cherokees allowed them to purchase land where they now reside. The Delawares comprise approximately 10,000 people today.

Eli's Country Inn is on Route 36, Greenwood 19950-0779. Call (302) 349–4265, (800) 594– 0048, or (302) 349–9340.

Do be warned that the local Greenwood police like to park at the intersection of U.S. Route 13 and State Route 16, just waiting for out-of-state drivers to speed by.

There's no telling where you might think you are when you go through ***Trap Pond State Park.*** This 2,000-plus acre park was once part of the large freshwater swampland of southwestern Sussex County. The pond was created in the early 1800s for a sawmill that processed the bald cypress trees from the area. The park has the northernost publicly owned stand of bald cypress in the country.

In the 1930s the federal government purchased the area and the Civilian Conservation Corps developed the recreation site. Within the park are bald cypress trees, wetlands, wildflowers, wildlife, a nature preserve, a picnic area, a playground, a primitive camping area for youngsters, more than 7 miles of hiking trails, a canoe trail (perhaps the only marked canoe trail on the Eastern Shore), camping, and a rent-a-camp program that lets you rent equipment to see if you like the experience before investing in all the gear.

Birders can spy on great blue herons, owls, hummingbirds, robins, mockingbirds, cardinals, finches, warblers, bald eagles, and pileated

From POWs to Pickles

The Kendzierski family apparently owns the only known privately owned fort in the United States. Fort Saulsbury is 6 miles east of Milford, near the town of Slaughter Beach, in the northeast corner of Sussex County. Constructed in 1917 and 1918, the location was selected as protection of the mouth of the Delaware Bay and River during World War I, and the fort was named for Delaware's U.S. Senator (1859–71) and Attorney General (1850–55) Willard Saulsbury Sr. The casements were 14 feet thick, steel-reinforced concrete, with 6 feet of earth on top for camouflage. Since completion came so close to the November 1918 armistice, the fort wasn't fully staffed as a defensive facility until World War II, and then only until Fort Miles at Cape Henlopen was completed in 1942. The fort then became a POW camp for German and Italian soldiers. The fort was deactivated on January 11, 1946, sold to the Kendzierski family, then served as a pickle processing and storage operation for the Liebowitz Pickle Company. It later was a storage spot for the Milford Salvage Company. It's unused today, but thought to be the only surviving World War I–era fort that is essentially unchanged.

woodpeckers. Pets are permitted in some areas of the park, but they must be kept on a leash and attended to at all times. Bicycles and horses are permitted on designated trails.

Motorboats (electric only) are permitted in some areas of the pond and are limited to a no-wake speed of 5 miles per hour. Rowboats, pedal boats, and canoes may be rented in the summer. The park is part of a trash-free program, which means you carry out everything you carry in.

There is a small entrance fee during the summer and on weekends and holidays in May, September, and October. The park is on County Road 449 near Laurel. Call (302) 875–5153 or (302) 875–2392 (campground).

A must-stop is at ***Lewes*** (pronounced Lewis), the Delaware side of the Lewes–Cape May, New Jersey, ferry. The hour-plus ride is a great way to avoid driving up the New Jersey Turnpike and then down to the beach towns of southern New Jersey or Atlantic City. The fare is $20 per car May through October and $18 the rest of the year, plus a passenger fee (from $2.00 to $6.00, depending on age and time of the year). Call (302) 645–6313 or (800) 64–FERRY or log on to www.capemaylewesferry.com.

If you drive the 20 miles along the beach from the Maryland border to Lewes (the first town in the first state), you may notice seven ***concrete towers*** rising up about 80 feet. They've been there for a number of years, since the days when German U-boats were a threat to our shores. They belong to the state, but there have been days when people were ready to tear them down. After all, they weren't being used. But there was never enough money, so they still stood. Now, people (perhaps the same ones) have decided the towers are historic.

That means you may climb the 115 steps of the ***Cape Henlopen State Park tower*** to the top for a lovely view that stretches from the Rehoboth boardwalk to Gordons Pond, taking in the Atlantic Ocean, Delaware Bay, and the outlying salt marsh. It's open seven days a week during the summer season in good weather. The rest of the year, it's open on weekends. The admission price is $2.50 for state residents and $5.00 for out-of-staters. Call (302) 645–8983.

But there are other reasons to come to Lewes, which is the northernmost of the coastal towns and is actually on the Delaware Bay rather than on the Atlantic Ocean. You can't miss the ***Zwaanendael Museum*** (Valley of the Swans), a Dutch Renaissance building that is an adaptation of the town hall at Hoorn in the Netherlands. No, it wasn't brought over stone by stone, and it wasn't built three centuries ago.

Instead, it was built in 1931 (the tercentenary of the founding of Lewes). Inside are exhibits of historic military and maritime artifacts from 1631 to the War of 1812 and about the H.M.B. *DeBraak*, a British brig that sank near Lewes in 1798.

Zwaanendael Museum

The Zwaanendael Museum, 102 King's Highway, Lewes 19958, is open Tuesday through Saturday from 10:00 A.M. to 4:30 P.M. and Sunday from 1:30 to 4:30 P.M. It is closed on holidays. There is no admission charge. (302) 645–9418.

Also to be seen, depending on whether you want nature or history, are the ***Prime Hook National Wildlife Refuge,*** (302) 684–8419, and the ***Seaside Nature Center,*** at Cape Henlopen State Park, (302) 645–6852.

At the ***Lewes Historical Society Complex*** is a furnished country store from the early years of this century, the 1798 Burton-Ingram House with period Chippendale and Empire antiques, and other historic

The Zwaanendael Merman

It's said the first "mermen" (no, not the current surfing music group) to reach American shores came from the Japanese in 1822 and that by 1842 P.T. Barnum displayed his first merman as the "Feejee Mermaid." Many fine museums own a merman specimen, but few choose to exhibit it. Therefore, because you get so few opportunities, one of the things you're sure to want to see at the Zwaanendael Museum is the merman. This one is about a foot long, and in 1941 it was loaned to the museum by a prominent local family who received it from a sea captain. The last family member died in 1985, and the museum collected $250 in donations to buy the merman from the estate. Although the museum has tried to provide the best exhibits on maritime history, the public won't allow the removal of the merman from display.

Trivia

The sand dunes at Cape Henlopen can reach 80 feet, and the Great Dune is the highest sand dune between North Carolina's Cape Hatteras and Cape Cod in Massachusetts.

buildings that were moved to Lewes. They include the blacksmith shop (now an extension to the gift shop), the Hiram Burton House, a doctor's office, an early plank house (early Swedish-style construction), the Ellegood House (the gift shop), and the Rabbit's Ferry House. Walking tours begin at the Thompson Country Store, which was operated by the Thompson family from 1888 to 1962, at Shipcarpenter and West Third Street. Reservations are required for groups. The complex is open Tuesday through Saturday, mid-June until Labor Day; tours are available by appointment. Tours are $6.00 for adults; children under twelve are free. It's located at 110 Shipcarpenter Street, Lewes 19855. For additional information, call the Lewes Historical Society at (302) 645–7670.

For curiosity's sake, stop by the ***Cannonball House*** at 118 Front Street, Lewes 19958, to see a cannonball in the foundation of the building, a souvenir of the War of 1812.

If you're in the area on the first Saturday of November, you should stop by the Eagle Crest Aerodrome to witness the ***Punkin Chunkin' contest***. It's just what it sounds like, a contest to see who can hurl pumpkins the farthest distance by the use of catapults and other odd contraptions. Because this is apparently the *only* punkin chunkin' contest anywhere, these people are setting world records.

For information contact the Lewes Chamber of Commerce and Visitor's Bureau at 120 Kings Highway, Lewes 19958; (302) 645–8073 or www.punkinchunkin.com.

While meandering along west of Cape Henlopen on Route 36, if you get a yen for a little fishing, stop by ***Abbott's Mill Nature Center,*** on County road 620 near Milford. It's one of a number of lakes and ponds in the area, but the nature center also has a historic gristmill, trails meandering through pine woods and along a stream, and canoeing and fishing. An Autumn at Abbott's Mill Festival is held the third Saturday in October. Year-round family programs, particularly for children from three to eighteen, but also for adults and families, are highlighted. For information call (302) 422–0847.

Places to Eat in Delaware

Bethany
Sedona,
26 Philadelphia Avenue,
(302) 539–1200

DiFebo's,
789 Garfield Parkway,
(302) 539–4914

Mango's 97 Garfield
Parkway,
(302) 537–6621,
www.mangomikes.com

Parkway,
114 Garfield Parkway,
(302) 537–7500

Dover
Tango's Bistro,
1570 North DuPont
Highway,
(302) 678–8500

Fenwick Island
Captain Pete's,
700 Coastal Highway,
(302) 537–5900

Libby's Restaurant,
Ocean Highway,
(302) 539–7379

Mancini's,
907 Coastal Highway,
(302) 537–4224

Lewes
A Taste of Heaven,
107 Second Street,
(302) 644–1992

Aurora Cafe,
329 Savannah Road,
(302) 645–2327

Buttery,
102 Second Street,
(302) 645–7755

King's Homemade Ice
Cream Shop,
201 Second Street,
(302) 645–9425

Kupchick's,
3 East Bay Avenue,
(302) 645–0420

Lighthouse Restaurant,
Fisherman's Wharf,
(302) 645–6271

Rose and Crown,
108 Second Street,
(302) 645–2373

Milford
Banking House Inn,
112 Northwest Front Street,
(302) 422–5708

Newark
Ashley's,
100 Continental Drive,
(302) 454–1500

New Castle
Arsenal on the Green,
30 Market Street,
(302) 328–1290

Lynnhaven Inn,
154 North DuPont
Highway,
(302) 328–2041

Salty Sam's Pier 13,
130 South DuPont
Highway,
(302) 323–1408

Rehoboth
Back Porch Cafe,
59 Rehoboth Avenue,
(302) 227–3674

Big Fish Grill,
4117 Highway 1,
(302) 227–9007

Blue Moon,
35 Baltimore Avenue,
(302) 227–6515

Chez La Mer,
210 Second Street,
(302) 227–6494

Cultured Pearl,
19 Wilmington Avenue,
(302) 227–8493

Espuma,
28 Wilmington Avenue,
(302) 227–4199

Fusion,
50 Wilmington Avenue,
(302) 226–1940

Garden Gourmet,
4121 Highway 1,
(302) 227–4747

LaLa Land,
22 Wilmington Avenue,
(302) 227–3887

Our Place,
37 Baltimore Avenue,
(302) 227–4143

Planet X,
35 Wilmington Avenue,
(302) 226–1928

Plumb Loco,
10 North First Street,
(302) 227–6870

Third Edition,
59 Lake Avenue,
(302) 227–9063

Tijuana Taxi,
207 Rehoboth Avenue,
(302) 227–1986

Victoria's,
2 Olive Avenue,
(302) 227–0615

Woody's,
2 Christian Street,
(302) 227–2561

Yum Yum,
37 Wilmington Avenue,
(302) 226–0400

SMYRNA
Thomas England House,
1165 South DuPont Highway,
(302) 653–1420

WILMINGTON
Brandywine Room,
11th and Market Streets,
(302) 594–3156

Columbus Inn,
2216 Pennsylvania Avenue,
(302) 571–1492

Green Room,
11th and Market Streets,
(302) 594–3155

PLACES TO STAY IN DELAWARE

There are dozens of hotel, condominiums, motels, apartments, houseboats, and other accommodations along the beaches of Dewey, Fenwick, Bethany, and Rehoboth. Some offer weeklong (Saturday to Saturday or Sunday to Sunday) rentals, weekends, or one-night options. Some are open only seasonally. Some are on the ocean, some are several blocks away. Note that accommodations statewide usually are full the first weekend after Memorial Day and the third weekend after Labor Day, due to the NASCAR races at Dover Downs.

BETHANY
Journey's End Guest House,
101 Parkwood Street,
(302) 539–9502

BRIDGEVILLE
Teddy Bear Bed and Breakfast,
303 Market Street,
(302) 337–3134

CAMDEN
Rose Tower Bed and Breakfast,
228 East Camden-Wyoming Avenue,
(302) 698–9033

CLAYMONT
Darley Manor Inn Bed and Breakfast,
3701 Philadelphia Pike,
(302) 792–2127

Wilmington Hilton,
I–95 and Namen's Road,
(302) 792–2700

DAGSBORO
Becky's Country Inn,
401 Main Street,
(302) 732–3953

DELAWARE CITY
Olde Canal Inn,
30 Clinton Street,
(302) 832–5100

DEWEY BEACH
Atlantic Oceanside Motel,
1700 Highway 1,
(302) 227–8811

Barry's Gull Cottage Bed and Breakfast,
116 Chesapeake Street,
(302) 227–7000

Bay Resort,
126 Bellevue Street,
(302) 227–6400

Bellbouy Inn,
21 Van Dyke Street,
(302) 227–6000

Chesapeake Landing,
101 Chesapeake Street,
(302) 227–2973

Cool Pines Bed and Breakfast,
108 Houston Street,
(302) 227–8164

Old Farmhouse Bed and Breakfast,
204 Saulsbury Street,
(302) 227–2359

DOVER
Dover Inn,
428 North DuPont Highway,
(302) 674–4011

Tudor House Bed and Breakfast,
228 North State Street,
(302) 736–1763

Sheraton Inn and Conference Center-Dover,
1570 North DuPont Highway,
(302) 678–8500

Greenwood
Eli's Bed and Breakfast,
P.O. Box 779, Route 36,
(302) 349–4265

Laurel
Heron's Nest Bed and Breakfast,
172 Lakeside Drive,
(302) 875–9230

Spring Garden Bed and Breakfast,
Delaware Avenue,
(302) 875–7015

Lewes
1897 House Bed and Breakfast,
801 Savannah Road,
(888) 227–1897

Bay Moon Bed and Breakfast,
128 King's Highway,
(302) 644–1802

Beachcomber's Haven,
7 Cape Henlopen Drive,
(888) 645–5459

Blue Water House,
407 East Market Street,
(302) 645–7832 or
(800) 493–2080

Country Lane Bed and Breakfast,
7 Country Lane,
(302) 945–1586

Inn at Canal Square,
122 Market Street,
(302) 644–3377 or
(888) 644–1911

John Penrose Virden House Bed and Breakfast,
217 Second Street,
(302) 644–0217

King's Inn,
151 Kings Highway,
(302) 645–6438

Little Mermaid,
425 King's Highway,
(302) 644–0551 or
(800) 592–9442

Savannah Inn,
330 Savannah Road,
(302) 645–5592

Summer Breeze Bed and Breakfast,
510 King's Highway,
(302) 645–7653

Wild Swan Inn,
525 King's Highway,
(302) 645–8550

Milford
Banking House Inn,
112 Northwest Front Street,
(302) 422–5708

Causey Mansion,
2 Causey Avenue,
(302) 422–0979

Towers Bed and Breakfast,
101 Northwest Front Street,
(302) 422–3814

Milton
Captain William Russell Bed and Breakfast,
320 Union Street,
(302) 684–2504

The Hollies,
313 Reed Street,
(302) 684–8905

Montchanin
Inn At Montchanin Village,
Route 100 and Kirk Road,
(302) 888–2133

Newark
Armitage Inn,
2 The Strand,
(302) 328–6618

Christiana Hilton Inn,
100 Continental Drive,
(302) 454–1500

McIntosh Inn of Newark,
100 McIntosh Plaza,
(302) 453–9100

New Castle
Armitage Inn,
Delaware Street and The Strand,
(302) 328–6618

Terry House Bed and Breakfast,
130 Delaware Street,
(302) 322–2505

William Penn Guest House,
206 Delaware Street,
(302) 328–7736

Rehoboth
Abbey Inn,
31 Maryland Avenue,
(302) 227–7023 or
(302) 923–1176

At Melissa's Bed and Breakfast,
36 Delaware Avenue,
(800) 396–8090

Beach House Bed and Breakfast,
15 Hickman Street,
(800) 283–INNS

Boardwalk Plaza,
2 Olive Avenue,
(302) 227–7169 or
(800) 332–3224

Corner Cupboard Inn,
50 Park Avenue,
(302) 227–8553

Delaware Inn Bed and Breakfast,
55 Delaware Avenue,
(302) 227–6031

Dinner Bell Inn,
2 Christian Street,
(302) 227–2561

Gladstone Inn,
3 Olive Avenue,
(302) 227–2641

Henlopen Hotel,
511 North Boardwalk,
(800) 441–8450

Lighthouse Inn Bed and Breakfast,
20 Delaware Avenue,
(302) 226–0407

Lord and Hamilton Seaside Inn,
20 Brooklyn Avenue,
(302) 227–6960

Mallard Guest House,
60 Baltimore Avenue,
(302) 226–3448

Melbourne Guest House,
14 Brooklyn Avenue,
(302) 227–2007

Pelican Loft Bed and Breakfast,
45 Baltimore Avenue,
(302) 226–5080

Pleasant Inn Lodge,
31 Olive Avenue,
(302) 227–7311

Royal Rose Inn,
41 Baltimore Avenue,
(302) 226–2535

Silver Lake Bed and Breakfast,
133 Silver Lake Drive,
(302) 226–2115

Three Maples Bed and Breakfast,
137 Old Landing Road,
(302) 227–2419

Shelbyvile

Victorian Rose Bed and Breakfast,
22 Church Street,
(302) 436–2558

Wilmington

Boulevard Bed and Breakfast,
1909 Baynard Boulevard,
(302) 656–9700

Hotel DuPont,
100 West 11th Street,
(302) 594–3100

Other Attractions Worth Seeing in Delaware

Abbott's Mill Nature Center,
Milford,
(302) 422–0847

Allee House,
Smyrna,
(302) 653–6872

Anna Hazard Museum,
Rehoboth Beach,
(302) 226–1119

Ashland Nature Center,
Hockessin,
(302) 239–2334,
www.dca.net/naturesociety

Assawoman Wildlife Area,
Bethany,
(302) 539–2100

Barratt's Chapel and Museum,
Frederica,
(302) 335–5544

Bellevue State Park,
Wilmington,
(302) 577–3390

Bowers Beach Maritime Museum,
North Bowers Beach

Brandywine Creek State Park,
Wilmington,
(302) 577–3534

Brandywine Park Zoo,
Wilmington,
(302) 571–7747

Brick Hotel Gallery,
Odessa,
(302) 378–4069

Bridgeville Firehouse Museum,
Bridgeville,
(302) 739–5318

Cape Henlopen State Park,
Lewes,
(302) 645–8983

Christ Episcopal Church,
Dover,
(302) 734–5731

Christ Episcopal Church,
Milford,
(302) 422–8466

Collins-Sharp House,
Odessa,
(302) 378–4069

Corbit-Sharp House,
Odessa,
(302) 378–4069

Delaware Archaeology Museum and Museum of Small Town Life,
Dover,
(302) 739–4266

Delaware Center for the Contemporary Arts,
Wilmington,
(302) 656–6466

Delaware Children's Theater,
Wilmington,
(302) 655–1014

Delaware History Museum,
Wilmington,
(302) 655–7161,
www.hsd.org

Delaware Museum of Natural History,
Wilmington,
(302) 658–9111

Delaware Seashore State Park,
Rehoboth Beach,
(302) 227–2800

Delaware Supreme Court,
Dover,
(302) 739–4155

Distinctly Delaware/ Delaware History Center,
Wilmington,
(302) 656–7161

Dover Art League,
Dover,
(302) 674–0402

Elsie Williams Doll Collection,
Georgetown,
(302) 856–9033

Fenwick Island State Park,
Millville-Oceanview,
(302) 539–9060

First USA Riverfront Arts Center,
Wilmington,
(302) 777–1600 or
(888) 395–0005

Fisher-Martin House,
Lewes,
(302) 645–8073

Fort Christina,
Wilmington,
(302) 652–5629

Fort Delaware State Park,
Delaware City,
(302) 834–7941

Fort DuPont State Park,
Delaware City,
(302) 834–7941

Fox Point State Park,
Wilmington,
(302) 577–3390

The Green,
Dover,
(302) 739–4266

Golden Fleece Tavern,
Dover,
(302) 739–4266

Governor Ross Mansion and Plantation,
Seaford,
(302) 628–9500

Greenbank Inn,
Wilmington,
(302) 999–9001

Hale-Byrnes House,
Newark,
(302) 998–3792

Harrington Museum,
Harrington,
(302) 398–3698

Harrington Railroad Museum,
Harrington,
(302) 398–3698

Hearn and Rawlins Mill,
Seaford,
(302) 629–4083

Heart Education Center,
1096 Old Churchmans Road,
Newark,
(302) 633–0200

Historic Houses of Odessa,
Main Street,
Odessa,
(302) 378–4069

Holts Landing State Park,
Millville-Oceanview,
(302) 539–9060

Holy Trinity (Old Swedes) Church and Hendrickson House Museum,
Wilmington,
(302) 652–5629,
www.oldswedes.org

Immanuel Episcopal Church,
New Castle,
(302) 328–2413

Indian River Lifesaving Station,
Bethany Beach,
(302) 227–0478

Iron Hill Museum of Natural History,
Newark,
(302) 368–5703

Kalmar Nyckel Foundation,
1124 East Seventh Street,
Wilmington,
(302) 429–7447

Kent County Courthouse,
Dover,
(302) 739–4266

Killens Pond State Park,
Felton,
(302) 284–4526

Legislative Hall,
Dover,
(302) 739–4114

Lincoln Collection of the
University of Delaware,
Wilmington,
(302) 573 4468

Lums Pond State Park,
Bear,
(302) 368–6989

Lydia Ann B. Cannon
Museum,
Milton,
(302) 684–3256

Maull House,
Lewes,
(302) 645–7670

Milford Museum,
Milford,
(302) 422–5026

Nanticoke Indian Museum,
Millsboro,
(302) 945–7022

Nassau Valley Vineyards,
Lewes,
(302) 645–WINE

Nemours Mansion and
Gardens,
Wilmington,
(302) 651–6912

New Castle Courthouse,
New Castle,
(302) 323–4453

New Castle–Frenchtown
Railroad Ticket Office,
New Castle

New Castle Presbyterian
Church,
New Castle,
(302) 328–3279

Old Asbury Methodist
Church,
Wilmington,
(302) 655–7060

Old Christ Church,
Broadcreek,
(302) 875–3644

Old Drawyer's Church,
Odessa,
(302) 378–4069

Old Dutch House,
New Castle,
(302) 322–2794

Old Town Hall Museum,
Wilmington,
(302) 655–7161,
www.hsd.org

Parson Thorne Mansion,
Milford,
(302) 422–3115

Playhouse Theatre,
Wilmington,
(302) 656–4401 or
(800) 338–0881

Port Penn Interpretive
Center,
Port Penn,
(302) 836–2533

Prince George's Chapel,
Dagsboro,
(302) 732–6835 or
(302) 732–3440

Quaker Hill Historic
District,
Wilmington,
(302) 658–9295 or
(302) 658–4200

Queen Anne's Railroad,
Lewes,
(302) 644–1720

Robinson House,
Claymont,
(302) 792–0285

Rockwood Museum,
Wilmington,
(302) 761–4340 or
(302) 761–4340
www.rockwood.org

Seaford Museum,
Seaford,
(302) 628–9828

Trees of the States
Arboretum,
Georgetown,
(302) 856–5400

White Clay Creek State
Park,
Newark,
(302) 368–6900

Willingtown Square,
Wilmington,
(302) 655–7161,
www.hsd.org

Wilmington Blue Rocks,
Wilmington,
(302) 888–2015,
www.bluerocks.com

Wilmington Maritime
Center,
Wilmington,
(302) 984–0472

Wilmington State Park,
Wilmington,
(302) 577–7020

Wilmington & Western Railroad, Wilmington, (302) 998–1930

Wilson-Warner House, Odessa, (302) 378–4069

Winterthur Museum, Garden, and Library, Winterthur, (302) 888–4600 or (800) 448–3883

Woodburn, Dover, (302) 736–5656

Calendar of Annual Events in Delaware

January

Exercise Like the Eskimos, *Bethany Beach, (302) 539–2100*

February

African-American Heritage Day, *Wilmington, (302) 571–1699*

Delaware Antiquarian Book Show/Sale, *Wilmington, (302) 655–3055*

Valentine Tea, *Rockwood Museum, Wilmington, (302) 761–4340*

Wilmington International Exhibition of Photography, *Newark, (302) 478–6392*

March

Chocolate Festival, *Rehoboth Beach, (302) 227–8259*

Easter in the Garden, *Wilmington, (302) 888–4600*

ICCD St. Patrick's Day Parade, *Wilmington, (302) 45–IRISH*

St. Patrick's Day Parade, *Dover, (302) 678–9112*

St. Patrick's Tea, *Rockwood Museum, Wilmington, (302) 761–4340*

April

Cherry Blossom 5K Run/Walk, *Wilmington, (302) 571–7788*

Earth Day Celebration of Brandywine Zoo, *Wilmington, (302) 571–7850*

Easter Promenade, *Rehoboth Beach, (800) 441–1329 or (302) 227–2233*

Easter Egg Hunt, *Bethany Beach, (302) 539–8011*

Governor's Annual Easter Egg Hunt, *Dover, (302) 739–5656*

Great Delaware Kite Festival, *Lewes, (302) 645–8073*

Historic Houses of Odessa Spring Exhibit, *Odessa, (302) 378–4069*

Ocean to Bay Bike Tour, *Fenwick/Bethany Beach, (302) 539–2100*

Seaford Bicycle Race, *Seaford, (302) 629–9690*

Spring Fling at the Brandywine Zoo, *Wilmington, (302) 571–7850*

May

A Day in Old New Castle, *New Castle, (302) 328–1832*

Blessing of the Fleet, *Lewes, (302) 645–5297*

Brandywine Zoo Mother's Day, *Wilmington, (302) 671–7788*

Delaware Agricultural Museum and Village Herb Festival, *Dover, (302) 734–1618*

Delmarva Hot Air Balloon Festival, *Milton, (302) 684–8404*

Milford Memorial Hospital Fair, *Milford, (302) 422–3904*

Old Dover Days, *Dover, (302) 734–1736*

Calendar of Annual Events in Delaware (Cont'd)

Spring Surf Fishing Tournament, *Fenwick/Bethany Beach, (302) 539–2100 or (800) 962–7873*

Wilmington Garden Day, *Wilmington, (302) 428–6172*

Winterthur Point to Point Races, *Wilmington, (800) 448–3883*

June

Brandywine Zoo Father's Day, *Wilmington, (302) 571–7788*

Delaware State Fair, *Harrington, (302) 398–3269*

Delmarva Chicken Festival, *Millsboro, (302) 937–6777*

Delmarva chicken Festival, *Wilmington, (302) 856–9037*

Great Delaware Kite Festival, *Lewes, (302) 645–8073*

Lewes Garden Tour, *Lewes, (302) 645–8073*

Separation Day, *New Castle, (302) 323–4453*

July

African-American Family Reunion Festival, *Wilmington, (302) 671–1699*

Beach an Bay Cottage Tour, *Bethany Beach, (302) 537–5828*

Caribbean Festival and Parade, *Wilmington, (302) 648–4095*

Cottage Tour, *Rehoboth Beach, (302) 227–8408*

Delaware Seashore Sandcastle Contest, *Dewey Beach, (302) 227–2800*

Delmarva Horseshoe Tournament, *Dover, (302) 734–1618*

Drive for Safety Golf Tournament, *Newark, (302) 654–7786*

Fourth of July Parade, *Bethany Beach, (302) 539–8011 or (302) 539–8011*

Hagley's Italian Fiesta, *Wilmington, (302) 658–2400*

Haneef's Annual Artisan Festival and Parade, *Wilmington, (302) 657–2108*

Independence Day Celebration, *Wilmington, (888) 3–CULTURE*

July Fourth Celebration, *Dover, (302) 734–7513*

Liberty Day, *Newark, (302) 366–7036 or (302) 366–7060*

Lunchtime on the Green, *Dover, (302) 734–1618*

Members' Fine Art Exhibit, *Rehoboth Beach, (302) 227–8408*

Nanticoke River Festival, *Seaford, (302) 629–9696*

Old-Fashioned Independence Day Celebration, *Laurel, (302) 422–3904*

Rehoboth Art League Cottage Tour, *Rehoboth Beach, (302) 227–8408*

Rehoboth Beach Fireworks, *Rehoboth Beach, (302) 227–2772*

State Fair, *Dover, (302) 398–3269*

August

African-American Festival, *Seaford, (302) 628–1908 or (302) 337–8230*

Arden Fair, *Arden, (302) 475–3126 or (302) 475–3912*

Creekside Bluegrass Festival, *Laurel, (302) 875–3658*

Delaware State News Sand Castle Contest, *Rehoboth Beach, (302) 741–8204 or (302) 741–8210*

Garrison Days, *Delaware City, (302) 834–7941*

Meteor Shower, *Wilmington, (302) 655–5740*

Old Canal Fest, *Delaware City, (302) 832–1890*

Calendar of Annual Events in Delaware (Cont'd)

Olde-Tyme Peach Festival, *Middletown, (302) 378–2788*

Old Sussex Day, *Trap Pond State Park, (302) 834–7941*

Outdoor Fine Art and Fine Craft Exhibit, *Rehoboth Beach, (302) 227–8408*

Peninsula Bluegrass Festival, *Houston, (302) 875–3658*

Wyoming Peach Festival, *Wyoming, (302) 697–2966*

September

Arden Fair, *Arden, (302) 475–3912*

Art on the Green, *New Castle, (302) 322–6334*

Brandywine Arts Festival, *Wilmington, (302) 656–8364*

Canal Fest, *Delaware City, (302) 834–4573*

Craft Festival at Winterthur, *Wilmington, (302) 888–4600*

Georgetown Hispanic Festival, *Georgetown, (302) 947–9199*

Nanticoke Indian Pow Wow, *Millsboro, (302) 945–3400*

Smooth Jazz Festival, *Wilmington, (888) 3–CULTURE*

Towne and Country Fair, *Seaford, (302) 629–9690*

Woodland Ferry Festival, *Seaford, (302) 629–9690*

Zippity Zoo Days, *Wilmington, (302) 571–7788*

October

Autumn at Abbott's Mill, *Milford, (302) 422–0847*

Autumn Jazz Festival, *Rehoboth Beach, (800) 29–MUSIC*

Boast the Coast, *Lewes, (302) 645–8073*

Bridgeville Apple-Scrapple Festival, *Bridgville, (302) 337–8771 or (302) 337–8771*

Fall Harvest at Pepperbox, *Laurel, (302) 875–4971*

Coast Day, *Lewes, (302) 645–1539*

Greenbank Fiber Festival, *Wilmington, (302) 999–9001*

Halloween Hoot, *Wilmington, (302) 655–6483*

Newark Trick or Treat, *Newark, (302) 366–7060*

Sea Witch Halloween Festival and Fiddlers' Convention, *Rehoboth Beach, (800) 441–1329*

November

Avenue of Lights, *Rehoboth Beach, (302) 227–2233 or (800) 441–1329*

Delaware Antiques Show, *Wilmington, (302) 888–4600*

Delaware Music School Auction, *Milford, (302) 422–2043*

Festival of Lights, *Dover, (302) 736–7050*

Hagley's Festival of Museum Shopping, *Wilmington, (302) 658–2400*

Holiday Fair, *Rehoboth Beach, (302) 658–2400*

Nemours Mansion and Gardens Tours, *Wilmington, (302) 651–6912*

Rehoboth Beach Independent Film Festival, *Rehoboth Beach, (302) 645–9095*

Thanksgiving Ball, *Dewey Beach, (302) 644–2900*

World Championship Punkin Chunkin' Festival, *Millsboro, (302) 856–1444*

Yuletide in Odessa, *Odessa, (302) 378–4069*

Calendar of Annual Events in Delaware (Cont'd)

Yuletide at Winterthur, *Wilmington, (302) 888–4600 or (800) 448–3883*

December

Caroling on the Square, *Wilmington, (302) 654–6482*

Christmas at Eleutherian Mills, *Wilmington, (302) 658–2400*

Christmas in Lewes, *Lewes, (302) 645–8073*

Christmas Parade, *Seaford, (302) 629–9173*

Dino Days, *Wilmington, (302) 658–9111*

Farmer's Christmas, *Dover, (302) 734–1618*

First Night Dover, *Dover, (302) 674–4010*

First Night Wilmington, *Wilmington, (302) 658–YEAR*

Posadas, *Georgetown, (302) 947–9199*

Yuletide in Odessa, *Odessa, (302) 378–4069*

Index

A

Abbott's Mill Nature Center, 218
Accident, 5
Air Mobility Command Museum, 207
Alex Haley statue, 41
Allegany Arts Council, 10
American Dine Museum, 47
Amstel House, 201
Annie Oakley, 164
Annmarie Garden, 121
Antietam, 15
Arden, 200
Armel-Leftwich Visitors Center, 38
Ashland Furnace, 54
Ashly Acres, 159
Asian Arts Center, 53
Assateague Island National Seashore, 174
Atlantic Hotel, 173

B

Back Burner, 200
Backbone Mountain, 4
Baltimore and Ohio Viaduct, 8
Baltimore Rent-A-Tour, 47
Baltimore-Washington International Airport, 33
Banneker-Douglass Museum, 37
Battle Creek Cypress Swamp Sanctuary, 119
Bay 'n Surf, 91
Beach to Bay Indian Trail, 175
Beaver Creek House Bed and Breakfast, 18
Beaver Creek School, 19
bed-and-breakfasts
  Beaver Creek House Bed and Breakfast, 18
  Bike and Bed program, 214
  Eli's Country Inn, 214
  John S. McDaniel House Bed and Breakfast, 154
  Lake Pointe Inn, 1
  Mt. Savage Castle, 12
  Slo Horse Inn, 158
  Spring Garden Bed and Breakfast, 212
  Tallulah's on Main, 150
Belair Mansion, 87
Belair Stables Museum, 88
Bell Hill Farm Market and Orchard, 106
Benson-Hammond House, 35
Berlin walking tour, 172
BET Soundstage, 86
Bethel Market, 211
Bethesda Post Office mural, 99
Bethesda Triangle, 97
Bethesda Urban District, 97
Bike and Bed program, 214
Black Panther, 133
Blackwater National Wildlife Refuge, 164
Bladensburg Dueling Grounds, 86
Bollman Truss Bridge, 62
Bombay Hook National Wildlife Refuge, 204
Boonsboro cantaloupes, 18
Bowie covered bridge, 87
Bowie Railroad Station and Huntington Museum, 88
Brandywine Park, 197
Brooks Barrel Company, 163
Burn Brae Dinner Theatre, 96
BWI Airport, 33

C

C&O Canal, 102
C&O Canal National
  Historical Park, 16
C&O Canal National Historical Park
  Visitor Center, 10
Cabin John Regional Park, 100
Calvert Distilling Company
  Seagram's America, 50
Calvert Marine Museum, 124–26
Camden Yard, 44
Camp David, 107
Campgrounds
  Crow's Nest Lodge Campground, 107
  Maple Tree Campground, 16
  Old Mink Farm, 107
Cannonball House, 218
Cantler's, 42
Cape Henlopen State Park tower, 216
Capital Green, 205
Captain Salem Avery House, 43
Captain Tyler ferry, 132
Carroll County Farm Museum, 56
Casselman Bridge, 7
Casselman Inn, 7
Catoctin Furnace, 104
Catoctin Mountain Orchard, 105
Charlotte Hall Farmers Market, 132
Chesapeake & Delaware Canal, 147
Chesapeake & Ohio Canal, 102
Chesapeake & Ohio (C&O)
  Canal Park, 16
Chesapeake Bay Bridge Walk Day, 43
Chincoteague ponies, 174
Choptank Electric Cooperative, 158
churches in Frederick, 103
Cider Mill Farm, 62
circle labyrinth, 132
College Park Airport, 89
College Park Aviation Museum, 89
Concord Point Light, 58
concrete towers, 216
Conowingo Hydroelectric Plant, 146
Counties
  Allegany County, 9–15
  Anne Arundel County, 33–43
  Baltimore City, 43–51
  Baltimore County, 52–56
  Calvert County, 119–26
  Caroline County, 157–61
  Carroll County, 56–58
  Cecil County, 143–48
  Charles County, 126–29
  Dorchester County, 162–67
  Frederick County, 103–8
  Garrett County, 1–9
  Harford County, 58–61
  Howard County, 61–64
  Kent County, DE, 203–8
  Kent County, MD, 148–50
  Montgomery County, 93–103
  New Castle County, 197–203
  Prince George's County, 83–93
  Queen Anne's County, 150–52
  St. Mary's County, 129–33
  Somerset County, 178–79
  Sussex County, 208–18
  Talbot County, 152–57
  Washington County, 15–21
  Wicomico County, 167–72
  Worchester County, 172–78
Country House, 168
covered bridges
  Bowie covered bridge, 87
  Fair Hill covered bridge, 143
  Gilpin Falls covered bridge, 146
  Jericho covered bridge, 53
  Loy's Station covered bridge, 105
  Roddy Road covered bridge, 105
  Utica covered bridge, 105
Cranesville Sub-Arctic Swamp, 6
Crisfield Historical Museum, 178
Crow's Nest Lodge Campground, 107
Cumberland Narrows, 12

D

Day Basket Factory, 146
Deep Creek Lake, 1
Deer Park Hotel, 7
Delaware Agricultural Museum and Village, 206
Delaware Art Museum, 198
Delaware State Police Museum and Education Center, 205
Delaware Toy and Miniature Museum, 199
Delmarva Peninsula, 195
DiscoverSea, 209
Dorchester Arts Center, 162
Dorchester County Public Library, 162
Dover Air Force Base, 206
Drane House, 5
Drum Point Lighthouse, 124
Dutch House, 201
DuVall Tool Museum, 84

E

East New Market, 166
Eastern Shore Early Americana Museum, 178
Ed Kane's Water Taxi, 51
Eli's Country Inn, 214
Exercise Like the Eskimos, 210

F

factory tours
  Calvert Distilling Company Seagram's America, 50
  General Motors (Truck Group) Baltimore Assembly Plant, 50
Fair Hill, 143
Fair Hill Inn, 145
Fair Hill Nature and Environmental Center, 143
Fenwick Island Lighthouse, 209
ferries
  Captain Tyler Ferry, 132
  Laurel-Woodland Ferry, 211
  Oxford-Belleview Ferry, 155
  Upper Ferry, 177
  Whitehaven–Mt. Vernon Cable Ferry, 172
  White's Ferry, 101
Fitzgerald, F. Scott and Zelda, 100
Flag Ponds Nature Park, 122
Flamingo Flats, 154
Forest Glen metro station, 96
Freedom of Conscience statue, 131
Friendship House, 127
Fuller-Baker Log House, 8
furnaces
  Ashland Furnace, 54
  Catoctin Furnace, 104
  Lonaconing Iron Furnace, 14

G

G&M, 34
Garrett County Historical Museum, 5
General Motors (Truck Group) Baltimore Assembly Plant, 50
George Read II House, 202
Gilpin's Falls covered bridge, 146
gold, 99
Great Falls Tavern Museum, 99
Greenbelt, 89
Greenbelt Museum, 90

H

Hagerstown Post Office murals, 18
Hagerstown Suns, 20
Hagley Museum, 198
Hall of Records, 205
Hancock's Resolution, 35
Harriet Tubman birthplace, 163
Harry Rudnick and Sons, 148
Havre de Grace Decoy Museum, 59
Havre de Grace Historic District, 59
High Ball, 170

Historic St. Mary's City, 129
Hockessin, 199
Holly's Restaurant, 151
Horsehead Wetland Center, 151
horseshoe crabs, 207
Hyattsville Post Office mural, 93

I

Inn at Perry Cabin, 154
Irish Brigade, 16

J

Jack Lewis, 212
Jeff Hastings's farm market, 211
Jericho Covered Bridge, 53
John Dickinson Plantation, 207
John S. McDaniel House
Bed and Breakfast, 154
Johnson Victrola Museum, 206

K

Kent Museum, 149
Krispy Kreme doughnuts, 53

L

Larriland Farms, 63
Laurel Post Office mural, 91
Laurel-Woodland ferry, 211
LaVale Toll Gate House, 3
Lewes, 216
Lewes Historical Society Complex, 217
light-rail system, 51
lighthouses
Concord Point Light, 58
Drum Point Lighthouse, 124
Fenwick Lighthouse, 209
Piney Point Lighthouse
Museum, 133
LiLeons, 85
Liriodendron, 61
Little Wedding Chapel, 145
Lonaconing Iron Furnace, 14
Loy's Station, 105

M

Magnolia, 208
Maple Tree Campground, 16
Martinak State Park, 160
Maryland Dove, 130
Maryland Gold Mine, 99
Maryland Vietnam Veterans
Memorial, 48
Maryvale Preparatory School, 53
Mason-Dixon line, 170
Messick Agricultural
Museum, 208
MetroArts
New Carrollton, 87
Penguin Rush Hour Mural, 95
mibster capital, 9
Mitchell House, 145
Montgomery Farm Woman's
Cooperative Market, 98
Montpelier Arts Center, 90
Montpelier Mansion, 90
Mount Carmel Monastery, 127
Mount Olivet Cemetery, 103
Mt. Savage Castle, 12
Mt. Savage Museum and
Historical Park, 12
Mudd, Dr. Samuel, house, 128
Museum of Costume, 153
Museum of Rural Life, 158
museums
Banneker-Douglass Museum, 37
Calvert Marine Museum, 124
Captain Salem Avery House, 43
Carroll County Farm Museum, 56
College Park Aviation Museum, 89
Delaware Agricultural Museum
and Village, 206
Delaware Art Museum, 198

Delaware State Police Museum and Education Center, 205
Delaware Toy and Miniature Museum, 199
DuVall Tool Museum, 84
Eastern Shore Early Americana Museum, 178
Garrett County Historical Museum, 5
Greenbelt Museum, 90
Hagley Museum, 198
Havre de Grace Decoy Museum, 59
Johnson Victrola Museum, 206
Kent Museum, 149
Messick Agricultural Museum, 208
Mt. Savage Museum and Historical Park, 12
Museum of Costume, 153
Museum of Rural Life, 158
Ocean City Life-Saving Station Museum, 177
Old Library Museum, 202
Piney Point Lighthouse Museum, 133
Ripken Museum, 60
St. Clements Island Potomac River Museum, 130
St. Mary's Square Museum, 153
Sewell C. Biggs Museum of American Art, 205
Susquehanna Museum of Havre de Grace, 59
Taylor House Museum, 172
Thrasher Carriage Collection, 11
Top of the World observation deck and museum, 45
U.S. Army Ordnance Museum, 60
U.S. Naval Academy Museum, 39
Underground Railroad: Harriet Tubman Museum, 163
Ward Museum of Wildfowl Art, 169
Washington County Museum of Fine Arts, 17
Zwaanendael Museum, 216

N

Nabb Research Center for Delmarva History and Culture, 167
National Park Seminary, 95
Naval Academy
  Armel-Leftwich Visitors Center, 38
  U.S. Naval Academy Museum, 39
Neck Meeting House, 158
New Castle Court House, 202
Nick's Airport Inn, 19

O

Oakland Post Office mural, 5
Ocean City Life-Saving Station Museum, 177
Old Library Museum, 202
Old Mink Farm, 107
Old New Castle, 201
Old Wye Grist Mill, 150
Olney Theatre Center, 100
Oregon Ridge Park and Nature Center, 54
Original Captain's Galley Restaurant, 179
Oriole Park at Camden Yards, 44
Orrell House and Bakery, 156
Our Fathers House Log Church, 3
Oxford-Belleview Ferry, 155

P

painted screens, 49
Patuxent Wildlife Research Center, 91
Penguin Rush Hour Mural, 95
Penn Alps, 7
Phillips Crab House, 176

Piney Point Lighthouse Museum, 133
Pioneer Lady statue, 97
Plumpton Park Zoo, 147
Pocomoke River, 175
Point Lookout State Park, 132
Pope's Creek, 127–28
post office murals
  Bethesda Post Office mural, 99
  Catonsville Post Office mural, 55
  Hagerstown Post Office murals, 18
  Hyattsville Post Office, 93
  Laurel Post Office mural, 91
  Oakland Post Office mural, 5
  Power of Communication, 175
  Rockville Post Office mural, 100
  Silver Spring Post Office mural, 94
  Towson Post Office mural, 52
Prime Hook National Wildlife Refuge, 217
Prince George's Genealogical Library, 88
Pryor's Orchard, 106
Punkin Chunkin' contest, 218

R

Radio and Television Museum, 88
Red Byrd Restaurant, 18
restaurants
  Back Burner, 200
  Bay 'n Surf, 91
  BET Soundstage, 86
  Burn Brae Dinner Theatre, 96
  Cantler's, 42
  Captain's Galley Restaurant, 179
  Fair Hill Inn, 145
  Holly's Restaurant, 151
  Krispy Kreme doughnuts, 53
  LiLeons, 85
  Mitchell House, 145
  Nick's Airport Inn, 19
  Phillips Crab House, 176
  Red Byrd Restaurant, 18
  Roy's Place, 101
  Stoney's Seafood House, 121
  Toby's the Dinner Theatre of Columbia, 63
  Vera's White Sands, 123
Ridgell's Country Store, 131
Ripken Museum, 60
Rockville Post Office mural, 100
Roddy Road Covered Bridge, 105
Roy's Place, 101

S

Sailwinds Park, 162
Salisbury Pewter, 168
Salisbury Zoo and Park, 169
Scenic View Orchard, 106
Seaside Nature Center, 217
Sewell C. Biggs Museum of American Art, 205
Show Place Arena, 85
Sideling Hill, 20
Silver Spring Acorn, 94
Six Flags Amusement Park, 83
skipjacks, 171
Slo Horse Inn, 158
Smyrna, 204
Sotterley Plantation, 129
Spocott Windmill, 166
Spring Garden Bed and Breakfast, 212
Spruce Forest Artisan Village, 7
St. Clements Island Potomac River Museum, 130
St. Mary's Square Museum, 153
State House, 204
steeplechase track at Fair Hill, 144
Stoney's Seafood House, 121
Suitland Bog, 84
Susquehanna Museum of Havre de Grace, 59
Susquehanna Trading Company, 59

sweet potato houses, 213

T

Tallulah's on Main, 150
Taylor House Museum, 172
Taylor's Island General Store, 164
Teackle Mansion, 178
Thomas J. Hatem Memorial Bridge, 59
Thomas Viaduct, 62
Thrasher Carriage Collection, 11
Tidewater Inn and Conference Center, 155
Toby's the Dinner Theatre of Columbia, 63
Top of the World observation deck and museum, 45
Town-Wide Yard Sale, 212
Transpeninsular Line markers, 209
Transportation and Industrial Museum, 10
Trap Pond State Park, 215
treasure hunting, 210
Tuckahoe State Park, 161

U

U.S. Army Ordnance Museum, 60
U.S. Department of Agriculture Research Center, 92
U.S. Naval Academy, 38
  Naval Academy chapel, 40
U.S. Naval Institute and Bookstore, 40
U.S. Snails, 159
Underground Railroad: Harriet Tubman Museum, 163
Upper Ferry, 171
Upper Youghiogheny, 3
USS *324,* 177
USS *Constellation,* 46
USS *Torsk,* 46
Utica covered bridge, 105

V

Vera's White Sands, 123
Victorian Historic District of Cumberland, 9
Viewtrail, 175

W

War Correspondents Arch, 17
Ward Museum of Wildfowl Arts, 169
Washington County Museum of Fine Arts, 17
Washington Monument, 17
Western Maryland Scenic Railroad, 11
Western Maryland Station Center, 10
Westvaco Paper Company, 13
Whitehaven–Mt. Vernon Cable Ferry, 172
White's Ferry, 101
Wild Acres Trail, 55
William Preston Lane Jr. Bridge, 31
Wilson Bridge, 19
Wilson Village Old General Store, 19
Woodland, 211
World War II memorial, 33
Wye Oak Sculpture, 160
Wye Oak State Park, 157

Z

Zwaanendael Museum, 216

About the Author

Judy Colbert is a longtime resident of Maryland. An award-winning freelance writer and photographer, Judy's more than 600 articles and photographs have appeared in such publications as *Washingtonian, Maryland, AAA World, Home & Away, Frequent Flyer, McCall's, Lodging,* and *Washington Flyer.* She has appeared on television and radio programs, including *Good Morning America* and Arthur Frommer's *Almanac of Travel.*

Other titles that Judy has authored include *Virginia: Off the Beaten Path,* published by The Globe Pequot Press; *Country Towns of Maryland and Delaware,* published by Country Roads Press; and *Fun Places to Go with Children in Washington, D.C.,* published by Chronicle Books.